Text | Arrange

- Text Roll-Up...
- Character...
- Frame...

- Fit Text To Path...
- Align To Baseline
- Straighten Text

- Spell Checker...
- Thesaurus...

- Extract...
- Merge-Back...

Arrange | Display

- Layers Roll-Up...
- Align...

- To Front
- To Back
- Forward One
- Back One
- Reverse Order

- Group
- Ungroup

- Combine
- Break Apart

- Separate
- Convert To Curves

Display | Special

- Snap To Grid
- Grid Setup...
- ✓ Snap To Guidelines
- Guidelines Setup...
- Snap To Objects

- ✓ Show Rulers
- ✓ Show Status Line
- Show Color Palette

- Edit Wireframe
- Refresh Window
- ✓ Show Bitmaps

- Show Preview
- Preview Selected Only

Special

- Create Pattern...
- Create Arrow...

- Preferences...

Help

Contents	F1
Screen/Menu Help	Shift+F1
How To Use Help	
Search For Help On...	Ctrl+F1
Tutorial	
About CorelDRAW!...	

The SYBEX Instant Reference Series

Instant References are available on these topics:

AutoCAD Release 11
dBASE
dBASE III PLUS Programming
dBASE IV Programming
dBASE IV 1.1
DESQview
DOS
DOS 5
Excel 4 for Windows
Harvard Graphics 3
Harvard Graphics for Windows
Lotus 1-2-3 Release 2.3
Lotus 1-2-3 for Windows
Macintosh Software
Microsoft Word for the Macintosh
Microsoft Word for the PC
Norton Desktop for Windows
Norton Utilities 6
PageMaker 4.0 for the Macintosh
Paradox 3.5
Paradox 4.0
PC Tools 7.1
Quattro Pro 3
Windows 3.0
Windows 3.1
Word for Windows, Version 2.0
WordPerfect 5
WordPerfect 5.1
WordPerfect 5.1 for Windows

Computer users are not all alike.
Neither are SYBEX books.

We know our customers have a variety of needs. They've told us so. And because we've listened, we've developed several distinct types of books to meet the needs of each of our customers. What are you looking for in computer help?

If you're looking for the basics, try the **ABC's** series. For a more visual approach, select full-color **Teach Yourself** books.

Running Start books are two books in one: a fast-paced tutorial, followed by a command reference.

Mastering and **Understanding** titles offer you a step-by-step introduction, plus an in-depth examination of intermediate-level features, to use as you progress.

Our **Up & Running** series is designed for computer-literate consumers who want a no-nonsense overview of new programs. Just 20 basic lessons, and you're on your way.

SYBEX **Encyclopedias, Desktop References,** and **A to Z** books provide a *comprehensive reference* and explanation of all of the commands, features, and functions of the subject software.

Sometimes a subject requires a special treatment that our standard series don't provide. So you'll find we have titles like **Advanced Techniques, Handbooks, Tips & Tricks,** and others that are specifically tailored to satisfy a unique need.

You'll find SYBEX publishes a variety of books on every popular software package. Looking for computer help? Help Yourself to SYBEX.

SYBEX

For a complete catalog of our publications:

SYBEX Inc.
2021 Challenger Drive, Alameda, CA 94501
Tel: (510) 523-8233/(800) 227-2346 Telex: 336311
Fax: (510) 523-2373

SYBEX is committed to using natural resources wisely to preserve and improve our environment. This is why we have been printing the text of books like this one on recycled paper since 1982.

This year our use of recycled paper will result in the saving of more than 15,300 trees. We will lower air pollution effluents by 54,000 pounds, save 6,300,000 gallons of water, and reduce landfill by 2,700 cubic yards.

In choosing a SYBEX book you are not only making a choice for the best in skills and information, you are also choosing to enhance the quality of life for all of us.

CorelDRAW 3 Instant Reference

Gordon Padwick

San Francisco • Paris • Düsseldorf • Soest

Acquisitions Editor: David Clark
Developmental Editor: James A. Compton
Editor: Peter Weverka
Project Editors: Kathleen Lattinville, Barbara Dahl
Technical Editor: Richard Anderson
Word Processors: Ann Dunn, Chris Meredith
Book Designer: Ingrid Owen
Graphic Artist: Suzanne Albertson
Screen Graphics: Cuong Le
Page Layout/Typesetter: Stephanie Hollier
Production Assistant: Arno Harris
Indexer:Paul Kish
Cover Designer: Archer Design
Screen reproductions produced with Collage Plus.

Library of Congress Card Number: 92-82687
ISBN: 0-7821-1152-1

Manufactured in the United States of America

10 9 8 7 6 5 4 3 2 1

Sizing - Arrange, transform, size

To Melissa

Acknowledgments

Although there is only one name on the cover of this book, many people contributed to it. I particularly want to thank David Clark, Acquisitions Editor, and Jim Compton, Developmental Editor, for their help and guidance throughout the project, and Kathleen Lattinville for firmly, but kindly, keeping me on schedule and coordinating the efforts of all the people involved.

My thanks also go to Peter Weverka for his skillful editing, to Richard Anderson for his thorough technical review and helpful suggestions, and to John Corrigan for his help in solving screen-capture problems.

This book would not have been possible without the support of many people at Corel Systems Corporation, particularly Janie Sullivan, who always made sure I had up-to-date software to work with and put me in touch with the right people when I needed to ask questions.

Finally, a personal note of thanks to my wife, Kathy, for her encouragement and patience during the long hours I spent in front of my computer.

Table of Contents

Introduction

Part One

CorelDRAW

Part Two

CorelCHART

Part Three

CorelPHOTO-PAINT

Part Four

CorelSHOW

Part Five

CorelTRACE

Appendix A

CorelDRAW File Formats

Index

Introduction

If you have used earlier versions of CorelDRAW, you will be delighted with Version 3.0. For quite a while, CorelDRAW has been many people's favorite draw-type graphics package, despite a few shortcomings. Now, those shortcomings are gone, some exciting new capabilities are added, and you get three additional applications all for less cost than before.

Most graphics packages are quite a challenge to new users, not because they are particularly difficult to use, but because there is so much to learn. This certainly is the case with CorelDRAW. When you buy CorelDRAW, you get a complete package of six programs:

- CorelDRAW, an extremely versatile drawing program. CorelDRAW is covered in Part I of this book.
- CorelCHART, a program that allows you to produce many types of two-dimensional and three-dimensional charts and graphs. CorelCHART is covered in Part II.
- CorelPHOTO-PAINT, a paint-type graphics program you can use to create as well as enhance bitmap graphics, including color and black-and-white scanned images, by using photography-like retouching techniques. CorelPHOTO-PAINT is covered in Part III.
- CorelSHOW, a program that allows you to create slides and overhead transparencies and run a slideshow on your computer monitor. CorelSHOW is covered in Part IV.
- CorelTRACE, a utility that converts color and black-and-white bitmap images into vector images. CorelTRACE is covered in Part V.
- CorelMOSAIC, a utility that simplifies selecting objects to import into CorelDRAW. CorelMOSAIC is included in Part I, the CorelDRAW section.

While all these applications are quite well integrated into a single graphics package, their individual ancestry clearly shows. That is one reason why you will find this book particularly useful.

What This Book Contains

Within each Part, tasks and major features are listed in alphabetical order. Throughout the book, step-by-step procedures show you how to successfully complete a wide variety of tasks.

When you are working with one of the programs in the CorelDRAW Package, you will usually find it easy to turn to the relevant section of the book and locate information relating to your current activity. If that fails, turn to the comprehensive index at the back of the book to find the number of the page you need to read.

As its title suggests, this book provides a fast way for you to gain clear and specific information about the major tasks you will encounter while working with the CorelDRAW package. It is not intended to be a comprehensive reference, so it does not deal with alternative methods of accomplishing an objective. Be prepared to explore beyond what is covered in this book and you will find many hidden treasures. You will find a lot more about CorelDRAW in Steve Rimmer's *Mastering CorelDRAW*, also published by SYBEX.

Who Should Read This Book

Whether you use or plan to use CorelDRAW frequently, or infrequently, this book is for you. It is a book to keep by the side of your computer for ready access. Its step-by-step procedures will save you a great deal of time.

The book makes certain assumptions about you. It assumes you have a job to do and a limited time in which to get it done; it assumes you know what you want to do, but are uncertain how to do it with CorelDRAW. The book assumes that you have some experience with computer graphics, perhaps with an earlier version of CorelDRAW or with another graphics package, and that you are comfortable working with Windows applications.

How to Use This Book

Use this book to help solve specific problems and also as a means of expanding your knowledge about CorelDRAW.

When you need to do something you are not sure about, look it up in the book. Generally, you will find a step-by-step procedure that tells you exactly what to do, or which you can easily modify to accomplish your specific task. Save yourself time in the future by marking the page where you found the information you used.

To expand your knowledge of CorelDRAW, open the book at random. Quite often you will come across something that is new to you. Look over the information so that you get a general idea of what is there. If you think it might be useful to you in the future, mark the page so that you can easily find it again.

Notes and Cross-References

Notes follow many procedures in this book. Notes provide information that supplements that given before or within a procedure. Make a habit of reading any notes that follow a procedure you are using.

To avoid unnecessary repetition, the book makes frequent use of cross-references. Cross-references to alphabetical entries are set in italics for easy identification. When a cross-reference is to an entry in another Part in the book, that Part is identified; otherwise the cross-reference is to an entry in the same section.

In some cases, references are made to headings within an alphabetical entry. In these cases, the heading name being referred to appears in quotation marks. Refer to the heading for further information.

Part I

CorelDRAW

ALIGNING AND SHAPING TEXT

CorelDRAW provides specific tools for aligning and shaping text. These tools supplement the tools you can use to align and shape both text and graphic objects. See *Alignment and Placement Aids*.

Aligning Paragraph Text within Margins

You can choose among five ways of aligning paragraph text within a frame. To align paragraph text:

1. Use the **Pick** tool to select the text.
2. Select **Edit ➤ Edit Text**.
3. In the Paragraph Text dialog box, click one of the five buttons in the **Justification** box

BUTTON	ALIGNMENT
Left	Left-aligned with a ragged right margin.
Center	Centered within the frame.
Right	Right-aligned with a ragged left margin.
Full	Aligns the text on both the left and right margins, inserting extra space between words if necessary.
None	Retains the current alignment and allows you to use the **Shape** tool to change the position and size of individual characters.

• **NOTES** You can also change text alignment from the Text roll-up.

Aligning Text to the Baseline

If you have accidentally moved individual characters off the baseline, you can realign characters to it.

1. Use the **Pick** tool to select the text.
2. Select **Text ➤ Align To Baseline**.

Fitting Text to a Path

You can fit text to a closed or open path.

1. Use the **Pick** tool to select the text and the path.
2. Select **Text ➤ Fit Text To Path**.
3. In the Fit Text To Path roll-up, select a character orientation, a position relative to the path, and a position along the path.
4. Click the **Apply** button.

• NOTES You can specify the exact distance of the text from the path and its exact placement along the path. To do so, click the **Edit** button to see the Fix Text to Paths Offsets dialog box.

To remove a path, select the text and the path, and choose select **Arrange ➤ Separate**. Then, with just the path selected, select **Edit ➤ Delete**.

Fitting Text within an Envelope

You can fit artistic text, but not paragraph text, within a closed shape. See *Shaping and Reshaping Objects*.

ALIGNMENT AND PLACEMENT AIDS

CorelDRAW! has several ways to help you align and place objects exactly. The information in this entry applies to graphic and text objects. See *Aligning and Shaping Text* for information about manipulating text objects only.

Finding the Cursor Position

The status line shows the position of the cursor in *x* and *y* coordinates. See *Screen* for information about how to display the status line.

Aligning Objects with the Crosshair Cursor

Use the crosshair cursor to align objects vertically and horizontally. You can place the crosshair cursor at any point and read its coordinates at the left end of the status line.

1. Select **Special ➤ Preferences**.
2. In the Preferences dialog box, click the **Cross Hair Cursor** check box.
3. Click **OK**.
4. After using the crosshair cursor, repeat steps 1 through 3 to return to the arrow cursor.

Placing Objects with the Grid

Use the non-printing grid to place objects where you want them. With the snap-to grid turned on, you can place objects at exact grid points.

1. Select **Display ➤ Grid Setup**.
2. In the Grid Setup dialog box, define the horizontal and vertical grid origin, and define the horizontal and vertical grid frequency.
3. If the **Show Grid** check box does not contain a check mark, click that check box.
4. If necessary, click the **Snap To Grid** check box to enable or disable the snap-to grid.
5. Click **OK**.

● **NOTES** To avoid clutter, not all grid points are shown on the screen. However, objects are snapped to invisible grid points as well as those that are visible.

After you have set up the grid, you can subsequently turn the snap-to grid on or off from the Display menu by clicking on **Snap To Grid**.

Aligning Objects with Guidelines

Use guidelines to align objects. You can place horizontal and vertical guidelines on the screen by eye, or by typing exact coordinates. The guidelines will not appear when you print your drawing.

To place guidelines by eye:

1. Make sure the rulers are displayed (see "Displaying Rulers" below).
2. To place a horizontal guideline, point into the horizontal ruler; to place a vertical guideline, point into the vertical ruler.
3. Press the mouse button and drag down from the horizontal ruler, or to the right from the vertical ruler, until the guideline is correctly placed. You can see the guideline coordinates at the left end of the status line.

To place guidelines on exact coordinates:

1. Select **Display ➤ Guidelines Setup**.
2. In the **Guidelines** dialog box, click either the **Horizontal** or **Vertical** check box.
3. Define the guideline position either by clicking on the arrows next to the Ruler Position text box, or by typing the value.
4. If necessary, click the **Snap To Guides** check box.
5. Click **Next** and repeat Step 3 if you want to add another guideline. If you do not want to add another guideline, click **Add**.

To move an existing guideline by eye:

1. Use the **Pick** tool to point onto the guideline you want to move.
2. Drag the guideline to the new position.

To remove a guideline:

1. Use the **Pick** tool to point onto the guideline you want to remove.
2. Drag the guideline up, or to the left, into the ruler.

Nudging Objects into Position

You can nudge an object to move it vertically or horizontally by an incremental distance you choose.

1. Select **Special ➤ Preferences**.
2. In the Preferences dialog box, define the nudge increment.
3. Click **OK**.
4. Use the **Pick** tool to select the object you wish to nudge.
5. Press the ↑, ↓, →, or ← key according to the direction you wish to nudge the object.

• **NOTES** You can nudge an object, even if it has been snapped.

Displaying Rulers

You can display a horizontal ruler at the top of the drawing area and a vertical ruler at the left of the drawing area. You can choose zero points for the rulers and the unit of measurement they display. To display or hide the rulers, select **Display ➤ Show Rulers**.

• **NOTES** The ruler zero points and measurement units are the same as those for the grid (see "Placing Objects with the Grid" above).

Snapping Objects to the Grid and to Guidelines

When you are placing objects, moving them, or reshaping them, you can do so with precision by snapping them to the grid or to guidelines.

1. Create a grid or guidelines as required (see above).
2. Select **Display ➤ Snap To Grid**, or **Display ➤ Snap To Guidelines**.
3. Place, move, or reshape the object.

• **NOTES** When you are close to a grid point or to a guideline, the object will snap to it. If you have both **Snap-To-Grid** and **Snap-To-Guidelines** enabled, Snap-To-Guidelines has priority.

Snapping to Objects

The snapping to objects capability allows you to accurately position one object, the moving object, relative to another, the stationary object.

1. Decide which node on the stationary object you want to snap the moving object to. See the "Notes" section below for information about selecting a node.
2. Select **Display ➤ Snap To Objects**.
3. Use the **Pick** tool to point to the moving object at the exact point you want to snap it to the stationary object. In Full-Color mode, you can select a point anywhere on a filled object. In Wireframe mode and in Full-Color mode for unfilled objects, you must select a point on the object's outline.
4. Drag the moving object until it is close to a node on the stationary object.

• **NOTES** The stationary object has nodes to which you can snap the moving object. If necessary, you can add nodes to the stationary object. See the Snap To Objects command (Display menu) in the CorelDRAW online **Help** feature for illustrations that show the positions of snap nodes.

Aligning Objects to Each Other

1. Use the **Pick** tool to select two or more objects. Select the object you want to align others to last.
2. Select **Arrange ➤ Align**. The Align dialog box appears.
3. Click one of the vertical alignment buttons or one of the horizontal alignment buttons, or one of each.
4. Click **OK**. The objects move to align with the last object you selected.

• **NOTES** You can also use **Arrange ➤ Align** to align an object to the center of the page or to the nearest grid point.

Creating Guides from Objects

You can create an object on the guides layer and use it as an alignment aid for precise drawing on other layers.

1. Select **Arrange ➤ Layers**.
2. In the Layers Roll-up, select **Guides**.
3. Draw the objects you want to use as guides. Objects you draw on this layer appear as dashed outlines.
4. Select a drawing layer. You can still see the dashed outline on the guide layer.
5. If necessary, turn on **Snap To Guidelines**.
6. Draw an object. It snaps to the guide object.

AUTOJOIN

AutoJoin helps you connect two straight lines, two curves, or a straight line and a curve. It also helps when you want to start and end a curve at the same point and create a closed curve.

Here's how to join lines or curves with the AutoJoin feature:

1. Draw a line or curve.
2. If necessary, use the **Pick** tool to select the first line or curve.
3. Using the **Freehand Pencil** tool, point to within the AutoJoin distance (see "Notes" below) of one end of the selected lines.
4. Draw a line or curve.

• NOTES The default AutoJoin distance is five pixels. You can change this default. See *Preferences*.

BLENDING OBJECTS

With the blend roll-up, you can blend one object into another through a series of intermediate steps. Blending creates a number of intermediate objects that progressively change their shape and properties from those of one object to those of the other. The blend can follow a straight line or a path.

Figure I.1 shows the Blend roll-up on the left, a blend along a straight line from a rectangle to an ellipse in the upper-right, and a blend along a curve from a rectangle to an ellipse in the lower-right.

Basic Blending

The basic technique for blending is as follows:

1. Use the **Pick** tool to select the two objects to be blended.
2. Select **Effects ➤ Blend Roll-Up**.
3. In the Blend roll-up, specify the number of blend steps and the rotation of the blend.
4. Click **Apply**.

Blending along a Path

1. Draw a path for the blend.
2. Follow steps 1 through 3 as in "Basic Blending" above.
3. In the Blend roll-up, click the **Path** button, the button in the lower-right with a curved line and a pointer.

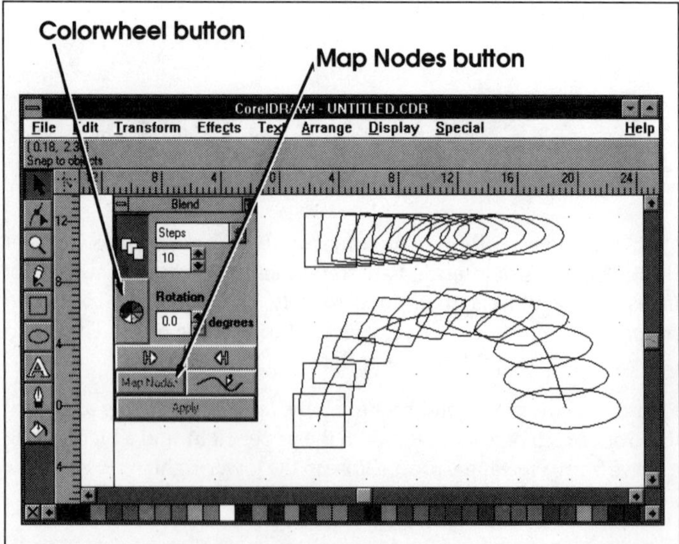

Figure I.1: The Blend roll-up, with a blend on a straight line and a blend on a curved line

4. In the flyout menu, choose **New Path**.
5. Use the new down-pointing arrow to select the blend path.
6. Click **Apply**.

Blending Colored Objects

Even two objects that have different color fills or outlines can be smoothly blended from one to the other. You can preview the color blend.

1. Do steps 1 through 3 as in "Basic Blending" above.
2. In the Blend roll-up, click the **Colorwheel** button. The straight line in the colorwheel indicates the color changes that will occur in the blend.
3. If you wish, click the **Rainbow** button. Then click either color-direction button to choose between the shortest or longest path around the colorwheel.
4. Click **Apply**.

• **NOTES** When you select a blend, the two arrow buttons in the Blend roll-up are black; when a blend is not selected, they are white. Click the left-arrow to identify the object that is the start of the blend, or the right-arrow to identify the end object.

Changing the Starting and Ending Objects

1. Use the **Pick** tool to select the blended object.
2. In the Blend roll-up, click the arrow on the left (it points to the right).
3. Click **New Start**.
4. Move the arrow so it points onto the new start object, and click the object to select it.
5. Click **Apply**.

Selecting Nodes on Starting and Ending Objects

CorelDRAW automatically selects the first node on the starting and ending objects as the basis of a blend. You can change the blend by selecting another node on each object.

1. Use the **Pick** tool to select the blended object.
2. In the Blend roll-up, click the **Map Nodes** button.
3. Point to and click on the node you want to use on the starting or ending object (whichever is selected).
4. Point to and click on the node you want to use on the other object.
5. Click **Apply**.

Clearing a Blend

1. Use the **Pick** tool to select the blend.
2. Select **Effects ➤ Clear Blend**.

Chaining a Blend

Chaining allows you to select any object in a blend, including an intermediate object, and blend that object with another object.

1. Start with a blend and another, separate object.
2. Hold down the Ctrl key, and use the **Pick** tool to select an object in the existing blend.
3. Hold down the Shift key and use the **Pick** tool to select the separate object.
4. If necessary, select **Effects ➤ Blend Roll-Up**.
5. Set the blend parameters in the Blend roll-up, as explained above.
6. Click and set the blend parameters in the Blend roll-up, as explained above.

7. Click **Apply**. A blend is created between an object in the first blend and the separate object.

CHARACTER ATTRIBUTES

There are three ways to set and change text attributes. You can use the Text menu or the Text roll-up, or you can copy the attributes from existing text.

Setting Character Attributes from the Text Roll-up

1. Use the **Text** tool to select the text characters.
2. Select **Text ➤ Text Roll-Up**.
3. In the Text roll-up, click the appropriate alignment icon.
4. Open the list of fonts, using the scroll bar if necessary, and click on a font name.
5. If necessary, open the Measurement-Units box and select the units you want.
6. Click the arrows adjacent to the font size until the correct number appears. Alternatively, type the font size.
7. Click the **Style** and **Placement** buttons to turn them on or off. From left to right, the buttons apply bold, italic, superscript, or subscript attributes to the text.
8. Click the **Character Kerning** button to change character spacing. See *Kerning Text* for additional information.
9. For paragraph text, click the **Frame** button to change the frame attributes. See *Creating Text* for additional information.
10. Click **Apply**.

Setting Character Attributes from the Text Menu

The Text menu provides separate submenus for changing the same attributes as you can from the Text roll-up. It is generally more convenient to use the roll-up. One advantage of the Text menu, however, is that you can see what fonts look like before you apply them.

1. Use the **Text** tool to select the characters.
2. Select **Text ➤ Character**.
3. Select a font, measurement unit, size, style, and placement for your text.
4. Click **OK**.

Copying Text Attributes

You can copy the attributes of selected text to other text.

1. Use the **Pick** tool to select the text you wish to change.
2. Select **Edit ➤ Copy Style From**.
3. In the Copy Style dialog box, select **Text Attributes**.
4. Click **OK**.
5. Click on the text with the attributes you wish to copy.

CLEARING TRANSFORMATIONS

In one operation you can reset all rotation and skew transformations to zero, restore all scaling and stretching operations, and clear all envelope and perspective transformations made from the Effects menu.

1. Use the **Pick** tool to select one or more objects.
2. Select **Transform ➤ Clear Transformations**.

• **NOTES** This operation does not affect any changes you have made to an object's position. In the case of a group, transformations that apply to the group as a whole are cleared; transformations made to individual objects within the group are not affected.

CLIP ART

See *Importing Objects* for information about clip art.

CLOSING OPEN PATHS

A path must be completely closed before you can fill it.

1. Use the **Pick** tool to select the open-path object.
2. Use the **Shape** tool to marquee-select the nodes at the two open ends of the path. The status line confirms that there are two selected nodes. (See *Selecting and Deselecting Objects* for information about marquee selection.)
3. Double-click one of the open nodes.
4. In the Node Edit pop-up menu, click **Join**.

• **NOTES** You may be unable to fill what appears to be a closed path. This usually happens because what appears to be a single node is in fact two separate nodes that are not joined. You can solve this problem by using this procedure to close open paths.

COLOR

You can draw lines in color and fill objects with color. The detailed steps here refer specifically to lines but apply also to fills.

You can select colors from

- the color palette at the bottom of the screen;
- the flyout color palette available from the Outline roll-up;
- the Outline Color dialog box, which is shown in Figure I.2.

In each case, you apply color to selected objects by clicking on one of the displayed colors. The Outline Color dialog box provides the most flexibility. See *Filling Objects* and *Outlining Objects* for additional information.

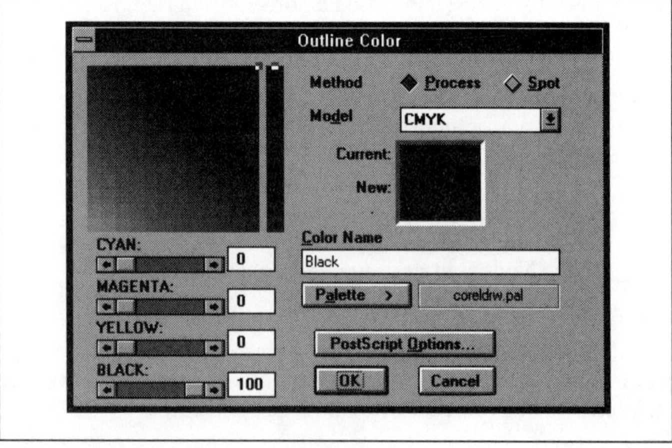

Figure I.2: The Outline Color dialog box

Choosing a Color Method

Click the **Process** or **Spot** button to select process colors or spot colors.

After you select **Process**, you choose colors from one of three color models (see "Selecting a Color Model" below). After you select **Spot**, you choose from Pantone colors.

Selecting a Color Model

With Process color selected, pull down the **Model** list box to choose among these color options:

- **CMYK**: the four-color method used in the printing industry. With this method, colors are formed by mixing percentages of cyan, magenta, yellow, and black.
- **RGB**: a three-color method in which colors are formed by mixing percentages of red, green, and blue.
- **HSB**: a method of defining colors in terms of hue, saturation, and brightness.

Click on whichever model you wish to use.

In the Outline Color dialog box, you can also

- click **Palette** to select specific color palettes supplied with CorelDRAW or color palettes you have created; or
- click **Names** to choose colors by name.

With Spot color selected, open the **Model** list box to choose between

- **PANTONE Palette**, which allows you to choose colors by their appearance on the screen; or
- **Names**, which allows you to choose colors by their Pantone names.

• NOTES When you choose a model that displays colors, the name of the selected color appears in the **Color Name** text box. When you use a model that allows you to choose a color by name, the **Color Name** text box changes to a Search String text box you can use to search for colors by name. Just type the first one or two characters of the color you want, and CorelDRAW will scroll through the box to the letters you typed.

Choosing a Color Palette

The text box adjacent to the **Palette** button shows the name of the current palette. To select another palette:

1. Click the **Palette** button.
2. Click **Load New Palette**.
3. Choose from the palettes displayed in the Open Palette dialog box.
4. Click **OK** to return to the Outline Color dialog box with the new palette selected.

• **NOTES** CORELDRAW.PAL. is the default process-color palette. Several other process-color palettes are supplied with CorelDRAW. PURE100.PAL is identical to CORELDRW.PAL and is available in case you make changes to the default palette. The default spot-color palette is CORELDRW.IPL.

You can use **Palette** to add or delete colors from existing palettes, create new palettes, and set a specific palette as the default.

Selecting Colors

Which colors the Outline Color dialog box displays depends on the color method and model you select. For process colors, you choose the color you want to apply to selected objects by

- clicking on the displayed color you want to use;
- setting the percentages of the color components in the slider boxes at the bottom-left of the Outline Color dialog box (you can set these percentages either by dragging or by typing values);
- selecting a color by name.

For spot colors, you choose a color by

- clicking on the displayed color you want to use, and adjusting its tint in the slider box at the bottom-left of the Outline Color dialog box;
- Selecting a color by name.

The sample box under the Model text box shows the present color of the selected object. If you select two or more objects, the sample box shows the color of the most recently applied color. After you select a color, the top part of the sample box continues to show the current color of the selected object, and the bottom shows the new color you selected.

PostScript Options

If you are using a PostScript-equipped printer, you can click the **PostScript Options** button to specify halftone screens. You can also enable **Overprint**, an option that slightly overlaps color separations to compensate for small misalignments that might occur during commercial multicolor printing.

Applying Color to Objects

After you have set the Outline Color dialog box, click the **OK** button to apply color to the selected objects.

COLORING MONOCHROME BITMAP OBJECTS

You can change the black pixels of a black-and-white bitmap to any outline color, and you can change the white pixels to another color. You cannot color a gray-scale bitmap object.

1. Use the **Pick** tool to select the bitmap object.
2. In the Outline tool flyout menu, click the **Colorwheel** icon.
3. In the Outline Color dialog box, click the outline color you want.
4. Click **OK**.
5. In the Fill tool flyout menu, click the **Colorwheel** icon.
6. In the Uniform Fill dialog box, click the fill color you want.
7. Click **OK**.

COMBINING OBJECTS AND BREAKING OBJECTS APART

You can combine several objects, connected or not, into a single object. You can also break a single multipath curve object into several single-path objects so that you can change the attributes of some of the paths.

Combining Objects

1. Use the **Pick** tool to select all the objects that are to be combined. Alternatively, marquee-select the objects.
2. Select **Arrange ➤ Combine**.

Breaking Objects Apart

1. Use the **Pick** tool to select a multipath curve object.

2. Select **Arrange ➤ Break Apart**.

● **NOTES** Combining objects with the same attributes can conserve memory and increase drawing speed.

See also *Grouping and Ungrouping Objects*.

CONSTRAINING OBJECTS

In many cases you can constrain a CorelDRAW action by holding down the Ctrl key. For example, you can constrain straight lines to specific angles, constrain rectangles to squares, and constrain ellipses to circles. See *Drawing Objects* for additional information.

You can also place constraints on the process of moving and transforming objects. See *Moving Objects* and *Transforming Objects* for additional information.

CONVERTING OBJECTS TO CURVES

You can convert rectangles, ellipses, and artistic text objects to curves so that you can reshape them. See *Shaping and Reshaping Objects*.

Converting Rectangles and Ellipses to Curves

1. Use the **Pick** tool to select a rectangle or a curve.

2. Select **Arrange ➤ Convert to Curves**.

Converting Text to Curves

1. Use the **Pick** tool to select one or more artistic text characters.
2. Select **Arrange ➤ Convert to Curves**.

• NOTES These steps convert each text character to a single-line curve object. You cannot edit the curve objects as text. You can convert the curve objects to text characters. See the discussion of creating custom fonts in the *Fonts* entry.

COPYING OBJECTS

You can use the Clipboard to copy graphic and text objects within a drawing or from one drawing to another. You can also duplicate objects. See *Duplicating Objects*.

Copying an Object within a Drawing

1. Use the **Pick** tool to select the object to be copied.
2. Select **Edit ➤ Copy** to copy the object and its attributes to the Clipboard.
3. Move the original object to a different place on the drawing.
4. Select **Edit ➤ Paste**.
5. Move the object to its correct position on the drawing.

Step 4 pastes the object into its original position in the drawing. If you do not perform step 3, the object will be placed exactly on top of the original object. Although you have two objects, you can see only one.

• NOTES When you copy an object to the Clipboard, you may see the message "Metafile too large to put on Clipboard" or "CorelDRAW Clipboard format too large to put in Clipboard." To overcome this problem, break the object into parts and copy it part by part. Alternatively, you can save the object as a file and then import it into the drawing.

You can use the Clipboard to copy complete artistic or paragraph text objects. To copy individual characters from an artistic or paragraph text object, select those characters with the Text tool.

Copying an Object from One Drawing to Another

1. Use the **Pick** tool to select the object to be copied.
2. Select **Edit ➤ Copy** to copy the object and its attributes to the Clipboard.
3. Open the drawing into which the object is to be copied.
4. Select **Edit ➤** Paste.
5. Move the object to the proper position on the drawing.

Copying an Object from Another Windows Application into CorelDRAW

Use the same general procedure as described above under "Copying an Object from One Drawing to Another." The following formats may be pasted from the Clipboard into CorelDRAW:

- CorelDRAW native format (CF-CORELDRAW)
- Windows Metafile
- ASCII text
- Windows bitmaps

Copying an Object from CorelDRAW into Another Windows Application

Use the same general procedure described above under "Copying an Object from One Drawing to Another." Objects containing PostScript textures, pattern fills, and bitmaps cannot be pasted into other applications.

CREATING TEXT

Unlike previous versions, CorelDRAW Version 3.0 allows you to create and edit text directly on your drawing, no matter whether it is artistic text (previously called "headline text") or paragraph text. You can also create and edit text in a dialog box.

Artistic text consists of up to 250 characters that are not constrained within a frame. Paragraph text consists of up to 4000 characters that are constrained within a predefined frame. You can perform a greater variety of manipulations on artistic text than you can on paragraph text.

Creating Artistic Text

1. Select character attributes for the text. See *Character Attributes*.
2. Select the **Text** tool.
3. Move the cursor to the place on your drawing where you want the text to begin and click the mouse button.
4. Type the text.

Creating Paragraph Text

1. Select character attributes for the text. See *Character Attributes*.
2. Select the **Text** tool.

3. Move the cursor where the top-left corner of the paragraph frame is to be.
4. Press the mouse button and drag down and to the right to create a frame for the paragraph.
5. Release the mouse button.
6. Type the text. Whenever the text reaches the right edge of the frame, it is wrapped to the next line.

• **NOTES** Only the text that fits within the frame shows on the screen. If you type more text than can fit into the frame, you can subsequently stretch the frame to make the extra text visible. See *Stretching and Shrinking Objects*.

Pasting Text

You can create text in a Windows application, copy it into the Clipboard, and then paste it into your drawing as artistic or paragraph text.

1. Create text in a Windows application.
2. Copy the text into the Clipboard.
3. Open your CorelDRAW drawing.
4. Use the **Pick** tool to select existing artistic or paragraph text. See the note below about pasting in a new piece of artistic text or a new paragraph.
5. Select **Edit ➤ Edit Text**.
6. In the Artistic Text or Paragraph Text dialog box, click on **Paste**.

• **NOTES** You must have some artistic text or paragraph text in position on your drawing before you can begin pasting. To paste text into a new position, first create either artistic text or paragraph text containing at least one character. Then paste the text. Finally, if necessary, delete the character you originally typed.

Importing Text

You can create text in a word processor or text editor, including non-Windows applications, and then import it into your drawing as paragraph text, but not as artistic text.

1. Create text in a word processor or text editor.
2. Write the text to disk as an ASCII file. It must not contain word-processing codes.
3. Open your CorelDRAW drawing.
4. Use the **Pick** tool to select existing text. See the note under "Pasting Text" for information about importing the text as a new paragraph.
5. Select **Edit ➤ Edit Text**.
6. In the Paragraph Text dialog box, click on **Import**.
7. In the Import Text dialog box, select the text file and click on **OK**.

Using Special Characters

CorelDRAW provides many special characters that you can see on your screen and print. All these characters are shown on the Character Reference Chart that is supplied with CorelDRAW.

To place a special character on your drawing or in a Text dialog box:

1. Find the special character on the Character Reference Chart.
2. Note the character's number in the column on the chart to the left of the symbol, and the font name at the top of the column containing the character.
3. If necessary, select the appropriate font. Do this either from the Text roll-up or from the Character Attributes dialog box.
4. Press and hold down the Alt key.
5. Type the three- or four-digit number that identifies the special character. You must type the leading zero.

6. Release the Alt key and the special character appears on your screen.

• NOTES If the special character's number is in the range 033 through 0126, you can select a special character by selecting the font and then just typing the equivalent keyboard character listed in the Windows column.

CROPPING BITMAP OBJECTS

1. Use the **Shape** tool to select the bitmap object.
2. Point to one of the handles around the object.
3. Press the mouse button and drag to crop the object.
4. Repeat steps 2 and 3 to crop in other directions.

• NOTES You can uncrop a previously cropped object by dragging its handles out.

CUSTOMIZING CORELDRAW

You can customize CorelDRAW by setting various preferences. See *Preferences*.

You can also customize it by making certain changes to your WIN.INI, CORELDRW.INI, and CORELDRW.DOT files. The installation procedure makes necessary additions to your WIN.INI file and also creates a CORELDRW.INI file and a CORELDRW.DOT file. For information about these files and how you can modify them to customize the program, do the following:

1. With no menu selected, press **F1** to access online help.
2. Click the **Reference** icon.
3. Click **Software-related Information**.
4. Click on the name of the item you wish to reference.

See *Help* for more information about using online help.

• **NOTES** Always make a copy of your original WIN.INI, CORELDRW.INI, and CORELDRW.DOT files before editing them. Then, if you make a mistake, you still have the originals.

DELETING OBJECTS

1. Use the **Pick** tool to select an object.
2. Select **Edit ➤ Delete**. Alternatively, press the Delete key.

DISPLAY MODES

You can create and edit drawings in two modes: Wireframe (Outline) mode and Full-Color (Preview) mode. Previous Corel versions allowed you to view, but not to create or edit, in Preview mode. You will probably work most often in Full-Color mode because it allows you to see the full effect of what you are doing. Wireframe mode has the advantage of allowing you to focus on object outlines. Also, in the case of complex drawings with filled objects, screen redrawing is much faster in Wireframe mode than in Full-Color mode.

To switch between Wireframe and Full-Color modes:

- Select **Display ➤ Edit Wireframe** to change from the default Full-Color mode to the Wireframe mode, or vice-versa.

• **NOTES** When you open the **Display** menu, the check mark adjacent to **Edit Wireframe** indicates that Wireframe mode is selected. The absence of a check mark indicates that Full-Color mode is selected.

Previewing Your Drawings

You can also select the Preview mode. In this mode, all menus, rulers, and tools are removed from the screen and you just see an enlarged view of your drawing or selected objects.

To preview your entire drawing:

1. Select **Display ➤ Show Preview** to preview the entire drawing.
2. Press F9 to leave Preview mode.

To preview only selected objects:

1. Use the **Pick** tool to select the objects you wish to preview.
2. Select **Display ➤ Preview Selected Only**.
3. Select **Display ➤ Show Preview**.
4. Press **F9** to leave Preview mode.

Displaying and Hiding Bitmap Objects in Full-color Mode

Bitmaps, particularly those that are complex and in color, can slow the process of redrawing the screen. The Display menu shows whether bitmaps are currently hidden or not. If **Show Bitmaps** is checked in the Display menu, bitmaps will be shown; if it is not checked, bitmaps will not be shown. Click on **Show Bitmaps** to change from one to the other.

DRAWING OBJECTS

With CorelDRAW's tools you can draw rectangles, ellipses, straight lines, and curves.

Drawing Rectangles and Squares

1. Select the **Rectangle** tool.
2. Point to where you want to place a corner.
3. Press the mouse button and drag to the opposite corner.
4. Release the mouse button.

• **NOTES** The status bar shows the dimensions of the rectangle.

To constrain the rectangle to a square, hold down the Ctrl key while you drag. Keep the Ctrl key pressed until you have released the mouse button.

Instead of drawing a rectangle from corner to corner, you can enlarge it from the center out by holding down the Shift key while you drag. Keep the Shift key pressed until you have released the mouse button.

To draw a square from the center out, hold down the Ctrl and Shift keys while you drag.

Drawing Rounded Rectangles and Squares

1. Draw a rectangle. Follow steps 1 through 4 in "Drawing Rectangles and Squares," if necessary.
2. Use the **Shape** tool to select the rectangle.
3. Point to a corner node and press the mouse button.

4. Drag the node along an edge to achieve the rounding effect you want. The rounding applies to all four corners.
5. Release the mouse button.

• NOTES The status line shows the corner radius.

You can adjust the rounding with the Shape tool. Point it to one of the nodes and drag it in either direction along an edge.

If you round the corners of a stretched rectangle, the corner rounding effect is elliptical.

Drawing Ellipses and Circles

1. Select the **Ellipse** tool.
2. Point to where you want a corner of the rectangular frame that encloses the ellipse to be.
3. Press the mouse button and drag to the opposite corner of the frame.
4. Release the mouse button.

• NOTES Refer to the explanation of drawing rectangles and squares for information about using the Ctrl key to constrain an ellipse as a circle, and about using the Shift key to draw an ellipse from its center.

Drawing Arcs and Wedges

You draw an arc or a wedge by modifying an ellipse or circle.

1. First, create an ellipse or circle. Follow steps 1 through 4 under "Drawing Ellipses and Circles" if necessary.
2. Using the **Shape** tool, select the ellipse by pointing onto it and clicking.
3. Point to the node on the ellipse.
4. Press and hold down the mouse button.

5. Drag outside the ellipse to create an arc, or drag inside the ellipse to create a wedge.
6. Release the mouse button.

• **NOTES** The status line shows the angle included in the arc or wedge.

Hold down the Ctrl key while you drag to constrain the angle of the arc or wedge to certain increments. See *Preferences* for information about setting this angle.

Drawing Straight Lines in Freehand Mode

CorelDRAW provides two line-drawing modes: Freehand and Bézier. The toolbox shows which of the two is currently available. If the Freehand pencil is available, the toolbox shows the Freehand pencil icon; if the Bézier pencil is available, the toolbox shows the somewhat smaller Bézier pencil icon. When you select the Pencil tool, the status bar tells you whether you are in the Freehand or Bézier mode.

To switch between freehand and Bézier modes:

1. Point to the **Pencil** tool.
2. Press and hold down the mouse button until a flyout menu with two pencil icons appears.
3. Click the left icon to select Freehand mode, or click the right icon to select Bézier mode.

Now you are ready to draw straight lines.

1. Select the freehand **Pencil** tool.
2. Check the status bar to verify you have the freehand Pencil tool.
3. If necessary, change from Bézier to Freehand mode (see above).
4. Point to where you want the line to begin and click.
5. Point to where you want the line to end and click. You can see the line as you position the end-point

6. If you want to draw a second straight line connected to the first, point to one end of the existing line, within the AutoJoin distance, and click. See *Preferences* for information about setting the AutoJoin distance. If you want to draw a second straight line which is not connected, point to a new position on the screen and click.
7. Point to where you want the new line to end and click.
8. Repeat steps 6 and 7 to draw additional connected or unconnected lines.
9. Terminate line drawing by selecting the **Pick** tool or another drawing tool.

• **NOTES** You can constrain a straight line to be horizontal, vertical, or at an incremental angle by holding down the Ctrl key while you drag the end-point of a line. See *Preferences* for information about setting the constraint angle.

You can also use Bézier mode to draw single and multiple straight lines. In Bézier mode, you don't see a line as you stretch it to its end-point. When you want to create several connected straight lines, just click at the successive end-points. To draw disconnected straight lines, press the spacebar twice after you have finished one line and before you start the next.

Drawing Curves in Freehand Mode

You can draw curves in Freehand or Bézier mode. See "Drawing Straight Lines in Freehand Mode" above for information about selecting freehand or Bézier mode. Also see "Drawing Curves in Bézier Mode" below.

1. Select the freehand **Pencil** tool.
2. Check the status bar to verify you are in Freehand mode.
3. Point to where you want the curve to begin.
4. Press and hold down the mouse button.
5. Drag the cursor to create the curve.
6. Release the mouse button at the end of the curve.

7. If you want to draw a second curve and join it to the first, point within the AutoJoin distance to one end of the existing curve and repeat steps 3 through 6. See *Preferences* for information about setting the AutoJoin distance.
8. If you want to draw a second curve that is not joined to the first, point to a new place on the screen and repeat steps 3 through 6.

• **NOTES** You can make corrections to your curve before you release the mouse button. At any time, with the mouse button still held down, press the Shift key and trace back along the curve you have drawn. The curve is deleted portion by portion as you retrace it. Release the Shift key, and continue to draw the curve.

You can subsequently change the shape of a curve with the Shape tool. See *Shaping and Reshaping Objects*.

Drawing Curves in Bézier Mode

Unlike Freehand mode, Bézier mode allows you to control where nodes are placed on your curve, so that you can produce smooth curves.

1. Select the Bézier **Pencil** tool.
2. Check the status bar to verify you are in Bézier mode.
3. Point to where you want the curve to begin.
4. Press and hold down the mouse button. A node appears at this point.
5. Drag the cursor in the direction you want the first segment of the curve to be drawn. As you drag, control points move in opposite directions from the node.
6. Release the mouse button when the control points are in the correct position.
7. Point to where you want the curve segment to end.
8. Press and hold down the mouse button. A node appears at this point.

9. Drag the cursor in the direction you want the next segment of the curve to be drawn. As you drag, control points move in opposite directions from the node.
10. Release the mouse button when the control points are in the correct position.
11. Repeat steps 7 through 10 to draw additional curve segments.

• **NOTES** These steps produce connected curve segments. To draw curve segments that are not connected, press the spacebar twice after completing one segment and before starting the next.

You can subsequently use the Shape tool to change the shape of the curve. See *Shaping and Reshaping Objects*.

You can constrain the angular position of control points by holding down the Ctrl key while you drag. See *Preferences* for information about setting the constraint angle.

DUPLICATING OBJECTS

You can duplicate an object on your drawing. The duplicate appears offset up and to the right of the selected object. See *Preferences* for information about setting the position of the duplicate. After the duplication operation, the duplicate is automatically selected.

1. Use the **Pick** tool to select the object to be duplicated.
2. Select **Edit ➤ Duplicate**.
3. Position the duplicate on your drawing.

• **NOTES** See *Copying Objects* for an alternative way of duplicating objects.

EDITING TEXT

You can edit artistic and paragraph text in two ways: directly on your drawing or in a text dialog box. For lengthy text it is more convenient to extract the text first. That way you can edit it with a text editor or word processor and then merge it back into your drawing. See *Extracting and Merging Back Text*.

Editing Text on a Drawing

1. If necessary, use the **Zoom** tool to magnify the text so that you can clearly see the characters.
2. Select the **Text** tool.
3. Point to the position in the text where you want to edit.
4. Click to create an insertion point.
5. Press the Backspace key to delete characters to the left of the insertion point, or press Delete to delete characters to the right. Alternatively, use the **Text** tool to highlight a number of characters, and press Delete to delete them all.
6. Type characters to insert them at the insertion point.

• **NOTES** You can copy text on a drawing or copy text from one drawing to another. See *Copying Objects*.

If you have applied perspective or an extrusion to text, you can only edit the text in a text dialog box.

Editing Text in a Dialog Box

1. Use the **Pick** tool to select artistic or paragraph text.
2. Select **Edit ➤ Edit Text**.
3. In the Artistic Text or Paragraph Text dialog box, use the techniques in "Editing Text on a Drawing" to delete or insert text.

• **NOTES** You can change character attributes in the Artistic Text and Paragraph Text dialog boxes.

EMBEDDING AND LINKING OBJECTS

CorelDRAW allows you to exchange information with files containing objects created in Windows applications that support Object Linking and Embedding (OLE).

Embedding Objects into a CorelDRAW File

You can embed (insert) an object created in another Windows application into a CorelDRAW drawing. The exact procedure varies slightly from application to application. The following steps assume you are embedding an application created in CorelPHOTO-PAINT. If you use a different application to create the object, consult its documentation for precise information.

1. Create and save an object in CorelPHOTO-PAINT.
2. Open your CorelDRAW file.
3. Select **File ➤ Insert Object**.
4. In the Insert Object dialog box, select **CorelPhoto-Paint! Picture.**
5. Click **Insert** to open CorelPHOTO-PAINT.
6. If you see the Create a New Picture dialog box, click **OK**.
7. In the CorelPHOTO-PAINT **Edit** menu, choose **Paste From**.
8. In the Paste a Picture from Disk dialog box, select the name of the file you want to paste into CorelDRAW.
9. Click **OK**.

10. Make sure the picture you want to paste is displayed. In the CorelPHOTO-PAINT **File** menu, choose **Update CorelDRAW!**.
11. In the CorelPHOTO-PAINT **File** menu, choose **Exit & Return to CorelDRAW!**.

Now the object is embedded into your CorelDRAW drawing.

Editing an Embedded Object

You can move and resize an embedded object within a CorelDRAW drawing. These operations do not change the fundamental object, they just affect the way CorelDRAW acts on the object.

Also, from within CorelDRAW, you can use the application in which you created the object to perform other editing operations. The following steps apply specifically to an object created in CorelPHOTO-PAINT. Objects created in other applications may require slightly different procedures.

1. Within CorelDRAW, select the embedded object.
2. Select **Edit ➤ Edit CorelPHOTO-PAINT! Picture**.
3. Wait until you see the object you have embedded into CorelDRAW displayed in the CorelPHOTO-PAINT window.
4. Make changes to the object using CorelPHOTO-PAINT tools.
5. In the CorelPHOTO-PAINT File menu, choose **Update CorelDRAW!**.
6. Again in the CorelPHOTO-PAINT File menu, choose **Exit & Return to CorelDRAW!**.

• **NOTES** With these steps, your changes affect only the object embedded in CorelDRAW, not the original object in CorelPHOTO-PAINT. Also, if you use CorelPHOTO-PAINT to make changes directly to the original object, the object embedded in your

CorelDRAW drawing is not affected. Contrast this with what happens with linked objects, where the changes to the original object do affect the linked copy.

Linking Objects into a CorelDRAW File

You can link an object created in another application into a CorelDRAW drawing. The exact procedure varies slightly from application to application. The following steps assume you are linking an object created in CorelPHOTO-PAINT. If you use a different application to create the object, consult its documentation for precise information about linking.

1. Create and save an object in CorelPHOTO-PAINT.
2. If necessary, open the CorelPHOTO-PAINT file that contains the object you want to link into your CorelDRAW drawing.
3. Use the CorelPHOTO-PAINT **Box Selection** tool (or another tool) to select the object you wish to link.
4. In the CorelPHOTO-PAINT Edit menu, choose **Copy** to copy the object into the Clipboard.
5. If you wish, you can now minimize or close CorelPHOTO-PAINT.
6. Open CorelDRAW.
7. Select **Edit ➤ Paste Special**.
8. In the Paste Special dialog box, select **CorelPhoto-Paint! Picture**.
9. In the Paste Special dialog box, click **Paste Link**.

Now the object is displayed as part of your CorelDRAW drawing.

Editing a Linked Object

You can move and resize an object linked into a CorelDRAW drawing. These operations do not affect the fundamental object, just the way CorelDRAW acts on it.

Also, from within CorelDRAW, you can use the application in which you created the object to perform other editing operations. The following steps apply specifically to an object created in CorelPHOTO-PAINT. Objects created in other applications may require slightly different procedures.

1. Within CorelDRAW, select the linked object.
2. Select **Edit ➤ Edit CorelPHOTO-PAINT! Picture**.
3. Wait until you see the object you have embedded into CorelDRAW displayed in the CorelPHOTO-PAINT window.
4. Make changes to the object using CorelPHOTO-PAINT tools.
5. In the CorelPHOTO-PAINT File menu, choose **Save** to save the changes to a file.
6. In the CorelPHOTO-PAINT File menu, choose **Exit**.
7. If necessary, update your CorelDRAW drawing. See "Automatic and Manual Updating" below.

• **NOTES** With these steps, your changes affect the object in CorelPHOTO-PAINT. Moreover, if you linked the object to other CorelDRAW files or to files in another application, the changes you make here will affect those files as well. Also, if you use CorelPHOTO-PAINT to make changes directly to the original object, your changes will affect not just your CorelDRAW drawing, but any other CorelDRAW drawings or other application files to which the CorelPAINT object is linked. By contrast, with enbedded objects, changes made to the original object do not affect the embedded one.

Automatic and Manual Link Updating

When you enable the automatic update feature for the link between your CorelDRAW file and the linked file, changes you make to the linked file are immediately visible in the CorelDRAW drawing. With manual update enabled, you must manually update your CorelDRAW drawing after you make changes to the linked file. To change a link from manual to automatic, or from automatic to manual:

1. Use the **Pick** tool to select the object in your CorelDRAW drawing for which you want to change the updating method.
2. Select **Edit ➤ Links**.
3. In the Link Properties dialog box, click **Automatic** or **Manual**.

• **NOTES** Changing from manual to automatic update does not affect previously made changes to the linked object.

Manually Updating a Link

If manual update is enabled for the link between your CorelDRAW drawing and the linked object, you must do a manual update to apply the changes made to the linked object to the version that appears in your drawing.

1. Use the **Pick** tool to select the object in your CorelDRAW drawing that you want to update manually.
2. Select **Edit ➤ Links**.
3. If necessary, in the Link Properties dialog box, select the link you want to update.
4. In the Link Properties dialog box, click **Update Now**.

Manually Updating All Links

To manually update all links to a file:

1. Select **Edit ➤ Select All**.
2. Select **Edit ➤ Links**.
3. In the Link Properties dialog box, click **Update Now**.

Canceling a Link

When you cancel a link to an object, the object remains in your CorelDRAW drawing in the form it was when you last updated it, but there is no longer any link to the application in which the object was created. The effect is the same as if you had copied the object to the Clipboard and then pasted it into your drawing. To cancel a link:

1. Use the **Pick** tool to select the object in your CorelDRAW drawing for which you want to cancel the link.
2. Select **Edit ➤ Links**.
3. If necessary, in the Link Properties dialog box, select the link you want to cancel.
4. In the Link Properties dialog box, click **Cancel**.

Link Changing and Updating

When you link an object to a CorelDRAW drawing, you establish a link between your CorelDRAW file and an object created in another application. Your CorelDRAW file accesses the object by way of this link. You should leave the linked object in place on disk so that CorelDRAW can access it. If you move the object to another directory, you must update the link. Use the steps below to do this. You can use the same steps to replace one linked object in your drawing with another.

1. Use the **Pick** tool to select the object in your CorelDRAW drawing for which you want to change or update the link.
2. Select **Edit ➤ Links**.
3. If necessary, in the Link Properties dialog box, select the link you want to change.
4. In the Link Properties dialog box, click **Change Link**.
5. In the Change Link dialog box, select the file you want to link instead of the existing one.
6. Click **OK**.

EXPORTING OBJECTS

You can export CorelDRAW files in a variety of formats. CorelDRAW supports many file formats so that you can import your files into other applications, including word processors, desktop publishing programs, presentation programs, and other graphics programs. See Appendix A for a list of file formats supported by CorelDRAW.

You can either export to a file or, if you are going to use your drawing in another Windows application, you can export to the Clipboard.

Exporting Objects to a File

1. Use the **Pick** tool to select the objects you wish to export.
2. Select **File ➤ Export**.
3. In the Export dialog box, select an export format in the **List Files of Type** box.
4. In the **Directories** list box, select a destination disk and directory.
5. Indicate which file should receive the object by selecting a file name in the **File Name** list box or by typing a file name in the **File Name** text box. An extension is not necessary unless you want to use a non-standard extension.
6. If necessary, click the **Selected Only** check box to select it.
7. Click **OK**.
8. Open the target application and import the file into it. See the target application's documentation for detailed instructions.

• **NOTES** To export your entire drawing, omit steps 1 and 6. Alternatively, if certain objects in the drawing are selected, make sure the **Selected Only** check box is not checked. If you forget to remove the check mark, only the selected objects in the file are exported.

Exporting Objects by Way of the Clipboard

You can use the Clipboard to copy objects from one CorelDRAW drawing to another, from a CorelDRAW drawing to another Windows application, or from another Windows application to a CorelDRAW drawing.

To copy from one CorelDRAW drawing to another:

1. Select the object or objects you want to export.
2. Select **Edit ➤ Copy**.
3. Open the file into which you want to import the object.
4. **Select Edit ➤ Paste**.

• **NOTES** Use almost the same procedure to copy objects from one application to another. The only difference is that steps 1 and 2 apply to the application you are copying from, and steps 3 and 4 apply to the application to which you are copying.

If your object is too large for the Clipboard, you will see an error message. In this case you have to export the object as a file and subsequently import it into the other application.

Different Windows applications handle the Clipboard in different ways. Therefore, your CorelDRAW objects may look different in other applications. See the Reference section of CorelDRAW's on-line **Help** for information.

EXTRACTING AND MERGING BACK TEXT

You can edit artistic or paragraph text in a drawing by saving it as a text file, editing the text file with a word processor or text editor, and subsequently merging the edited text back into your drawing. Some, but not all, attributes of the original text are applied to the merged back text.

Extracting Text

You do not need to select the text you wish to extract because the procedure extracts all the text in your drawing.

1. Save your current drawing. This step is necessary because you must have the file in order to use the Merge Back command.
2. Select **Text ➤ Extract**.
3. In the **Extract** dialog box, either accept the file name for the extracted text that CorelDRAW proposes by clicking on **OK**, or type a new name and then click **OK.**

You can now minimize or close CorelDRAW and open a word processor or text editor such as Windows Notepad, open the file containing the extracted text, and edit it. Unless you specify otherwise, your text file will be kept in the CORELDRW\DRAW subdirectory.

Editing Extracted Text

It is very important that you change only the text, not the surrounding codes, in the text file. CorelDRAW needs the codes to identify the file from which the text was extracted and the position of the text in the file.

The text strings in the text file are shown in the reverse order to that in which you placed them into your drawing. Each text string starts with an identifying code and ends with the <CDR> delimiter.

Edit the text strings and save the file. If you use a word processor, make sure you save the file as a text file so that it does not include any word processing codes.

Merging Back Edited Text

1. Open CorelDRAW.
2. Open the drawing from which you extracted the text.
3. Select **Text ➤ Merge Back**.

4. If necessary, select the edited text file.
5. Click **OK**.

EXTRUDING OBJECTS

Extruding gives three-dimensional effects to objects. You can extrude objects to give them a perspective effect, or you can extrude them orthogonally. Figure I.3 shows the Extrude roll-up on the left, an orthogonal extrusion in the middle, and below it a perspective extrusion. See *Perspective* for information about making one-point and two-point perspective views of objects.

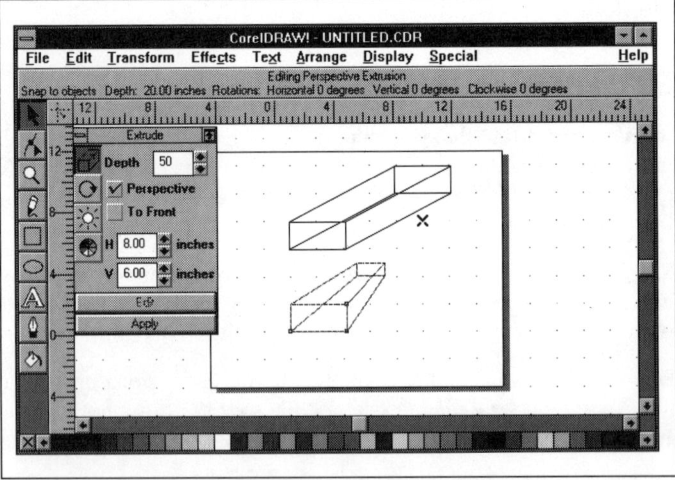

Figure I.3: The Extrude roll-up with depth enabled and an orthogonal extrusion (above) and a perspective extrusion (below) on-screen

Selecting Perspective and Orthogonal Extrusions

1. Click the **Perspective** check box to change between perspective and orthogonal extrusions. After you click, the changed extrusion is shown as a dashed outline.
2. Click **Apply** to make the change effective.

Starting an Extrusion

1. Use the **Pick** tool to select the object you wish to extrude.
2. Select **Effects ➤ Extrude Roll-Up**.
3. In the Extrude roll-up, click **Apply**.

The current extrusion settings are applied to the object.

Removing an Extrusion

1. Use the **Pick** tool to select the extruded object.
2. Select **Effects ➤ Clear Extrude**.

Changing the Extrusion Depth

The Depth option controls the depth of a perspective extrusion as a percentage of the distance between the object and its vanishing point. Depth does not affect orthogonal extrusions.

1. Click the **Depth** icon at the top-left of the Extrude roll-up.
2. Change the number to the right of the depth icon, either by clicking on the arrows by the side of the number or by typing a new number.
3. Click **Apply** to make the change effective.

Moving the Vanishing Point

The vanishing point is shown by an *X* on your drawing.

1. If necessary, click the **Depth** icon.

2. Either use the arrows by the side of the **H** value or type a new value to change the horizontal position of the vanishing point.
3. Use the arrows by the side of the **V** value or type a new value to change the vertical position of the vanishing point.

• **NOTES** You can also move the vanishing point interactively. To do so, point to the X on your drawing, press and hold down the mouse button while you drag the vanishing point to another position, and click **Apply** when you are satisfied with the new position.

Altering the Spacial Orientation of a Perspective Extrusion

You can rotate the extruded object in three-dimensional space by increments of five degrees.

1. Select the second icon from the top in the Extrude roll-up to display the **Extrude Rotator**, which is shown in Figure I.4.
2. Click on the arrows around the outside of the rotator to rotate the object about its horizontal axis.

Figure I.4: The Extrude roll-up with the Rotator, Light Source Direction, and Extrusion Coloring icons selected

3. Click on the horizontal arrows inside the rotator to rotate the object about its vertical axis.
4. Click on the vertical arrows inside the rotator to rotate the object along an axis perpendicular to your screen.
5. Click **Apply** to make the changes effective.

Altering the Spacial Orientation of an Orthogonal Extrusion

You can rotate the extruded object in three-dimensional space by increments of five degrees.

1. Select the second icon from the top in the Extrude roll-up to display the **Extrude Rotator** (see Figure I.4).
2. Click on the arrows around the outside of the rotator to rotate the extruded surface around the original object.
3. Click on the horizontal arrows inside the rotator to move the extruded surface horizontally.
4. Click on the vertical arrows inside the rotator to move the extruded surface vertically.
5. Click **Apply** to make the changes effective.

Lighting an Extruded Object

You can produce shading affects to simulate the appearance of an object being illuminated by a light source.

1. Select the third icon from the top in the Extrude roll-up to display the **Light Source Direction** icon (see Figure I.4).
2. If necessary, click the **Switch** icon to turn the light on.

The Extrude roll-up now contains a sphere inside a cubic wireframe. The sphere represents your object. The line intersections on the wireframe represent possible positions for the light source; and the *X* at one intersection shows the current position of the light source.

3. Click on one of the line intersections on the cube to position the light source. Notice the shading effect on the sphere.
4. Drag the marker on the **Intensity** bar to change the intensity of the light.
5. Click **Apply** to apply the light changes to your object.

Coloring an Extruded Object

You can control the color of surfaces on an extruded object.

1. Select the bottom of the four icons in the extrude roll-up to display the **Extrusion Coloring** icon (see Figure I.4).

    - If you want to apply the original surface fill to all surfaces of the extruded object, click **Use Object Fill**.
    - If you want to apply a different fill to the extruded surfaces, click **Solid Fill**. Then click on the flyout color box, and choose a color from the color matrix.
    - If you want to blend one color into another on the extruded surfaces, click **Shade**. Then click **From** to choose the color closest to the original surface, and **To** to choose the color remote from the original surface.

2. Click **Apply** to apply the color changes to your object.

Editing Extrusions

1. Use the **Pick** tool to select the object.
2. Select **Arrange ➤ Separate**.
3. Proceed with normal node editing. See *Shaping and Reshaping Objects*.

FILES

See Appendix A for a list of file types that you can import into CorelDRAW, and for the file types CorelDRAW can export.

Opening a New File

- To open a new file, select **File ➤ New**. CorelDRAW opens a new drawing page.

Opening an Existing File

1. Select **File ➤ Open**.
2. In the Open Drawing dialog box, select the directory where the file you want is stored.
3. If necessary, drop down the **List Files of Type** box and select the file type.
4. From the list of file names, select the one you want to open. If **Preview** is enabled (see below), you will see a miniature view of the selected file in the window at the right side of the Open Drawing dialog box.
5. Click **OK**.

At any time before you click OK, you can click the options button. This allows you to

- choose whether or not you want to preview drawings,
- display file names sorted by name or date,
- find a file by searching for keywords,
- use CorelMOSAIC to help you find a file,
- see any keywords or notes you have attached to files.

Saving a File with Its Existing File Name

- Select **File ➤ Save**.

• NOTES When you use this command to save a file you have already named, the file is saved immediately and the existing file with the same name is updated to include your new work. When you use the Save command with a file you have not named yet, it will act as a **Save As** command. (See below.)

Saving a File with a New Name

1. Select **File ➤ Save As**.
2. If necessary, in the Save Drawing dialog box, select the directory into which you want to save the file.
3. If necessary, drop down the **List Files of Type** box and choose the type of file you wish to save.
4. If necessary, in the **File Name** text box, type the file name. Do not type an extension unless you want it to be different from the extension CorelDRAW automatically supplies. The list box under the file name box shows the files already in the selected directory. If you have already named the file, that name appears in the **File Name** text box. Type another name if you wish to save the original file.
5. If you wish, add keywords and notes in the appropriate boxes.
6. If you wish, you can change the size of the image header. See the note below.
7. Click **OK**.

• NOTES The image header is a miniature representation of your drawing which is used when you open an existing file or when you search for files with CorelMOSAIC. The detail shown in these miniatures depends on the size of the image header. Increase the size of the image header if you need more detail, but remember that this increases the size of the drawing file.

If you try to save a file to a directory that already contains a file with the same name, CorelDRAW warns you that you are about to write over an existing file.

Closing Files

There is no Close command in the File menu. When you open a new or existing file, CorelDRAW automatically closes the current one. CorelDRAW warns you if you are about to close a file you haven't saved yet, and gives you the opportunity to save it before you close it.

Importing and Exporting Files

See *Importing Objects* and *Exporting Objects*.

Inserting Objects

See *Embedding and Linking Objects*.

Backup Files

CorelDRAW has two ways of creating backup files, Automatic and Normal.

- Automatic backups, by default, are made every ten minutes and are written as .ABK files in your CORELDRAW \AUTOBACK subdirectory.
- Normal backup files, by default, are made every time you save a file with the Save or Save As command and are written as .BAK files in the subdirectory in which you are currently saving files. These files are automatically deleted when you exit CorelDRAW.

• **NOTES** Both backup methods are controlled by entries in your CORELDRAW.INI file, so you can turn both forms of backup on or off. You can also change the time interval at which automatic backups occur and the directory into which .ABK files are written.

See "Specifying Backup File Creation Options" in the CorelDRAW online **Help** for information.

Opening a Backup File

1. Select **File ➤ Open**.
2. In the **File Name** text box, replace the .CDR extension with .ABK or .BAK.
3. Proceed with steps 2 through 5 under "Opening an Existing File" above.
4. After opening a backup file, save it with a .CDR extension.

• **NOTES** In step 2, you can specify several extensions. For example, to list all .CDR, .ABK, and .BAK files, the text box would contain ***.CDR,*.ABK,*BAK**. Note the commas that separate the terms.

Printing Files

See *Printing Drawings*.

Temporary Files

CorelDRAW creates temporary files while it is running. These files start with ~WAL and have the .TMP extension. Some of these files can be quite large, so you should make sure that you have several megabytes of free space on your hard disk before using CorelDRAW.

Under normal circumstances, CorelDRAW automatically erases all temporary files at the end of each session. However, if CorelDRAW terminates abnormally—for example when a power outage occurs—you may be left with temporary files on your disk. Check your hard disk from time to time and delete any unnecessary temporary files.

FILLING OBJECTS

You can fill closed objects with patterns, various shades of gray, or color. If you print on a PostScript-equipped printer, you can also fill with textures and halftone screens. This entry describes the various fills you can use.

Fills appear on your screen when you are working in Full-Color mode, but not when you are working in Wireframe mode. The status line tells you the current fill when a single object is selected, but not when more than one object is selected.

If you combine closed and open objects with the Combine command in the Arrange menu and subsequently fill the combined object,

- each closed object is filled as normal, and
- each open object is filled as if a straight line joined its ends.

You can fill objects either from the Fill flyout or from the Fill roll-up. The following explanations assume you are using the roll-up.

You can create your own fill patterns.

Removing the Fill from Objects

1. Select the object or objects from which you want to remove the fill.
2. Click the **Fill** tool to display the Fill roll-up, which is shown in Figure I.5.
3. Click the **X** icon in the fill flyout.

Filling Objects with Uniform Colors

1. Select the **Fill** tool to display the flyout.
2. Click the Fill roll-up icon to display the roll-up shown in Figure I.5.

3. To fill one or more objects with color, use the **Pick** tool to select the objects.
4. Click on a color in the Fill roll-up.

• **NOTES** If you do not select an object before you click on a color, a dialog box will appear with options for filling all objects, filling all text objects, or filling all objects other than text objects.

See *Color* for additional information about colors.

You can fill selected objects with color by clicking on the color palette at the bottom of the screen.

Filling Objects with a Two-Color Pattern

1. Select the **Fill** tool to display the fill flyout.
2. Click the **Fill** icon to display the roll-up.
3. Click the **Two-Color Pattern** icon, the third from the top, to display a sample fill pattern.
4. Click on the sample pattern to display a palette of available patterns.
5. Click on the pattern you want to use.
6. Click **OK** to select the pattern.

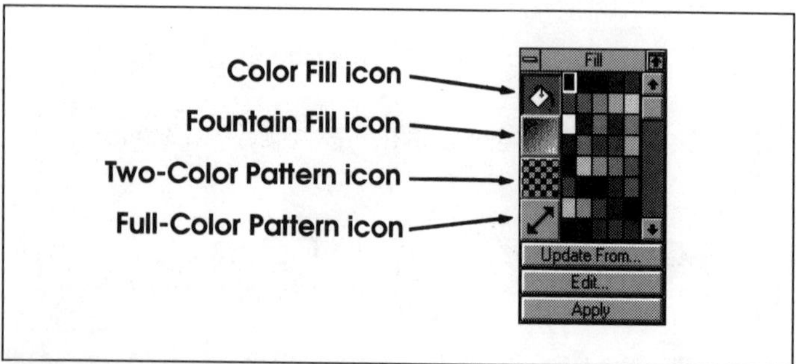

Figure I.5: The Fill roll-up

7. Skip to step 16 if you do not want to make any changes to the pattern.
8. To modify the pattern, click the **Edit** button to display the Two-Color Pattern dialog box, which is shown in Figure I.6.
9. Click the **Back** button to display a palette of background colors.
10. Click on the background color you want to use.
11. Click the **Front** button to display a palette of foreground colors.
12. Click on the foreground color you want to use.
13. Click the **Small**, **Medium**, or **Large** button to select a pattern size.
14. If you wish, click on the arrows by the parameter boxes to adjust the pattern. You can see the effect of the changing values in the sample pattern.
15. Click **OK** to return to the pull-up.
16. Click **Apply** to apply the pattern to the selected objects.

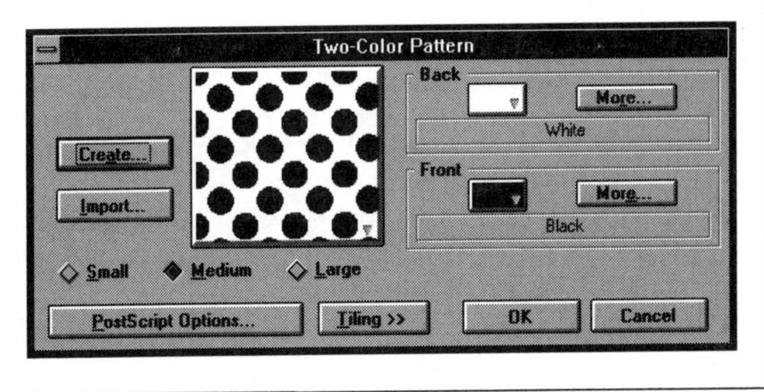

Figure I.6: The Two-Color Pattern dialog box

• NOTES To import patterns in any of the formats CorelDRAW supports, click the **Import** button in the Two-Color Pattern dialog box. This gives you an Import dialog box in which you can select a file.

To create your own patterns, click the **Create** button in the Two-Color Pattern dialog box. This brings up the Bitmap Pattern Editor dialog box. Point to cells and click the mouse button to create a pattern.

If you are using a PostScript-equipped printer, you can fill objects with halftone screens. Click the **PostScript Options** button in the Two-Color Pattern dialog box to access this capability.

Filling Objects with Full-Color Patterns

1. Select the **Fill** tool to display the fill flyout.
2. Click the **Fill** icon to display the Fill roll-up.
3. Click the **Full-Color Pattern** icon, the fourth from the top, to display a sample fill pattern.
4. Click on the sample pattern to display a palette of available patterns.
5. Click on the pattern you want to use.
6. Click **OK** to select the pattern.
7. Skip to step 12 if you do not want to make any changes to the pattern.
8. To modify the pattern, click the **Edit** button to display the Full-Color Pattern dialog box, which is shown in Figure I.7.
9. Click on the **Small**, **Medium**, or **Large** button to select a pattern size.
10. If you wish, click on the arrows by the parameter boxes to adjust the pattern. You can see the effect of the changing values in the sample pattern.
11. Click **OK** to return to the Fill roll-up.
12. Click **Apply** to apply the pattern to the selected objects.

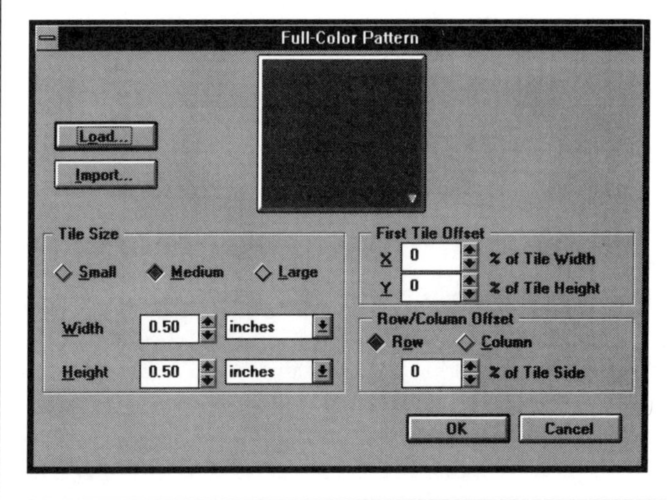

Figure I.7: The Full-Color Pattern dialog box

• **NOTES** To import patterns in any of the formats CorelDRAW supports, click the **Import** button in the Full-Color Pattern dialog box. This gives you an Import dialog box in which you can select a file.

To load patterns into the palette of available patterns, click the **Load** button in the Full-Color Patterns dialog box. This brings up a Load Full-Color Pattern dialog box in which you can select files to be loaded.

Filling Objects with Fountain Fills

1. Select the **Fill** tool to display the Fill flyout.
2. Click the **Fill** icon to display the Fill roll-up.
3. Click the **Fountain Fill** icon, the second from the top, to display a sample fountain fill.
4. Choose between a top-to-bottom or center-to-edge fountain by clicking on the appropriate button under the sample fountain fill.

5. Click the left color button to select the bottom (or edge) color from the flyout array of colors.
6. Click the right color button to select the top (or center) color from the flyout array of colors.
7. If you are satisfied with the fountain fill, skip to step 12.
8. To modify the fountain fill, click the **Edit** button in the pull-up to get the Fountain Fill dialog box, which is shown in Figure I.8.
9. If necessary, change the colors by clicking the **From** and **To** buttons. Alternatively, you can click the **More** buttons if you want to bring up a Fountain Fill dialog box with more colors. From this second dialog box you can also create custom colors. See *Color*.
10. If necessary, change the center offset (center-to-edge only), the angle (top-to-bottom only), and the edge pad.
11. Click **OK** to return to the pull-up.
12. Click **Apply** to apply the fountain fill to the selected objects.

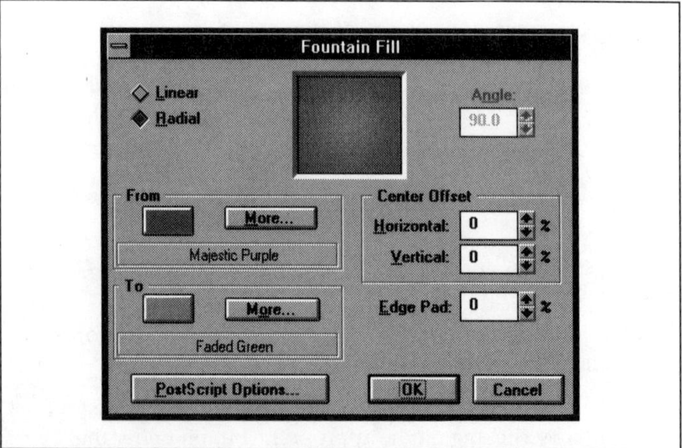

Figure I.8: The Fountain Fill dialog box

• **NOTES** If you are using a PostScript-equipped printer, you can fill your objects with fountain-fill halftone screens by clicking the **PostScript Options** button in the Fountain Fill dialog box.

Filling Objects with Gray

1. Select the **Fill** tool to display the fill flyout.
2. Click one of the seven squares in the bottom row of the flyout to fill the selected objects with white, black, or one of five shades of gray.

• **NOTES** You can fill selected objects with white, black, or a shade of gray by clicking on the color palette at the bottom of the screen.

An object on your screen filled with white appears the same as an object with no fill. However, an object filled with white is opaque and hides anything behind it, whereas an object with no fill is transparent. Another difference is that an object filled with white can be selected anywhere on the outline or within the object, whereas an object with no fill can only be selected on the outline.

Filling Objects with Textures

You can only fill objects with textures if you are using a PostScript-equipped printer.

1. Select the **Fill** tool to display the Fill flyout.
2. Click the **PS** icon to display the PostScript Texture screen, which is shown in Figure I.9.
3. Select a texture and its parameters.
4. Click **OK** to apply the texture to the selected objects.

• **NOTES** CorelDRAW allows you to select textures and shows them on your screen even if you are not using a PostScript-equipped printer. However, when you print the drawing, textures appear as shades of gray.

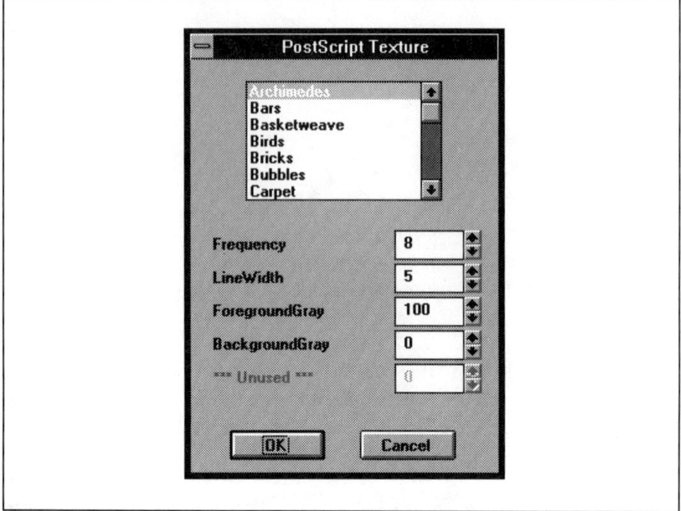

Figure I.9: The PostScript Texture dialog box

Copying Fills from One Object to Another

1. Use the **Pick** tool to select the object you want to fill.
2. Select the **Fill** tool to display the Fill flyout.
3. Click the **Fill** icon to display the Fill roll-up.
4. Click **Update From** in the roll-up.
5. Use the **From** arrow to point to the object with the fill you want to copy.
6. Click to copy the fill to the previously selected object.

• **NOTES** You can also copy fills using the **Copy Style From** command in the **Edit** menu.

FONTS

CorelDRAW is compatible with TrueType, Adobe Type 1, and WFN fonts. You can choose from the 153 fonts Corel provides as well as 103 more supplied on CD-ROM. You can purchase additional fonts, and you can use CorelDRAW to add special characters to existing fonts and to create your own complete fonts. You can use the fonts supplied with CorelDRAW in other Windows applications.

Choosing Fonts

See *Character Attributes* for information about choosing fonts for artistic and paragraph text.

Creating Custom Fonts

You can create fonts one character at a time using several methods. With CorelDRAW, you can

- modify characters in an existing font by converting them to curves and then using CorelDRAW to optimize them;
- use CorelDRAW to draw original characters; or
- use CorelTRACE to trace scanned drawings, and then optimize the characters with CorelDRAW.

For best results, follow these rules when you create custom forms:

- Work on each character in CorelDRAW at a size where the largest character almost fills an 8$^1/_2$ by 11-inch page.
- Make each character a single object or a combined (not grouped) object.
- Draw each character with no crossing lines. Corel recommends no intersections of any kind.
- Do not use any fill or outline color attributes and do not specify a line thickness.

• NOTES If you are modifying an existing font, make a copy and work with the copy, not the original. Then, if you make a mistake or subsequently want the existing font in its previous form, you will be safe.

Creating a Character

Proceed as follows to create a character:

1. Select **File ➤ Page Setup**.
2. In the Page Setup dialog box, select **Portrait** orientation, **Custom** page size, 750 **points** for the horizontal and vertical measurements, and click **OK**.
3. Select **Display ➤ Grid Setup.**
4. In the Grid Setup dialog box, set the horizontal and vertical grid origins to 30 **points**. This establishes a consistent base point for the characters you will create.
5. In the Grid Setup dialog box, set the horizontal and vertical grid frequency to 0.1 point.
6. Click **OK**.
7. If necessary, select **Display ➤ Show Rulers** to display the rulers. The displayed ruler units are in picas. (Twelve points equal 1 pica.)
8. Select **Display ➤ Guidelines Setup**.
9. Place a vertical guideline at 0.0 points and a horizontal guideline at 0.0 points. The horizontal guideline is the character's baseline. The vertical guideline is usually the leftmost edge of the character. You may want to add other horizontal guidelines to denote the height of lowercase characters (the x-height), the height of ascenders, or the depth of descenders. You could add other vertical guidelines to denote character width and other features.
10. Create the character. If you are modifying a character from an existing font, place it on the page and change its size to 720 points. If you are working from an original drawing, scale it to be consistent with other characters.

11. If you are modifying a character from an existing font, select **Arrange ➤ Convert To Curves**. If you are working from a scanned image, use CorelTRACE to trace it and then bring it into CorelDRAW.
12. Move the character so that it is aligned with the horizontal and vertical guidelines.
13. Use the **Shape** tool to modify and optimize the character. Make sure there are no crossing lines and that all objects are combined.
14. Before proceeding, print the character to verify your work.
15. Select **File ➤ Export**.
16. In the Export dialog box, open the **List Files of Type** list box.
17. Click either **Adobe Type 1 Font,*.PFB** or **TrueType Font,*.TTF**.
18. If necessary, select the directory where you wish to store the file.
19. Select the **File Name** text box and type a name for the file.
20. Click **OK**.
21. In the Adobe Type 1 Export dialog box, which is shown in Figure I.10, add or select the appropriate information. If you selected TrueType Font,*.TIF in step 17, you will get a similar dialog box. Initially, there is an insertion marker in the **Font Family Name** text box. Type a name for the family, and then press Tab.
22. Click one of the **Styles** buttons, and then press Tab.
23. If you are creating a non-standard character set with symbols that can be chosen from the CorelDRAW Symbols dialog box, click the **Symbol Font** check box to place an *X* in it. Do not place an *X* in this box if you are creating standard characters. Press Tab.
24. In the **Typeface Design Size** box, type the size at which you created the character. If you followed the preceding steps, type **720**. Press Tab.

25. Accept the suggested value for **Grid Size**, which is 512 for Adobe Type 1 fonts and 1000 for TrueType fonts. Press Tab.

26. Accept the suggested value for **Inter Word Spacing** to set the size of the space character. Press Tab.

27. Click the **Load Font Metrics** button to apply width and kerning information from an AFM file.

28. If necessary, select the appropriate **Character Number**. This should correspond to Windows 3.1 character numbers. See your Windows documentation.

29. If the **Auto Width** box is checked, the **Character Width** box is not available and the character width is set automatically by the original design, with an extra 5 percent to allow for inter-character spacing. If the **Auto Width** box is not checked, set the character width by typing a number in the **Character Width** box.

30. Click the **Delete Character** button if you want to delete the character from the font file.

31. Click the **Export Character** button to write the character to the file, or click the **Save Changes** button to return to your drawing.

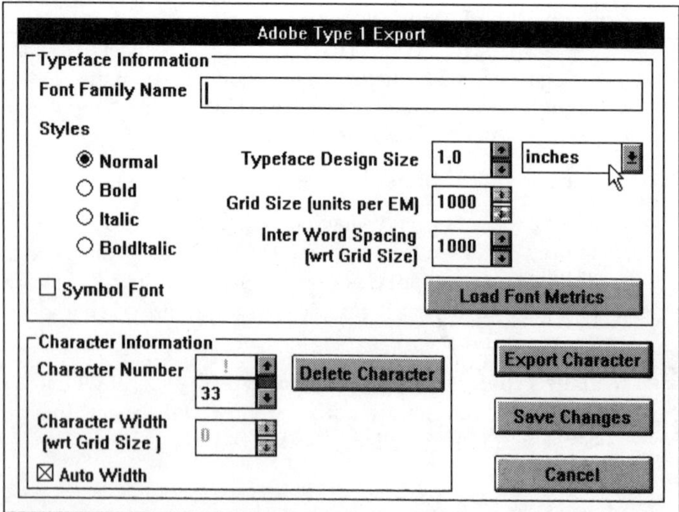

Figure I.10: The Adobe Type 1 Export dialog box

Using Custom Fonts

To use a custom TrueType font you have created:

1. In Windows, display the **Main** program group.
2. From the Main program group, select the **Control Panel**.
3. From the Control Panel, select **Fonts**.
4. In the Fonts dialog box, select **Add**.
5. In the Add Fonts dialog box, select the directory and enter the file name for your font.
6. Click **OK**.

To use a custom Adobe Type 1 font, follow the same steps, except select the **ATM Control Panel** in step 2.

Changing the Default Font

The default font is the one CorelDRAW uses in your drawings unless you choose a different one. Do the following to change the default font:

1. Exit from CorelDRAW.
2. In the Windows Program Manager window, choose Accessories. The **Accessories** window appears.
3. In the Accessories Window, choose **Notepad**. The Notepad window appears.
4. In the Notepad window, select **File ➤ Open**. The Open dialog box appears.
5. In the Open dialog box, select your CorelDRAW directory. Usually it is C:\CORELDRW\DRAW.
6. In the File Name text box, type **CORELDRW.INI**.
7. Click **OK**. The CORELDRW.INI file opens in the Notepad window.
8. Select **Search ➤ Find**. The Find dialog box appears.

9. In the Find What dialog box, type **DefaultFont**.
10. Click **Find Next** once. You see DefaultFont in the comments at the beginning of CORELDRW.INI.
11. Click **Find Next** once more. You see the line that defines the default font. If it has not been changed since CorelDRAW was installed, this line says

```
DefaultFont=Avalon,1,24
```

12. Delete the text to the right of the equals sign and replace it with a new font name, style, and size. See the notes below.
13. Select **File ➤ Save**.
14. Select **File ➤ Exit**.
15. Restart CorelDRAW.

• **NOTES** The default font is specified in the following format: <fontname>,<fontstyle>,<fontsize>. Font names are those you see in CorelDRAW's Character Attributes dialog box. Font styles are:

1	represents normal
2	represents bold
4	represents italic
8	represents bold italic

Some fonts are not available in all styles. The font size is stated in points in the range 0.7 through 1440.

Using Custom Symbols

See *Symbols*.

FORMATTING PARAGRAPH TEXT

You can control various attributes of all the paragraph text within a frame, including the spacing, horizontal alignment, and number of columns. You can also activate automatic hyphenation.

Establishing the Number of Columns

1. Use the **Pick** tool to select paragraph text.
2. Select **Text ➤ Frame** to display the Frame Attributes dialog box, which is shown in Figure I.11.
3. If necessary, open the **Units** list box and choose the measurement units you will use to define the gutter width and hyphenation zone.

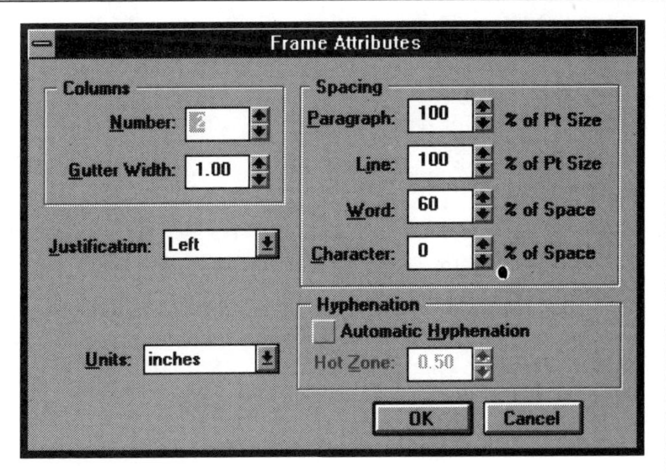

Figure I.11: The Frame Attributes dialog box

4. In the **Columns** box, select the number of columns and the gutter width. Gutter width is the space between columns.
5. Click **OK**.

Setting the Horizontal Alignment

1. After you've selected the paragraph text and chosen **Text ➤ Frame**..., pull down the **Justification** list box and choose the alignment.
2. Click **OK**.

• NOTES The procedure for aligning paragraph text within margins in the *Aligning and Shaping Text* entry has the same effect. See that entry for an explanation of the options.

Spacing Paragraph Text

1. After you have selected the paragraph text and chosen **Text ➤ Frame**..., use the arrows in the **Spacing** box, or type values, to select spacing parameters.
2. Click **OK**.

• NOTES Paragraph and line spacing are specified as percentages of point size. You can select zero or negative paragraph spacing to make paragraphs overlap, or zero line spacing to make lines overlap.

Word and character spacing are specified as percentages of the width of a space character. You can select zero word spacing to eliminate space between words. You can specify negative character spacing to bring characters closer together than normal.

Character spacing selected in this way affects all the characters in a paragraph. See *Kerning Text* for information about controlling the space between individual characters.

Automatic Hyphenation

CorelDRAW can automatically hyphenate paragraph text.

1. With some paragraph text selected, select **Text ➤ Frame**.

2. Click the **Hyphenation** box to turn hyphenation on.
3. Use the arrows in the **Hot Zone** text box, or type a value, to specify the hot zone. The hot zone measurement units are those selected in the Units box.
4. Click the **Automatic Hyphenation** check box to turn hyphenation on or off.

• **NOTES** A word that starts within the hot zone and is too long to fit within the right margin is wrapped to the next line. A word that starts to the left of the hot zone and is too long to fit within the right margin is automatically hyphenated, if possible.

GROUPING AND UNGROUPING OBJECTS

You can collect objects together to form a group. Then you can combine that group with other objects, or even with another group, to create a second level of grouping. You can proceed in this way to create up to ten levels of groups.

Grouping Objects

1. Use the **Pick** tool to select the objects you want to group. Alternatively, marquee-select the objects.
2. Select **Arrange ➤ Group**.

• **NOTES** See *Layering Drawings*.

Ungrouping Grouped Objects

1. Use the **Pick** tool to select the group.
2. Select **Arrange ➤ Ungroup**.

• NOTES When you ungroup groups of objects, the last group you made is ungrouped first, then the next to last, and so on.

There is a significant difference between grouping objects and combining objects. You group objects so that you can manipulate them as a single entity. You can combine lines and curves to create a single curve object. See *Combining Objects and Breaking Objects Apart*.

Also see *Layering Drawings*.

HALFTONE SCREENS

If you are using a PostScript-equipped printer, you can fill objects with halftone screens. See the explanation of filling objects with a two-color pattern under *Filling Objects*.

HELP

CorelDRAW has various Help facilities which are similar to those in many other Windows applications. You can access context-sensitive help, indexed help, and reference information.

There is a wealth of information in Help, some of which is not in the *User's Manual*. The following summarizes some of the more significant aspects of using Help. See your Windows documentation for more information.

To print help information displayed on your screen, select **File** in the CorelDRAW!–Help menu, and then click **Print Topic**.

To exit from help, select **File ➤ Exit**.

Context-Sensitive Help

There are two kinds of context-sensitive help. One is available when a dialog box is open or you have highlighted an item under one of the Main menu commands. To access this kind of help:

1. Open a dialog box or highlight an item under one of the Main menu commands.
2. Press **F1**. A help box appears with information relating to the dialog box or menu item.

The second kind of context-sensitive help is available when no dialog boxes are open and no menu items are highlighted.

1. Press **Shift-F1**. The cursor changes to an arrow with a question mark.
2. Point to the subject you want information about, such as a tool or a roll-up, and click. A help box appears with relevant information.

Help Menu

- Click **Help** in the menu bar. The Help menu allows you to choose **Contents**, **Using Help**, **Search for Keywords**, or **About CorelDRAW!**.

• NOTES If you choose **Contents**, you can select information about using help, the CorelDRAW screen, commands, tools, or the keyboard. You can also select a section of help about how to perform certain tasks, a glossary, and reference material.

Using Help provides information about using the help system.

Search for Keywords allows you to search for information by selecting or typing keywords. When you select this option, you get a Search dialog box. Choose from the list of keywords or type your own, and then click **Show Topics**. Choose from the list of topics, and then click **Go To** or double-click to display information on that topic.

About CorelDRAW! shows you the version of CorelDRAW you are using, together with the number of objects and groups in your current drawing and the amount of free space on your hard disk.

HIDING BITMAP OBJECTS

In Wireframe view, but not in Full-Color view, you can hide bitmap objects to reduce the time taken to redraw screens.

1. Select **Display** from the Main menu.
2. Click **Show Bitmaps** to switch between showing and hiding bitmaps.

• **NOTES** A check mark beside **Show Bitmaps** indicates that bitmaps will be shown on your screen. The absence of a check mark indicates that bitmaps will not be shown; their presence in the drawing is indicated by an empty box.

HYPHENATING TEXT

See the information about automatic hyphenation in the *Formatting Paragraph Text* entry.

IMPORTING OBJECTS

You can use the following methods to import objects into your drawing:

- Copy the object from another application into the Clipboard and then paste it into your drawing. See *Copying Objects*.
- Insert the object from another application by embedding or linking. See *Embedding and Linking Objects*.
- Use Mosaic to locate and then import an object. See "Using Mosaic to Import Objects" further down in this entry.
- Import the file through a CorelDRAW input filter. See "Installing Input Filters" and "Importing Objects from Other Applications" below.

For information about importing text, see *Creating Text*.

Installing Input Filters

You must have the appropriate input filters installed before you can import files. See the "Recommended formats for importing graphics from other applications" topic in online **Help** for information about the file formats you need to have installed.

If CorelDRAW was fully installed, all the filters will be available. If CorelDRAW was only partially installed, the filters you need may not be present. To verify which filters are present:

1. Select **File ➤ Import**.
2. In the Import dialog box, open the **List Files of Type** list box.
3. Scroll through the list of file types to verify that those you need are present.

If the filters you need are not present, do the following to install filters from your CorelDRAW distribution disks:

1. Minimize CorelDRAW and display the Windows Program Manager dialog box.
2. Select **File ➤ Run**.
3. Insert your CorelDRAW distribution disk 1 in a floppy disk drive.
4. Type either **A:SETUP** or **B:SETUP**, according to which disk drive you are using.
5. Click **OK**.
6. When the CorelDRAW! Setup dialog box appears, click **Continue**.
7. In the CorelDRAW! Installation Options dialog box, click **Custom Install**.
8. In the Set Destination Path dialog box, make sure the path is correct. If not, type the correct path.
9. Click **Continue**.
10. In the CorelDRAW! Custom Installation dialog box, click the **CorelDRAW! Some** button.
11. In the Installation Options for CorelDRAW! dialog box, click on each button except **Filters** so that only that one is checked.
12. Click **Continue**.
13. In the CorelDRAW! Custom Installation dialog box, click the **None** buttons for all applications except CorelDRAW.
14. Click **Continue**.
15. In the Set Program Manager Group dialog box, verify that the correct group is identified. If not, type the name of the correct group.
16. Click **Continue**.
17. In the CorelDRAW! dialog box, click **Install**.
18. Replace the CorelDRAW disk when requested to do so by a message on the screen.

19. When the CorelDRAW! Setup Exit dialog box appears, click **Continue**.
20. Maximize CorelDRAW.

Importing Objects from Other Applications

If you know the name and location of the file you want to import, you can import it directly. If you want to search for an image to import, use Mosaic to import files. See "Using Mosaic to Import Objects" below.

1. Select **File ➤ Import**.
2. In the Import dialog box, pull down the **List Files of Type** list box.
3. Select the type of file you want to import.
4. In the Directories list box, select the drive and directory that contains the file to be imported. A list of files of the type you specified appears in the **File Name** list box.
5. Select the required file name.
6. Click **OK**. After a few seconds, the object appears in your drawing.

Using Mosaic to Import Objects

With Mosaic you see a thumbnail image of an object before you import it.

1. Select **File ➤ Import**.
2. In the Import dialog box, click **Mosaic**.
3. In the CorelMosaic dialog box, select **File ➤ Open Directory**.
4. In the Open Directory dialog box, select the directory that contains the object you want to import. See the note below.
5. In the **List Files of Type** list box, select the type of file you want to import. See the note below. The names of all files

of the selected type in the directory are displayed in the **File Name** list box.

6. Click **OK**. Thumbnail images of all files in the selected directory will appear, provided those files have image headers, as shown in Figure I.12. See the note below.
7. Click the image you want to import into your drawing.
8. Select **Edit ➤ Import into Draw**. After a few moments Mosaic is minimized and the image you selected appears in your drawing.

• **NOTES** If you have installed all options and used the directory names supplied by CorelDRAW, you can find the supplied clip art images in subdirectories under C:\CORELDRW\DRAW\CLIPART. The clip art is in categories, each in a separate subdirectory. Each clip art object has a descriptive file name with a .CRD extension.

See the discussion of saving a file with a new name in the *Files* entry for information about image headers.

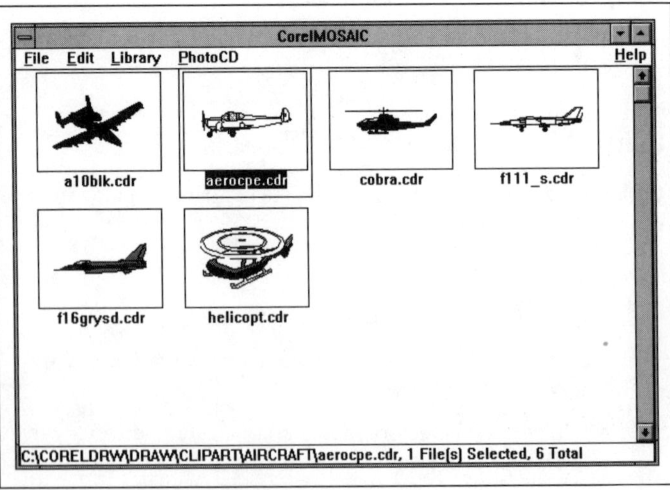

Figure I.12: Thumbnail images of clip art

Using Mosaic with Import Photo CD Images

CorelMOSAIC can open and export Kodak Photo CD images. To import Photo CD images into a drawing:

1. In the CorelMOSAIC Main Menu, select **PhotoCD ➤ Open Photo CD**. The Open Photo CD dialog box appears with OVERVIEW.PCD in the File Name text box.
2. Open the Drives list box and select the appropriate drive letter for your CD ROM drive.
3. Click **OK**. Thumbnails of images on the CD ROM appear.
4. Scroll if necessary and click the image you want to use.
5. Click **OK** to import the image into your drawing.

You can also use CorelMOSAIC to convert Kodak Photo CD images into BMP, EPS, PCX, and TIF formats. To do this, select **PhotoCD ➤ Export Photo CD Images**, select the images you want to convert, the format you want to convert them into, and the directory into which you want to write the converted files, and then click **OK**.

KERNING TEXT

Kerning is the process of adjusting the space between text characters to improve their appearance and legibility. You can adjust the spacing between all the characters in a paragraph from the Frame Attributes dialog box. See the discussion of spacing paragraph text in the *Formatting Paragraph Text* entry.

Changing Character Spacing in a Block of Text

1. Use the **Shape** tool to select artistic or paragraph text. Nodes appear next to each character, and spacing-control handles appear below the block, as shown in Figure I.13.

2. Point to the spacing-control handle at the right end of the block and press the mouse button.
3. Drag the spacing-control handle to the right to increase the spacing between all the characters, or to the left to decrease the spacing.

Changing Line Spacing in a Block of Text

1. Use the **Shape** tool to select artistic or paragraph text. Nodes appear next to each character, and spacing-control handles appear below the block, as shown in Figure I.13.
2. Point to the spacing-control handle at the left end of the block and press the mouse button.
3. Drag the spacing-control handle down to increase the spacing between all the lines, or up to decrease the spacing.

Figure I.13: A selected block of text with nodes and spacing-control handles

Changing the Spacing of Individual Characters

1. Make sure the snap-to grid, snap-to guidelines, and snap-to object are disabled.
2. Use the **Shape** tool to select artistic or paragraph text. Nodes appear next to each character, and spacing-control handles appear below the block.
3. Hold down the Ctrl key while you point to the node just to the left of a character.

4. Press the mouse button and drag the node horizontally to move the character to the left or right.
5. Release the mouse button and then release the Ctrl key.

Figure I.14 shows a word before kerning and, at the bottom, the same word after kerning.

• **NOTES** Having one or more of the snap options enabled may interfere with your ability to place characters exactly where you want. Usually, you should disable all snap options—the snap-to-grid, snap-to-guidelines, and snap-to-objects—before kerning.

While you move characters, constrain them on the baseline and avoid moving them vertically. If you accidentally move a character vertically, use the Align to Baseline command to restore its alignment. See *Aligning and Shaping Text* for further information.

If you want to move two or more characters at one time, select those characters.

You can also nudge characters. Use the **Shape** tool to select one or more character nodes, and press one of the cursor keys to move the character left, right, up, or down. The distance the character moves depends on the setting in the **Preferences** dialog box. See *Preferences*.

Figure I.14: A word before kerning (top) and after kerning (bottom)

LAYERING DRAWINGS

You can create your drawing on as many layers as you wish. Although you can simultaneously view and edit objects on any number of layers, you create objects on only one layer at a time. You can print any or all of the drawing layers.

Working with Layers

To access CorelDRAW's layering capabilities:

- Select **Arrange ➤ Layers Roll-Up**. The Layers roll-up appears, as shown in Figure I.15.

Selecting Layers

By default, a drawing has three layers:

- Layer 1, in which you initially create objects
- Guides, which contains guidelines
- Grid, which contains the grid

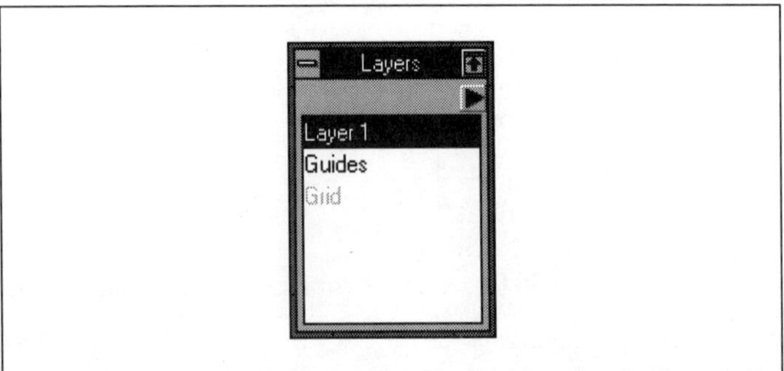

Figure I.15: The Layers roll-up with one layer for objects, one for guidelines, and one for the grid

To make a layer active:

1. Point to a layer in the **Layers** roll-up.
2. Click the mouse button.

• **NOTES** Guidelines exist in their own layer. You can hide this layer to remove and subsequently replace multiple guidelines. You can draw on and print this layer.

The grid exists in its own layer. You can hide this layer to remove and subsequently replace the grid on your screen. You cannot draw on this layer, but you can print it.

You can snap objects on any drawing layer to guidelines and to the grid.

Adding a Layer

1. Click the right-pointing arrow in the **Layers** roll-up. A flyout menu appears.
2. Click **New**.
3. In the Layer Options dialog box, click the four buttons as appropriate to make the layer visible or invisible, printable or not printable, locked or unlocked, or to have a color override or not. See the notes below.
4. If you want to name the layer, type a name in the text box.
5. Click **OK**.

• **NOTES** After you have added a layer, its name appears in the Layers roll-up.

If you make a layer visible, you can see it on your screen even if it is not selected as the active layer. Making a layer visible or invisible does not affect printing.

If you make a layer printable, it will be included when you print your drawing. Making a layer printable or not printable does not affect its visibility on the screen.

If you lock a layer you cannot subsequently select it. This prevents you from accidentally accessing that layer.

If you select **Color Override**, you can click on the color sample box to choose a color from an array of colors. Subsequently, all objects on that layer will appear as wireframes in the color you have chosen, even if you have are using the Full-Color display mode. This allows you to easily identify which objects are on each layer.

Editing a Layer's Attributes and Name

1. Click the right-pointing arrow in the **Layers** roll-up. A flyout menu appears.
2. Click **Edit**.
3. In the Layer Options dialog box, click the four buttons to select attributes and, if required, change the layer's name. See "Adding a Layer" above for information.

Deleting a Layer

1. Click the right-pointing arrow in the **Layers** roll-up. A flyout menu appears.
2. Click **Delete**.
3. In the CorelDRAW! dialog box, click **OK** if you wish to delete the layer and all objects on it. Otherwise, click **Cancel**.

Changing the Layer Stacking Order

Objects drawn in layers are stacked in the order shown in the Layers roll-up, the top layer in the list being the top layer in the stack. To change the stacking order in the drawing, you change the order in the list.

1. In the Layers roll-up, point to the name of the layer you want to move.
2. Press the mouse button and drag the name up or down to the layer that will be immediately below its new position on the list.
3. Release the mouse button.

• **NOTE** Refer to *Stacking Order* for additional information.

Activating and Deactivating Multilayering

Multilayering affects your ability to select and manipulate objects on inactive layers. When multilayering is active, you can select and manipulate objects on all layers. When multilayering is inactive, you can only select and manipulate objects on the active layer.

To activate or deactivate multilayering:

1. Click the arrow in the Layers roll-up.
2. Click **Multilayer** to change multilayering from active to inactive or vice-versa.

• **NOTES** Even when multilayering is inactive, you can still manipulate guidelines from another layer.

Copying and Moving Objects from One Layer to Another

1. Make sure multilayering is active. See "Activating and Deactivating Multilayering" above.
2. Use the **Pick** tool to select the object you want to copy or move.
3. Look at the status bar to see which layer the object is on. In the Layers roll-up, select that layer.
4. Click the arrow in the **Layers** roll-up.
5. In the flyout menu, click **CopyTo** or **MoveTo**.
6. Point with the arrow labeled " To" to the name of the layer on which you want to place the object, and click.

Combining and Grouping Objects on Different Layers

See *Combining Objects and Breaking Objects Apart* and *Grouping and Ungrouping Objects* for basic information. You can select objects in different layers for combining and grouping, provided multilayering is activated. When you select objects on different layers, all the combined or grouped objects move to the currently active layer. If you subsequently break apart or ungroup the objects, they will all remain on the layer in which you combined or grouped them.

• **NOTES** Group across layers to collect objects from various layers and move them all to a new layer.

When you combine objects, the combined object takes on the fill and outline attributes of the last object you selected.

LINKING OBJECTS

See *Embedding and Linking Objects*.

MAIN MENU BAR

The CorelDRAW Main menu bar provides access to nine individual menus. Refer to **Menus** in the CorelDRAW online **Help** for information about each menu and a general description of the items on it.

MARQUEE-SELECT

See *Selecting and Deselecting Objects* and *Shaping and Reshaping Objects*.

MASKS AND CLIPPING HOLES

You can create a transparent hole in a filled object and make anything behind the filled object visible.

Creating a Mask

The following steps create a circular hole in a filled rectangle. You can use these steps with other shapes.

1. Create a filled rectangle.
2. Create a circle, smaller than the rectangle, with no fill.
3. Move the circle on top of the rectangle.
4. Marquee-select both objects.
5. Select **Arrange ➤ Combine**. A circular hole appears in the rectangle. Now you have a mask.
6. Move the mask over another object.
7. If necessary, select the mask and then select **Arrange ➤ To Front**.
8. The object, or part of it, is visible through the mask.

• **NOTES** If you are going to print on a PostScript-equipped printer, your mask can have no more than about 125 nodes.

MIRRORING OBJECTS

You can flip graphic or text objects about their horizontal or vertical center lines to create mirror images.

Using the Mouse to Create a Mirror Image

1. Use the **Pick** tool to select the object.
2. Point to the handle at the center of the top, bottom, or side of the object's frame.
3. Drag horizontally across the object to beyond the opposite edge and release the mouse button.

• **NOTES** Hold down the Ctrl key while you drag to constrain the mirror image to an exact whole-number multiple of its original size. Release the Ctrl key after you have released the mouse button.

To retain the original object as well as create a mirror image, tap the + key on the numeric keypad before you release the mouse button.

Making Precise-Size Mirror Images

1. Use the **Pick** tool to select the object.
2. Select **Transform ➤ Stretch & Mirror**.
3. Select or type the percentage size of the horizontal or vertical mirror image relative to the original.
4. Click **Horizontal** or **Vertical**.
5. If you want to retain the original object, click **Leave Original**.
6. Click **OK**.

• **NOTES** When you select **Horizontal**, you flip the object on a horizontal surface about its vertical axis. When you select **Vertical**, you flip the object on a vertical surface about its horizontal axis.

MOVING OBJECTS

You can move an object to a different position on your screen by dragging it with your mouse, or you can move it with precision under keyboard control. See *Copying Objects* for information about moving objects between layers.

Moving an Object with the Mouse

1. Enable or disable snap-to options as appropriate. See *Alignment and Placement Aids.*
2. Use the **Pick** tool to select the object.
3. Point onto the object, and press and hold down the mouse button while you drag to a new position. A dashed rectangle shows the object's new position. The status line shows the distance you have moved the object.
4. Release the mouse button.

• **NOTES** To constrain the object and move it in a horizontal or vertical direction only, hold down the Ctrl key while you drag. Release the mouse button before you release the Ctrl key.

To move a copy of an object and leave the original in place, tap the + key on the numeric keypad before you release the mouse button.

Moving an Object a Specific Distance

1. Use the **Pick** tool to select the object.
2. Select **Transform ➤ Move**.
3. In the Move dialog box, make sure the **Absolute Coordinates** box is not checked.
4. Select the **Horizontal** and **Vertical** measurement units you want to use.
5. Select or type the **Horizontal** and **Vertical** distances you want to move the object. Positive values are up and to the right.
6. Leave the **Leave Original** box unchecked if you do not want to leave a copy of the original object in place; check the box if you do want to leave a copy of the original.
7. Click **OK**.

• NOTES You can also nudge an object to change its position by pressing the cursor keys. See *Preferences* for information about setting the nudge distance.

Moving an Object to a Specific Position

1. Make sure the rulers are displayed.
2. Use the **Pick** tool to select the object.
3. Select **Transform ➤ Move**.
4. In the Move dialog box, click the **Absolute Coordinates** box so that it is checked. A sample object frame appears. It has nine handles corresponding to the four corners of the frame, the four center points of the sides, and the center of the frame.
5. Click one of the nine handles to identify it as the point to be moved to the position you specify. The **Horizontal** and **Vertical** text boxes show the current position of the selected handle.
6. Select the **Horizontal** and **Vertical** measurement units you want to use.
7. Select or type the **Horizontal** and **Vertical** distances you want to move the object. Positive values are up and to the right on the screen.
8. Leave the **Leave Original** box unchecked if you do not want to leave a copy of the original object in place; check the box if you do want to leave a copy of the original.
9. Click **OK**.

NODES

To see an object's nodes, point onto it with the **Shape** tool and click. Figure I.16 shows nodes on typical objects. See *Shaping and Reshaping Objects*.

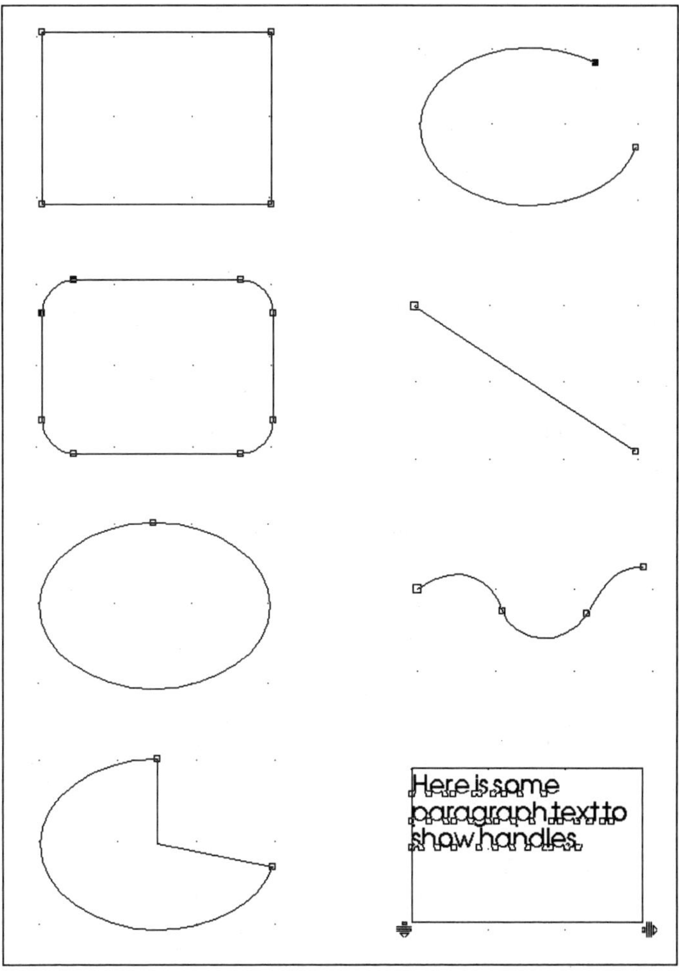

Figure I.16: Typical objects with their nodes revealed

NUDGING OBJECTS

You can nudge a selected object by tapping the cursor keys. See *Preferences* for information about setting the distance the object moves with each tap.

OUTLINING OBJECTS

You draw an object by creating an outline and, in the case of closed objects, filling it with a color, pattern, or texture. You can change the shapes of line endings and corners. You can also control the shape of the pen used to draw lines.

When you are working in Wireframe mode, you only see the outline as a thin, black line, but when you are in Full-Color mode you see the outline with thickness, color, and style, and you see the fill as well. See *Display Modes*.

Creating an Outline

See *Drawing Objects* for information about creating outlines.

Changing Line Thickness

There are three ways to select a line thickness:

- from the Outline tool flyout,
- from the Pen roll-up, or
- from the Outline Pen dialog box.

To use the Outline tool menu:

1. Use the **Pick** tool to select the object.
2. Select the **Outline** tool.

3. In the Outline tool flyout, click on the thickness you want. You can choose among ¼-, 2-, 8-, 16-, or 24-point thicknesses.

To use the Pen roll-up:

1. Use the **Pick** tool to select the object.
2. Select the **Outline** tool.
3. In the Outline tool flyout, click the **Outline Pen roll-up icon** (the second from the left on the top row).
4. Click the arrows next to the **Thickness** sample box to change the line thickness. Each click changes the thickness by 0.001 inch.
5. Click **Apply**.

To use the Outline Pen dialog box:

1. Use the **Pick** tool to select the object.
2. Select the **Outline** tool.
3. In the Outline tool flyout, click the **pen** icon (the leftmost icon in the top row).
4. In the Outline Pen dialog box, the **Width** text box shows the current line width. Change the width by clicking on the arrows next to the text box or by typing a width value.
5. Click **OK**.

Changing Line Color

See *Color* for information about choosing and applying colors to an outline.

Changing Line Style

CorelDRAW offers a variety of dashed and dotted line styles. You can choose them from either the Pen roll-up or the Outline Pen dialog box. You can also create custom line styles. To choose a line style from the Pen roll-up:

1. Select the object and display the Pen roll-up or the Outline Pen dialog box, as described under "Changing Line Thickness" above.
2. In either case, click the **Style** sample box to display a list box with the available line styles.
3. Scroll if necessary to show the style you want, and click on it.
4. Click **Apply** in the roll-up, or click **OK** in the dialog box.

• **NOTES** Refer to "CorelDRW.DOT File" in CorelDRAW online **Help** for information about creating your own line styles.

Changing Line-Ending Shape

You can select butt, round, or square line endings.

1. Select the object and display the Outline Pen dialog box, as described under "Changing Line Thickness" above.
2. Click one of the **Line Caps** buttons to select a shape.
3. Click **OK**.

Adding Arrowheads to Lines

1. Select the object and display the Outline Pen dialog box, as described under "Changing Line Thickness" above.
2. Click one of the arrow boxes under **Arrows** to display an arrow list box.
3. Click the arrowhead you want to use. It appears in the arrow box.

4. If necessary, click the second arrow box and choose an arrowhead.

5. Click **OK**.

• **NOTES** You can also use the Pen flyout to select arrowheads. Arrowheads are automatically created at a size proportional to line thickness. If you have a thin line and are displaying it without magnification, the arrowhead will probably be invisible. To see the arrowhead, magnify the screen image or make the line thicker. You can control the arrowhead size independently of the line width by using the arrowhead editor. See "Editing an Arrowhead or Line Ending Shape" in the CorelDRAW online Help system.

In the Outline Pen dialog box, the left arrowhead sample box illustrates the arrowhead at the beginning of the line, which is not necessarily the left end of the line. If you draw a line from right to left, the arrowhead you choose in the left sample box will appear at the right end of the line; even though the sample box shows it pointing to the left, it will point to the right on the line.

To create a new arrowhead, draw it as a normal object, select **Special ➤ Create Arrow**, and click **OK** in the Create Arrow dialog box. You can have up to one hundred arrowheads, including those supplied with CorelDRAW.

Changing Corner Styles

You can select miter, round, or bevel corners.

1. Select the object and display the Outline Pen dialog box, as described under "Changing Line Thickness" above.

2. Click one of the buttons under **Corners** to select a corner style.

3. Click **OK**.

• **NOTES** CorelDRAW squares a corner when two lines meet at less than a specified miter angle. See *Preferences* for information about specifying the miter angle.

Changing Pen Shapes

By default, CorelDRAW creates outlines with a square pen so that horizontal and vertical lines have the same width. You can change the pen size and shape to get a calligraphic effect.

1. Select the object and display the Outline Pen dialog box, as described under "Changing Line Thickness" above.
2. Click one of the arrows by the **Stretch** text box under **Calligraphy** to change the pen from a square to a rectangle, or type a percentage value that represents the width-to-height proportion.
3. Click one of the arrows by the **Angle** text box under **Calligraphy** to change the angle of the pen, or type a value for the angle.
4. Click **OK** to apply the new pen shape to the selected object.

• **NOTES** Be prepared to experiment to see the effect of various pen shapes.

To restore the default pen shape, click **Default** in the Calligraphy box.

Copying an Outline

To copy the attributes of an outline to another object:

1. Use the **Pick** tool to select the object with the outline you want to change.
2. Select **Edit ➤ Copy Style From**. In the Copy Style dialog box, click the **Outline Pen** button if you wish to copy the pen attributes with the exception of color.
4. In the Copy Style dialog box, click the **Outline Color** button if you wish to copy the pen color.
5. Click **OK**.
6. Point with the **From** arrow to the outline you want to copy.

Removing an Object's Outline

You can remove an outline from an object's displayed and printed image. When you do this, you are actually making the outline width zero. The outline is still there and can be filled.

1. Select the object and display the Outline Tool flyout, as described under "Changing Line Thickness" above.
2. Click **X**.

• **NOTES** If the object you select is not filled, or is filled with the background color, you will not see it in Full-Color mode after you remove its outline.

You can restore the outline so you can see it in Full-Color mode.by changing to Wireframe mode, selecting the object, and selecting a non-zero width.

PAGE SETUP

The Page Setup command lets you establish your page size, orientation, and background color. You can also add a printable background pattern or texture to your page.

Setting the Page Size, Orientation, and Background Color

1. Select **File ➤ Page Setup**.
2. Click the **Portrait** or **Landscape** button. Note that this affects only the displayed page. You must set the printer orientation separately. See *Printing Drawings*.
3. Click one of the **Page Size** buttons.
4. If you click the **Custom** button, select the Horizontal and Vertical dimensions, together with their measurement

units. If you click any other size button, the page dimensions are set automatically.

5. Click the **Paper Color** button.
6. Click a color in the Paper Color dialog box to select a background color. You can also select a color palette and select a color by name. See *Color*.
7. Click **OK** to leave the Paper Color dialog box.
8. Click **OK** to leave the Page Setup dialog box.

Adding a Background to a Page

You can use a pattern, texture, fountain fill, or another object as a page background.

1. Select **File ➤ Page Setup**.
2. Click the **Add Frame Page** button.
3. Click **OK**.

This draws a rectangle the same size as the page and places it behind all objects on the screen. You can fill the rectangle the same way you fill any other object. See *Filling Objects*.

PERSPECTIVE

You can create one-point and two-point perspective views of an object. Figure I.17 shows a rectangle containing text before perspective is applied, with one-point perspective, and with two-point perspective. These perspective views are different from those made as a perspective extrusion of an object. See *Extruding Objects*.

Creating a One-Point Perspective

See the Glossary in online **Help** for information about one-point and two-point perspective.

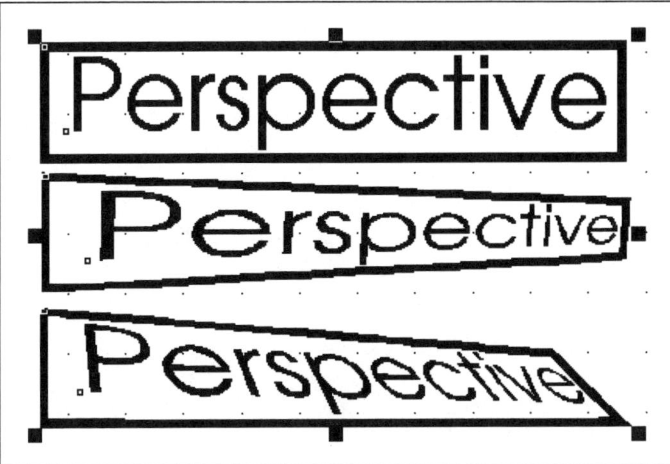

Figure I.17: The same object without perspective (top), with one-point perspective (middle), and with two-point perspective (bottom)

1. Draw an object.
2. If necessary, use the **Pick** tool to select the object.
3. Select **Effects ➤ Edit Perspective**. The object is outlined with a rectangular dashed frame with handles at each corner, and the cursor changes to a larger arrowhead.
4. Point onto one of the handles and the cursor changes to a cross.
5. While holding down the Ctrl key, press the mouse button and drag the handle vertically or horizontally. An *X* shows the position of the vanishing point.
6. Release the mouse button.

Creating a Two-Point Perspective

1. Follow step 1 through 4 of "Creating a One-Point Perspective" above.

2. Without pressing the Ctrl key, press the mouse button and drag the handle diagonally. An *X* at the left or right of the object represents the horizontal vanishing point. An *X* above or below the object represents the vertical vanishing point.
3. Release the mouse button.

• **NOTES** If you hold down the Shift key while you drag, the opposite handle of the object moves the same distance, but in the opposite direction.

After you have added perspective to an object, you might need to restore a rectangular frame so that you can perform additional transformations. Do this by selecting the object and then selecting **Effects ➤ Add New Perspective**.

Moving a Vanishing Point

1. Use the **Pick** tool to select the object.
2. Select **Effects ➤ Edit Perspective**.
3. Point onto a vanishing point. The cursor changes to a cross.
4. Press and hold down the mouse button while you drag the vanishing point to a new position.

Copying an Object's Perspective

1. Use the **Pick** tool to select the object to which you want to apply perspective.
2. Select **Effects ➤ Copy Perspective From**.
3. Point with the **From** arrow onto the object from which you want to copy perspective.
4. Click the mouse button.

Clearing an Object's Perspective

1. Use the **Pick** tool to select the object from which you want to clear perspective.
2. Select **Effects ➤ Clear Perspective**.

PLACING OBJECTS

See *Aligning and Shaping Text* and *Alignment and Placement Aids.*

PREFERENCES

You can alter many of the ways in which CorelDRAW works. Do this by changing values and making choices in the Preferences dialog box, and changing, adding, or deleting entries in the CORELDRW.INI file. You can also add files that in some cases enhance the performance of your monitor and printer.

Setting Preferences

1. Select **Special ➤ Preferences**.
2. Select or type new values for the duplicate placement distance, the nudge distance, the Constrain angle, and the miter limit.
3. Click buttons to enable or disable Auto-Panning, the crosshair cursor, and the interruptible display feature.
4. Click the **Curves** button to display the Preferences–Curves dialog box. Here, you can set preferences for freehand tracking, autotrace tracking, the corner threshold, the straight line threshold, and AutoJoin. Then click **OK** to return to the Preferences menu.

5. Click the **Display** button to display the Preferences–Display dialog box. Here, you can set the preview fountain stripes value, the point size below which text is greeked, the way colors are shown on your screen, the flatness of curves, and whether or not the page border is shown on your screen. Then click **OK** to return to the Preferences menu.
6. Click the **Mouse** button to display the Preferences–Mouse dialog box. Here, you can assign functions to the right mouse button. Then click **OK** to return to the Preferences menu.
7. Click **OK** to retain your new preferences.

• **NOTES** CorelDRAW online **Help** provides extensive information on the many preference choices available. Access Help information by displaying the appropriate preferences dialog box and pressing Shift-F1.

Enhancing Monitor and Printer Performance

Corel provides some files that enhance the performance of some monitors and printers. For information about these files:

1. Press **F1** to display the CorelDRAW!–Help dialog box.
2. Click **Reference** to see a list of reference topics.
3. Click **Hardware-related Information** to see a list of topics.
4. Click ***.PAN Files** to see a list of the enhancement files provided and get information about their use.

PRINTING DRAWINGS

CorelDRAW can print a drawing on any Windows-supported printer. It uses the same commands as many other Windows applications. Refer to your Windows documentation for information about installing printers and printing files.

Printer Setup

Check, and if necessary modify, the Print Setup dialog box before printing a drawing.

1. Select **File ➤ Print Setup** to display the Print Setup dialog box.
2. In the Printer box, verify that the correct printer is selected. If necessary, choose the printer you want to use.
3. In the Orientation box, click the **Portrait** or **Landscape** button to correspond with the page orientation. See the section about setting the page size, orientation, and color in the *Page Setup* entry.
4. In the **Paper** box, select the paper size and source.
5. Click the **Options** button to display the Options dialog box.
6. Modify the options as necessary. See your Windows documentation for information about the options.
7. Click **OK** to return to the Print Setup dialog box.
8. Click **OK** to make your printer setup information effective.

• **NOTES** The information here relates specifically to a LaserJet printer. The dialog boxes you see if you are using another printer may be somewhat different. For example, if you are using a PostScript-equipped printer, the Options dialog box offers you an **Advanced** button. Click this button to specify several PostScript-related parameters.

Printing a Drawing on a Non-PostScript Printer

1. Select **File ➤ Print**.
2. In the Print Options (Non-PostScript) dialog box, click buttons to enable the appropriate options (see below).
3. Click **OK**.

By clicking buttons, you can select the following options in the Print Options dialog box:

OPTION	EFFECT
Selected Objects Only	Prints only those objects on the drawing that you have selected. Otherwise, prints all objects on the drawing.
Fit To Page	Reduces the drawing to page-size. Check this box if your drawing is larger than the size of paper your printer can use.
Tile	Prints the drawing at full size, using as many tiles as are required to print it all. Check this box if your drawing is larger than the size of the paper your printer can use.
Scale	Enlarges or reduces your drawing by a percentage size you select or type in the adjacent text box.
Fountain Stripes	Specifies the numbers of stripes used to print and display fountain fills. You specify the number by selecting or typing a value in the adjacent text box. A low number makes the fountain fills course, but speeds printing and displaying. A high number enhances the appearance of the fountain fills, but shows printing and display. You may want to experiment with this parameter to achieve satisfactory performance. You can also set this number as a preference. See *Preferences.*
Copies	Determines the number of copies you want to print. You select or type the number in the adjacent text box.

OPTION	EFFECT
Destination	Confirms the printer you have selected in **Print Setup**. It also gives you the opportunity to print to file (see "Printing a Drawing to a File" below) and to access the Print Setup dialog box.

Printing a Drawing on a PostScript Printer

Printing a drawing on a PostScript-equipped printer is similar to the procedure described above in "Printing a Drawing on a Non-PostScript Printer," but more options are available. The additional options are:

OPTION	EFFECT
Print As Separations	Prints process-color or spot-color separations. When you click this button, the following three options—**Crop Marks and Crosshairs**, **Film Negative**, and **Print File Info**—are automatically enabled. You may disable any of them by separately clicking their buttons.
Crop Marks and Crosshairs	Prints crop marks and crosshairs automatically, provided the page size is smaller than the paper size.
Film Negative	Prints the drawing as a negative suitable for use on a phototypesetter that images directly onto film.
Print File Info	Prints the file name and the current date and time outside the page area, provided the page size is smaller than the paper size. When you print color separations, each component of the separation is identified.

OPTION	EFFECT
Within Page	Causes the file information to be printed inside the left margin of the drawing. To enable this option, you must have selected **Print File Info**. **Within Page** allows you to print the information even if the drawing area fills the entire page.
All Fonts Resident	Prints all text in your drawing with fonts resident in the printer, rather than with CorelDRAW fonts.
Set Flatness To	Allows you to increase the flatness value in order to simplify drawings that are too complex to print. You can select or type a flatness value into the text box. You can also set the flatness value in the CORELDRW.INI file. See *Preferences*. You may want to temporarily increase the flatness value in order to reduce the time taken to print proofs of your drawings.
Auto Increase	Increases the flatness value automatically until the drawing can be printed.
Default Screen Frequency	Prints halftone screens at your printer's default screen frequency.
Custom Screen Frequency	Lets you select or enter a specific halftone screen frequency.
For MAC	Writes a Macintosh-compatible file. To enable this option you must have checked **Print To File**.

Printing a Drawing to a File

Instead of using the printer connected to your computer, you can print your drawing to a file, transfer the file to another computer, and then print the file on a printer or other output device connected to that computer. To do this:

1. Use **Print Setup**... to specify the printer on which the drawing will eventually be printed. This printer does not have to be connected physically to your computer. See "Printer Setup" above.
2. Select **File ➤ Print**.
3. In the Print Options (Non-PostScript) or Print Options (PostScript) dialog box, click the **Print To File** button. Click any other appropriate option buttons.
4. Click **OK**.
5. In the Print To File dialog box, select the directory into which the file will be written, and choose or type a file name.
6. Click **OK**.
7. In the next dialog box, which has the name of the destination printer as a title, select or type appropriate responses.
8. Click **OK**.

• **NOTES** Consult the documentation for the target printer for details about the responses you should make in step 7.

Printing Directly from Windows

After you have printed your drawing to a file, you can print it using any computer that is running Windows 3.1 or later, even if CorelDRAW is not installed on that computer.

1. In the Windows Program Manager window, select **Main**.
2. In the Main window, select **Print Manager**.
3. Minimize the **Print Manager**.
4. In the Main window, select **File Manager**.
5. Select the directory that contains a CorelDRAW drawing file.
6. Point to the file name, press the mouse button, and drag the icon onto the **Print Manager** icon.

7. Release the mouse button.
8. Select the appropriate printing options and click **OK**.

Merge Printing

Merge printing allows you to replace text in your drawing with text from a text editor or word processor. You could merge print, for example, to print multiple copies of certificates or diplomas in which the names and other information differ from one copy to another.

Merged text has the same attributes and transformations as the text it replaces, unless the original text has been extruded or fitted to a path. However, the attributes of individual characters are not always transferred to the merged text.

In the following procedure, the original text in the drawing is called a "label"—it is the name of an item of text. Corel refers to the label as "primary text." Text to be merged into the drawing as replacements for labels is referred to as "secondary text."

Do the following to prepare the drawing into which text will be merged:

1. Prepare a CorelDRAW drawing as you normally would, except for the labels.
2. Create labels in each position where you want to merge secondary text. Each label must be a separate object and must be unique. Create the labels with the attributes you want for the merged text.
3. Optionally, print your drawing so that you can refer to the labels.
4. Save your drawing.

Do the following to prepare the merge document that contains the secondary text to be merged into the drawing:

1. Open a text editor or word processor.
2. On the first line, type the number of labels in your drawing.

3. On the second line, type a backslash (\), followed by the first label, and then another backslash. The text here must be exactly the same as the label in the drawing. See the note below.
4. On the next line, type the next label preceded and followed by a backslash.
5. Repeat step 4 until you have typed all the labels.
6. On the next line, type a backslash, the text that will replace the first label on the first printed drawing, and another backslash.
7. Repeat step 6 until you have typed text that corresponds to each label on the first printed drawing.
8. Repeat steps 6 and 7 to type the text that replaces labels on another printed version of your drawing.
9. Repeat step 8 for each drawing you want to print. You can have secondary text for as many printed drawings as you wish.
10. Save your secondary text as an ASCII file with a .TXT extension.

• **NOTES** The Corel documentation uses the term "primary text" where this book uses "label."

Labels in the merge document must be exactly the same as those in the drawing. Specifically, capitalization and line breaks must be the same. Also, there must be no spaces between the two backslashes other than those in the labels on the drawing.

Each set of secondary text must contain text to replace every label. If there is no text to replace a label, use two backslashes to represent an empty text string.

Printing a Merged Drawing

To print a merged drawing:

1. In CorelDRAW, open the drawing with which you want to merge text.

2. Select **File ➤ Print Merge**.
3. In the Print Merge dialog box, select the name of the file that contains the secondary text.
4. Click **OK**.
5. In the Print Options dialog box, select the appropriate print options. See note below.
6. Click **OK**.

• **NOTES** Set the number of copies in the Print Options dialog box to 1 if you want to print one copy of each drawing for which a set of secondary text exists in your merge document. If you specify more than one, you will print multiple copies of each drawing.

Printing Selected Layers

See the information about adding a layer under *Layering Drawings* for information about selecting layers to be printed.

REPEATING OPERATIONS

Do the following to perform the same operation repeatedly:

1. Use the **Pick** tool to select an object and perform an operation on it.
2. Keep the same object selected, or select another object.
3. Select **Edit ➤ Repeat**.

ROLL-UPS

CorelDRAW Version 3.0 has introduced roll-ups, a new kind of dialog box that remains on-screen in full or as an icon for as long as you wish. As with other dialog boxes, you can move roll-ups anywhere on your screen.

Roll-ups are available for such operations as outlining, filling, blending, extruding, selecting text attributes, and controlling layers.

Displaying and Using Roll-ups

You access some roll-ups from the Main menu and others from the toolbox. The Text roll-up is typical of one selected from the main menu. To select it:

1. Select **Text ➤ Text Roll-Up**. The Text roll-up appears.
2. Select choices in the roll-up as you would in any other dialog box.

The Pen roll-up is typical of one selected from the tool box. To select it:

1. Click the **Outline** tool. The Outline flyout appears.
2. Click the **Roll-up** icon, the second from the left in the top row. The Pen roll-up appears.
3. Select choices in the roll-up as you would in any other dialog box.

Minimizing and Restoring a Roll-up

1. To minimize a roll-up, click the arrow at the right end of its title bar. Only the title bar remains on your screen.
2. To restore a roll-up that you previously minimized, click on the arrow at the right end of the title bar.

Closing a Roll-up

To close a roll-up, double-click on the **Control-menu** box at the left end of its title bar.

• NOTES If you click just once on a roll-up's Control-menu box, you can choose to

- roll down the roll-up;
- roll up the roll-up;
- arrange the roll-up—that is, minimize it and move the remaining title bar to a corner of the drawing area;
- arrange all—that is, minimize all roll-ups and move all the remaining title bars to the corners of the screen;
- access online **Help** for information about using the roll-up;
- close the roll-up.

ROTATING OBJECTS

With the exception of imported bitmaps, you can rotate objects to any angle. Although you can rotate bitmaps, they are displayed as gray rectangles unless the rotation is exactly 0 or 180 degrees. You can print rotated bitmaps only on a PostScript-equipped printer.

Rotating an Object with the Mouse

1. Use the **Pick** tool to select the object to be rotated.
2. Use the **Pick** tool to point onto the selected object and click. The normal selection handles disappear and are replaced by rotation and skew handles, which are shown in Figure I.18.
3. Point onto one of the curved rotation handles at a corner of the object's frame. The cursor changes to a cross.
4. Press the mouse button and drag the rotation cursor around the object. As you drag, a dashed rectangle shows the amount of rotation, and the angular rotation appears in the status line.
5. Release the mouse button.

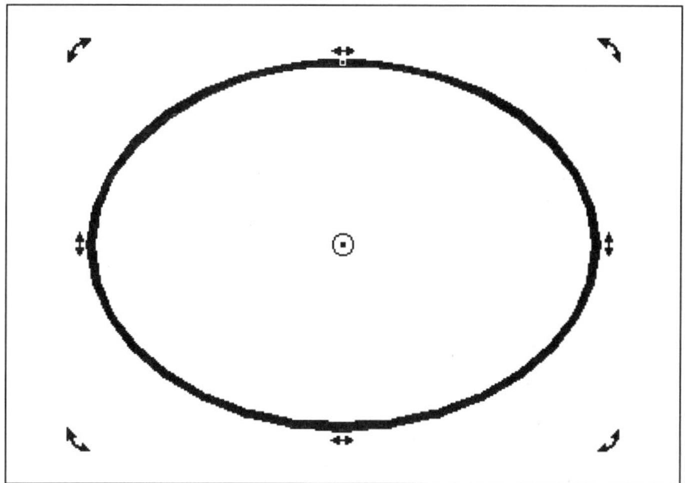

Figure I.18: Rotation handles (the curved two-headed arrows) and skew handles (the straight two-headed arrows). The dot and circle in the center represent the center of rotation.

• NOTES Tap the + key on the numeric keypad before releasing the mouse button if you want to leave an original, unrotated copy of the object.

Hold down the Ctrl key until after you have released the mouse button to constrain the rotation to specific angles. See *Preferences* for information about setting the constrain angle.

Rotating an Object with the Rotate and Skew Command

1. Use the **Pick** tool to select the object to be rotated.
2. Select **Transform ➤ Rotate & Skew**.
3. In the Rotate & Skew dialog box, select or type the rotation angle.
4. Click the **Leave Original** check box if necessary.

5. Click **OK**.

Moving an Object's Center of Rotation

1. Use the **Pick** tool to select the object to be rotated.
2. Use the **Pick** tool to point onto the selected object, and click. The normal selection handles disappear and are replaced by rotation and skew handles (see Figure I.18). The current center of rotation is shown by a dot surrounded by a small circle. By default, the center of rotation is at the center of the object's frame.
3. Point onto the center of rotation and press the mouse button.
4. Drag the center of rotation to a new position.
5. Release the mouse button.

• **NOTES** The new center of rotation applies to subsequent rotation of the object made with the mouse or from the **Rotate & Skew** command.

Restoring an Object's Original Angle

See *Clearing Transformations*.

SCALING AND STRETCHING OBJECTS

You can change an object's size while keeping its height and width in proportion, or you can independently change an object's height and width.

Stretching or Shrinking an Object Using the Mouse

1. Use the **Pick** tool to select the object.
2. Point onto one of the corner handles if you want to maintain the object's height-to-width ratio, to a center handle on a vertical edge of the object's frame to change its width, or to a center handle on a horizontal edge of the frame to change the height.
3. Press the mouse button, and drag the handle to a new position. A dashed rectangle on the screen shows the new size, and the status line shows the percentage change.
4. Release the mouse button.

• NOTES Tap the + key on the numeric keypad before releasing the mouse button if you wish to retain a copy of the object in its original size.

Hold down the Ctrl key until you have released the mouse button to stretch or shrink the object to an exact multiple of its original size.

Hold down the Shift key until you have released the mouse button to stretch or shrink the object in equal amounts from the center.

Stretching or Shrinking an Object Using the Stretch & Mirror Command

1. Use the **Pick** tool to select the object.
2. Select **Transform ➤ Stretch & Mirror**.
3. In the Stretch & Mirror dialog box, select or type the horizontal and vertical percentages.
4. Click **Leave Original**, if necessary.
5. Click **OK**.

SCREEN

Figure I.19 shows the CorelDRAW screen. The screen components are described in the table below.

COMPONENT	PURPOSE
Color Palette	Contains colors for outlining and filling objects.
Control-menu box	Provides commands for sizing and positioning the window.
cursor	Selects a specific point on the screen. The cursor changes shape according to the operation you are performing.
Editing window	The area in which you create your drawing.
menu bar	Provides access to pull-down menus.
Maximize/Restore button	Expands a window to fill the entire screen, or contracts the window to occupy only part of the screen.
Minimize button	Shrinks a window to an icon at the bottom of the screen.
printable page	The area of the drawing window that can be printed.
rulers	Used for sizing and positioning objects.
scroll bars	Used to view parts of a drawing that are not shown on the current screen.
status line	Provides information about selected objects and actions.
title bar	Displays the name of the current program and file.
toolbox	Contains the tools you use to create and edit drawings.

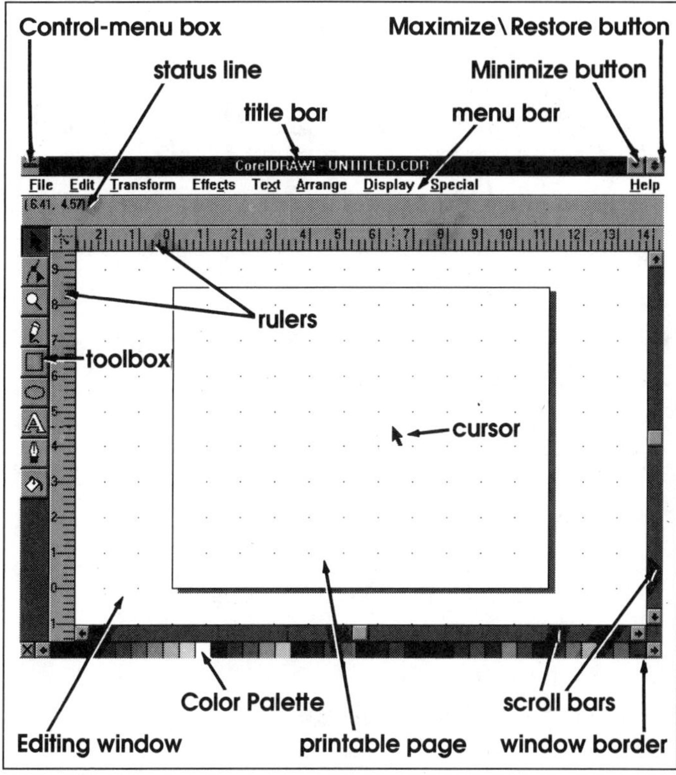

Figure I.19: The CorelDRAW screen

COMPONENT	PURPOSE
window border	Used to outline windows and to change their size.

See "Setting Up the CorelDRAW Screen" in online **Help** for information about the screen defaults and how you can change them.

SELECTING AND DESELECTING OBJECTS

You must select an object before you can make any changes to it. You can tell an object is selected when eight small boxes, called "handles," surround it.

Selecting and Deselecting the Most Recently Drawn Object

- Press the spacebar.

Selecting Any Other Object

1. Use the **Pick** tool to point anywhere onto the outline of the object, or within the object if it is filled.
2. Click the mouse button.

Selecting Multiple Objects

1. Use the **Pick** tool to point anywhere onto the first object.
2. Click the mouse button.
3. Point anywhere onto another object.
4. Hold down the Shift key while you click the mouse button.
5. Repeat steps 3 and 4 to select additional objects.

Selecting All Objects within a Rectangular Area

1. Use the **Pick** tool to point onto an unoccupied space in the drawing window above and to the left of all objects to be selected.

2. Press and hold down the mouse button while you drag down and to the right. Drag until a dotted rectangle encloses all the objects.
3. Release the mouse button. Handles appear around the selected group of objects.

• **NOTES** This technique is known as marquee-selection. Marquee-selection temporarily groups objects only as long as the group remains selected. See *Grouping and Ungrouping Objects* for information about permanent grouping.

Selecting All Objects in a Drawing

- Select **Edit ➤ Select All**.

Deselecting All Selected Objects

1. Use the **Pick** tool to point onto an unoccupied space in the Editing window.
2. Click the mouse button.

Deselecting One of Multiple Selected Objects

1. Use the **Pick** tool to point onto the outline of the object to be deselected, or within the object if it is filled.
2. While holding down the Shift key, click the mouse button.

Deselecting All Selected Objects

- Press the spacebar.

Reselecting Previously Selected Objects

- Press the spacebar.

Selecting an Object within a Group

1. Use the **Pick** tool to point anywhere on the outline of the object, or within it if it is filled.
2. Hold down the Ctrl key and click the mouse button.

• **NOTES** If you have nested groups—that is, groups within groups—you may have to click several times with the Ctrl key pressed to reach the object you want.

Selecting the Next and Previous Objects in a Drawing

Do the following to select objects in the order you drew them:

1. Select an object.
2. Press the Tab key to select the next object, or press Shift-Tab to select the previous object.

SHAPING AND RESHAPING OBJECTS

You can use the **Shape** tool to change the shape of lines or curves. You can also change the shape of a rectangle, an ellipse, and text objects, but you must first convert them to curves. See *Converting Objects to Curves*.

Selecting Nodes on a Line or Curve

1. Use the **Shape** tool to point onto an object.
2. Click the mouse button. The nodes on the object appear as small open squares, as shown in Figure I.20. The status line indicates the type of object selected and, in the case of a line or curve, the number of nodes it has.
3. Point onto the node you want to use.

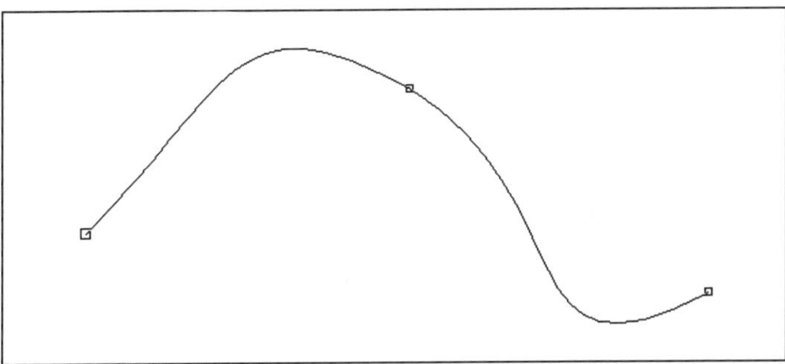

Figure I.20: Shaping nodes on a curve

4. Click the mouse button and the node turns black, as shown in Figure I.21. The status line shows the position of the node and its type. If the object is a curve, dashed lines extend from the node to control points.
5. If you want to select an additional node, point to that node.
6. Hold down the Shift key while you click the mouse button. The status line shows how many nodes are selected.
7. Repeat steps 5 and 6 to select more modes.

• **NOTES** Nodes are the small squares through which a curve passes. The part of a curve between two nodes is known as a "segment." The node at the beginning of the curve is slightly larger than the others.

Control points determine the angle at which the curve passes through nodes as well as its curvature.

You can use marquee-selection to select one or multiple nodes.

When you select a node, you also select the curve segment that precedes it. When you select a segment, you also select the node at its end.

With a curve selected, you can press the Home key to select the first node or the End key to select the last node.

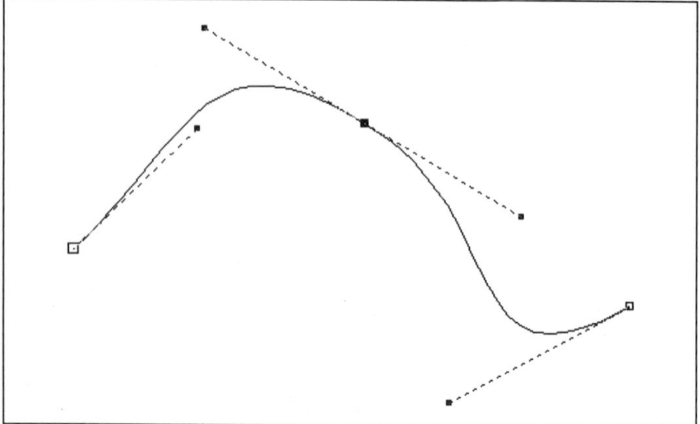

Figure I.21: Selected nodes with control points

Deslecting Nodes

Using the **Shape** tool, click on an unselected node without holding down the Shift key to select that node and, at the same time, to deselect all other nodes.

To deselect all nodes without selecting another, point with the **Shape** tool onto an unoccupied place in the drawing area and click the mouse button.

Changing the Path of a Curve

1. Use the **Shape** tool to point to a node.
2. Press the mouse button and drag the node to a new position. The curve changes shape so that it continues to pass through the node.
3. Release the mouse button.

• **NOTES** To move two or more nodes simultaneously, first select them, and then drag one of them to the new position. All selected nodes move the same distance.

Hold down the Ctrl key until you have released the mouse button to move nodes in horizontal or vertical directions only.

Changing the Shape of a Curve Close to a Node

1. Select a node.
2. Point onto a control point.
3. Press and hold down the mouse button while you drag the control point. The status line shows the distance and angle through which the control point moves.
4. Release the mouse button.

• **NOTES** Angular movement of a control point changes the angle at which the curve passes through a node. Moving the control point further from or nearer to a node increases or decreases the effect on the curvature close to the node.

Adding Nodes to Curves

1. Use the **Shape** tool to point onto the curve at the point where you want to add a node.
2. Double-click the mouse button. The Node Edit pop-up, shown in Figure I.22, appears.
3. Click **Add** in the Node Edit pop-up. A new node appears on the curve.

• **NOTES** If, in step 1 above, you click on an existing node other than the first one, the new node is created at the mid-point of the preceding curve segment. If you select two or more segments, new nodes are created at the mid-point of each selected segment.

Deleting Nodes from a Curve

1. Using the **Shape** tool, double-click on the node you want to delete. The Node Edit pop-up appears.
2. Click **Delete** in the Node Edit pop-up.

• **NOTES** To delete multiple nodes, use the **Shape** tool to select those nodes, and then double-click on one of the selected nodes. You can also press Delete on your keyboard to delete selected nodes.

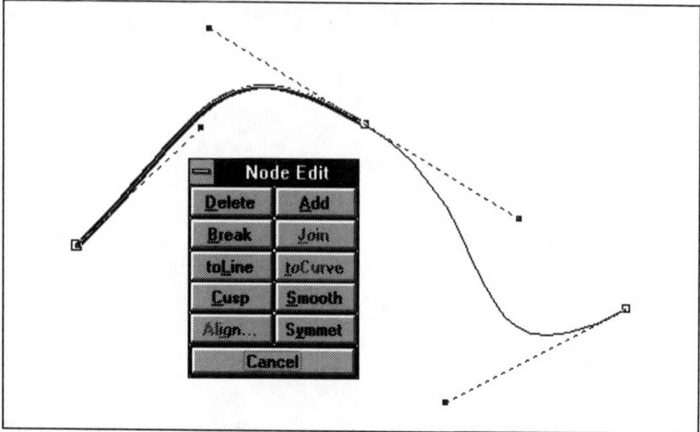

Figure I.22: The Node Edit pop-up

Aligning Nodes

1. Use the **Shape** tool to click the first node you want to align.
2. Hold down the Shift key and click the second node you want to align.
3. Check the status line to verify that two nodes are selected.
4. Double-click one of the selected nodes.
5. Click **Align**... in the Node Edit pop-up. The Node Align dialog box appears.
6. Click either the **Align Horizontally** or the **Align Vertically** check box.
7. Click **OK**.

• **NOTES** You can align nodes on the same path, or on different subpaths in the same object.

If you need to align nodes in different objects, first combine the objects, then align the nodes, and then break the objects apart.

You can use the same technique to align control points.

Joining Nodes on a Curve to Form a Closed Path

1. Use the **Shape** tool to click the first end node you want to join.
2. Hold down the Shift key and click the second end node you want to join
3. Check the status line to verify that two nodes are selected.
4. Double-click one of the selected nodes.
5. Click **Join** in the Node Edit pop-up. The two select nodes move to the mid-point between them and become one node.

• **NOTES** You can also marquee-select the two nodes.

After you have joined the beginning and ending node of a curve, you have a closed path that you can fill.

Joining Nodes to Form a Single Curve from Two Separate Curves

1. Use the **Pick** tool to select the first object.
2. Hold down the Shift key and use the **Pick** tool to select the second object.
3. With both objects selected, select **Arrange ➤ Combine**.
4. Follow steps 1 through 5 directly above in "Joining Nodes on a Curve to Form a Closed Path."

• **NOTES** The curves to be combined must be combined into a single object before you form a single curve from them. If the curves are already a single object, omit steps 1 through 3. If the selected curves are combined as a single object, the status line reports a single node.

After you select the Pick tool, the status line tells you how many subpaths (unconnected paths) exist in the selected object.

Breaking a Curve into Separate Paths

1. With the **Shape** tool, double-click at the place where you want to break the curve. The Node Edit pop-up appears.
2. Click **Break** in the pop-up to create superimposed starting and ending nodes.
3. Move the nodes as required.

• **NOTES** You can simultaneously break a curve at several nodes. Select the nodes, double-click on one of them, and click **Break**.

Using Smooth, Symmetrical, and Cusp Nodes

CorelDRAW has three types of nodes: smooth, symmetrical, and cusp.

- Smooth nodes are those in which the node and its two control points lie on a straight line. When you move one control point, the other moves to maintain the linear relationship. Curves are continuous at a smooth node.
- Symmetrical nodes are smooth nodes with the added property that the two control points are the same distance from the node. Curvature is the same on both sides of a symmetrical node.
- Cusp nodes have two independent control points. The node and its two control points are not necessarily on a straight line, and the two control points can be at different distances from the node. Curves are discontinuous at a cusp node.

When a single node is selected, the status line shows its type. The status line does not show node type when two or more nodes are selected.

There are two types of segments between each pair of nodes:

- A curve segment, which has two control points associated with it, one for the node at each end.
- A line segment, which has no control points associated with it.

Changing a Node's Type

1. Use the **Shape** tool to double-click on the node you want to change.
2. Click **Smooth**, **Symmet**, or **Cusp** in the Node Edit pop-up. The node type changes, the effect is shown on the screen, and the status line shows the node's new type.

• NOTES To change several smooth nodes simultaneously, select the nodes, double-click on one of them, and then click the new type of node.

Changing a Curve Segment to a Line Segment

1. Using the **Shape** tool, double-click on the curve segment or the node that follows it. The Node Edit pop-up appears.
2. Click **toLine** in the Node Edit pop-up.

• NOTES To change several curve segments to line segments simultaneously, select the curve segments, double-click on one of the associated nodes, and then click **toLine**.

Changing a Line Segment to a Curve Segment

1. Using the **Shape** tool, double-click on the line segment or the node that follows it. The Node Edit pop-up appears.
2. Click **toCurve** in the Node Edit pop-up.

• NOTES To change several line segments to curve segments simultaneously, select the line segments, double-click on one of the associated nodes, and then click **toCurve**.

Shaping Objects with Envelopes

CorelDRAW allows you to select an artistic text object or a graphics object and shape it to fit within another object (an envelope). You cannot fit paragraph text into an envelope. Do the following to fit an object into an envelope:

1. Create an object, such as the artistic text shown at the top of Figure I.23.
2. Use the **Pick** tool to select the text.
3. Select **Effects ➤ Edit Envelope**. The flyout shown in Figure I.24 appears. It allows you to choose one of four envelope modes.
4. Click the top envelope mode. The differences between the modes are explained in the notes below. After you select the mode, your object has a dashed, rectangular frame with nodes at the four corners and at the mid-points of the sides, top, and bottom.
5. Point onto one of the nodes, press the mouse button, and drag to change the shape of the frame. You can drag the nodes at the center of the top and bottom vertically, and those at the center of the sides horizontally. You can drag each corner node either vertically or horizontally.

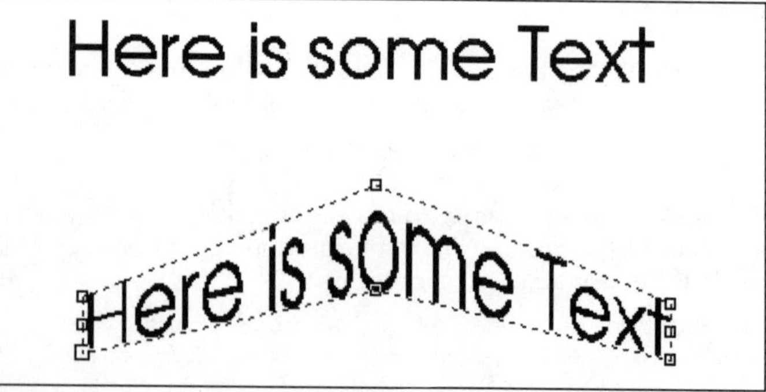

Figure I.23: An artistic text object before being shaped by an envelope (top) and after being shaped (bottom)

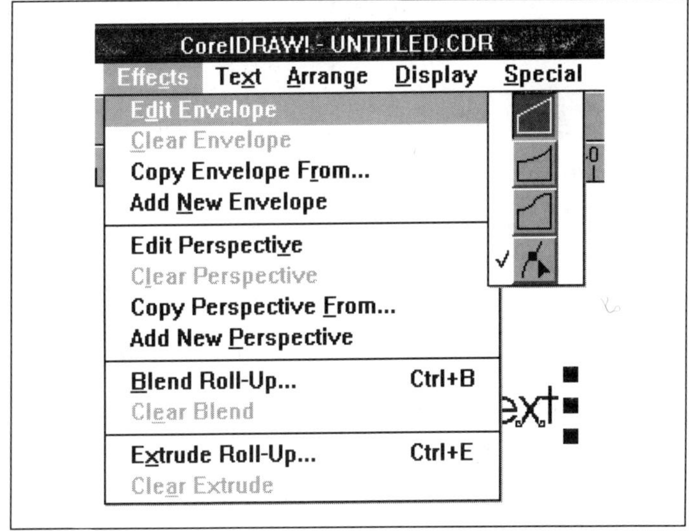

Figure I.24: The flyout for choosing one of four envelope modes

6. Release the mouse button and the object changes shape to fit the envelope, as shown at the bottom of Figure I.23.

• **NOTES** The top envelope mode, which is used in this example, creates an envelope with straight edges. The second allows each edge of the envelope to be a single curve. The third allows each edge to be a double curve. The fourth mode allows you to manipulate nodes freely, including moving control points to change the curvature of the envelope.

Hold down the Ctrl key while you drag a node to make that node and the one opposite it move in the same direction. Hold down the Shift key while you drag a node to make that node and the one opposite it move in opposite directions. If you want to expand or contract the object, hold down the Ctrl and Shift keys while you drag a corner node to make all four corner nodes move. You can also expand or contract the object by holding down the Ctrl and Shift keys while you drag a center node to make all four center nodes move.

If you have a selected object within an envelope and select **Effects ➤ Add New Envelope**, you place an envelope around the existing envelope. You can shape this outer envelope as you shaped the first.

Copying an Envelope from One Object to Another

1. Use the **Pick** tool to select the object to which you want to copy an envelope.
2. Select **Effects ➤ Copy Envelope From**. The From arrow appears.
3. Point onto the envelope you want to copy and click the mouse button. The object you first selected changes shape to fit within a copy of the envelope.

Clearing an Envelope

1. Use the **Pick** tool to select an object enclosed within an envelope.
2. Select **Effects ➤ Clear Envelope**. The object returns to the shape it had before the envelope was applied.

• **NOTES** If you had used the **Add New Envelope** command to put several envelopes around an object, each time you select **Effects ➤ Clear Envelope**, you remove the topmost envelope. To remove all envelopes surrounding an object in one step, select **Transform ➤ Clear Transformations**.

SHORTCUT KEYS

Most procedures in this book are described in terms of selecting from menus. However, CoralDRAW provides shortcuts to speed certain actions. Look at the shortcut keys on the dialog boxes you use most often to familiarize yourself with how to use the shortcuts.

Tables I.1, I.2, and I.3 list various shortcuts you can use to speed up your work with CorelDRAW.

Table I.1: Function Key Shortcuts

KEY	USE
F1	Gets help on the currently selected command or the currently open dialog box.
Shift-F1	Gets help on the screen item or active command.
F2	Displays the Zoom-in cursor.
F3	Zooms out by a factor of two.
F4	Changes the magnification so that all objects fit within the drawing window.
F5	Selects the Pencil tool.
F6	Selects the Rectangle tool.
F7	Selects the Ellipse tool.
F8	Selects the Text tool.
F9	Toggles between the Normal and Preview display modes.
Shift-F9	Toggles between the Full-Color and Wireframe display modes.
F10	Selects the Shape tool.
F11	Opens the Fountain Fill dialog box.
Shift-F11	Opens the Uniform Fill dialog box.
F12	Opens the Outline Pen dialog box.
Shift-F12	Opens the Outline Color dialog box.

Table I.2: Speed Key Shortcuts

KEY	USE
Ctrl-1	Opens the Layers roll-up.
Ctrl-2	Opens the Text roll-up.
Ctrl-A	Opens the Align dialog box.
Ctrl-B	Opens the Blend roll-up.
Ctrl-C	Executes the Combine command.
Ctrl-D	Executes the Duplicate command.
Ctrl-E	Opens the Extrude roll-up.
Ctrl-F	Opens the Fit Text To Path dialog box.
Ctrl-G	Executes the Group command.
Ctrl-J	Opens the Preferences dialog box.
Ctrl-K	Executes the Break Apart command.
Ctrl-L	Opens the Move dialog box.
Ctrl-N	Opens the Rotate & Skew dialog box.
Ctrl-O	Opens the Open Drawing dialog box.
Ctrl-P	Opens the Print Options dialog box.
Ctrl-Q	Opens the Stretch & Mirror dialog box.
Ctrl-S	Saves the drawing under the current file name.
Ctrl-T	Opens the Edit Text dialog box.
Ctrl-U	Executes the Ungroup command.
Ctrl-V	Executes the Convert To Curves command.
Ctrl-W	Executes the Refresh Window command.
Ctrl-X	Exits CorelDRAW.
Ctrl-Y	Turns the snap-to grid on or off.
Ctrl-Z	Executes the Align To Baseline command.
Alt-Enter	Re-executes the most recent action.

Table I.2: Speed Key Shortcuts (continued)

KEY	USE
Alt-F4	Exits CorelDRAW.
Shift-Insert	Executes the Paste command.
Ctrl-Insert	Executes the Copy command.
Delete	Executes the Delete command.
Shift-Delete	Executes the Cut command.
Alt-Backspace	Undoes the most recent action.
Page Down	Executes the Back One command.
Shift-Page Down	Executes the To Back command.
Page Up	Executes the Forward One command.
Shift-Page Up	Executes the To Front command.

Table I.3: Other Shortcuts

ACTION	RESULT
Double-click on the border of printable page	Opens the Page Setup dialog box.
Double-click on a guideline	Opens the Guidelines dialog box.
Double-click on a ruler	Opens the Grid Setup dialog box.
Double-click on a character node	Opens the Character Attributes dialog box.

Table I.3: Other Shortcuts (continued)

ACTION	RESULT
Press the spacebar	Selects the most recently selected (or drawn) object, or deselects the currently selected object. Also switches between the Pick tool and the most recently used drawing tool.
Press Esc	Deselects all selected objects.

SKEWING OBJECTS

With the exception of imported bitmaps, you can freely skew objects horizontally and vertically. Figure I.25 shows an unskewed character and rectangle, grouped as a single object, at the top-left. The same object is shown skewed horizontally at the top-right, skewed vertically at the bottom-left, and skewed in both directions at the bottom-right.

Bitmaps can be skewed at any angle, however, after being skewed, they are displayed only as rectangles filled with gray. Skewed bitmaps can only be printed with a PostScript-equipped printer.

Skewing an Object with the Mouse

1. Use the **Pick** tool to select the object to be skewed.
2. Use the **Pick** tool to point onto the selected object, and click. The normal selection handles disappear and are replaced by rotation and skew handles.
3. To skew horizontally, point onto one of the straight skew handles at the top or bottom of the object; to skew vertically, point onto one of the straight skew handles at the

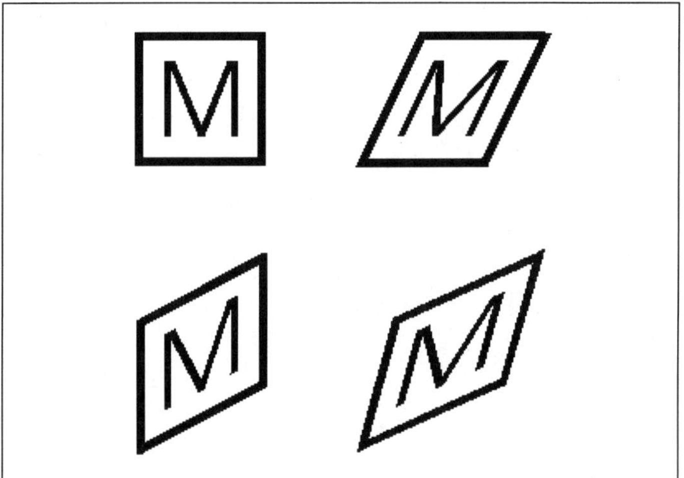

Figure I.25: An object before being skewed (top-left), skewed horizontally (top-right), skewed vertically (bottom-left), and skewed in both directions (bottom-right)

side of the object. The cursor changes to a cross when it is on one of the handles.

4. Press the mouse button and drag the handle in the direction you want the object to be skewed. As you drag, a dashed outline shows the skews, and the status line indicates the skew angle.
5. Release the mouse button.

• **NOTES** Tap the + key on the numeric keypad before releasing the mouse button if you want to keep an unskewed version of the object. Hold down the Ctrl key until you have released the mouse button to constrain the skew to specific angles. See *Preferences* for information about setting the constraint angle.

Skewing an Object with the Rotate & Skew Command

1. Use the **Pick** tool to select the object to be skewed.
2. Select **Transform ➤ Rotate & Skew**.
3. In the Rotate & Skew dialog box, select or type a skew angle in the **Skew Horizontally** and **Skew Vertically** text boxes.
4. Click the **Leave Original** box if necessary.
5. Click **OK**.

Unskewing an Object

See *Clearing Transformations*.

SPELL CHECKING

You can check the spelling of individual words before you place them into a drawing, and of words or groups of words in artistic or paragraph text as well. In addition to using CorelDRAW's built-in spelling dictionary, you can create your own dictionary.

Checking Spelling in Artistic and Paragraph Text

1. Use the **Text** tool to highlight the text you wish to check.
2. Select **Text ➤ Spell Checker**. The Spelling Checker dialog box appears.
3. If you want to compare words with those in a personal dictionary as well as with those in the CorelDRAW dictionary, pull down the **Personal Dictionary** list box and click on the name of the dictionary you want to use.

4. Click **Check Text**. CorelDRAW compares the selected text with words both in the standard dictionary and in a personal dictionary, if you are using one. When the spell checker finds a word in the selected text that is not in the dictionary or dictionaries, it displays that word in the Word Not Found box.
5. If you selected a personal dictionary, you can click **Add** to add the word in the Word Not Found text box to that dictionary. You cannot add words to the standard dictionary.
6. If you are satisfied your word is correct even though it is not in the dictionary, click **Ignore** to accept your spelling of the word, or click **Ignore All** to make CorelDRAW ignore all occurrences of the word in the selected text.
7. If you want to correct the spelling, click in the **Replace With** text box to create an insertion point, and then type the correct word. Alternatively, click the **Suggest** box and CorelDRAW will display a list of words with similar spellings. Click the correct word and it appears in the **Replace With** text box.
8. Click **Replace** to replace the incorrect word with the correct word. Alternatively, click **Replace All** to replace every occurrence of the incorrect word with the correct word.
9. Repeat steps 3 through 8 until the CorelDRAW dialog box displays the message "Spelling check finished."
10. Click **OK**.

• **NOTES** If you prefer CorelDRAW to always provide suggestions for correct spelling, click the **Always Suggest** button.

If you wish to terminate spell checking before all the text has been checked, click **Cancel**.

Checking the Spelling of Individual Words

1. Select **Text ➤ Spell Checker**. The Spelling Checker dialog box appears.
2. With an insertion marker in the **Word To Check** text box, type the word you want to check.

3. Click **Check Word**. The CorelDRAW! dialog box appears and displays either the message "Word Not Found" or "Word OK."
4. Click **OK**.
5. Type another word you want to check and repeat steps 3 and 4, or click **Cancel**.

• NOTES See the previous procedure for information about comparing the spellings with those in a personal dictionary and adding the word to a personal dictionary.

Creating a Personal Dictionary

1. Select **Text ➤ Spell Checker**.
2. Point into the unnamed text box in the **Create a personal dictionary** section of the Spelling Checker dialog box and click the mouse button.
3. Type a name for your dictionary. As soon as you type the first character, the Create button becomes available.
4. Click **Create**. The name of your personal dictionary appears in the Personal Dictionary text box.

• NOTES The name you choose for a personal dictionary becomes a file name with the extension .DIC. The name should follow DOS file name restrictions.

You can create as many personal dictionaries as you wish. However, you can only use the standard dictionary and one personal dictionary to check spelling.

STACKING ORDER

Filled objects are opaque. When they overlap, the more recently created object in a layer obscures part or all of the objects created earlier in the same layer. You can use various commands in the Arrange menu to alter the stacking order of objects in a layer and control which objects obscure others. The Arrange menu options are:

To Front	places selected objects on top of all others.
To Back	places selected objects behind all others.
Forward One	moves selected objects up one position.
Back One	moves selected objects down one position.
Reverse Order	reverses the stacking order of selected objects.

• NOTES With the exception of **Reverse Order**, select one or more objects before using these commands. In the case of **Reverse Order**, you must select at least two objects.

See *Layering Drawings* for information about placing objects on layers.

STARTING A NEW DRAWING

See the explanation of opening a new file in the *Files* entry.

STRETCHING AND SHRINKING OBJECTS

See *Scaling and Stretching Objects*.

SYMBOLS

The CorelDRAW package contains a large number of symbols that you can use in drawings. If you have installed the CD-ROM version of CorelDRAW, you have access to many thousands of symbols. Otherwise you can use only those supplied on disk. Refer to the "CD-ROM Clipart, Symbols & Flicks" catalog to see what symbols are available.

Symbols are in vector, not bitmapped, format. They are curves rather than text. You can manipulate symbols just as you can manipulate any other curve object.

Placing Symbols in a Drawing

1. Point to the **Text** tool.
2. Press and hold down the mouse button until a flyout menu appears, and then release the mouse button.
3. Click on the **Star** icon to select symbols. The Text tool in the toolbox is replaced by the Symbol tool.
4. Point onto your drawing where you want to place a symbol, and click. The Symbols dialog box appears.
5. If necessary, scroll the list box on the right to find the symbol category you want.
6. Click on the name of the symbol category. The preview window at the left shows the first symbol in the category you select.
7. Click the arrow at the bottom-right of the preview window. A symbol selection box appears, showing the symbols that are available in the selected category.
8. Scroll through the selection box to find the symbol you want, and then click that symbol. The symbol appears in the preview window.
9. If necessary, open the measurement units scroll box and select a new measurement unit for specifying the symbol size.

10. In the **Size** text box, select or type the size you want the symbol to be.
11. Click **OK**. The dialog disappears and the symbol appears on your drawing.

• **NOTES** Each symbol has a number within its category. This number appears in the Symbol # text box. If you know the number of the symbol you want, you can type the number in the text box instead of scrolling through the selection box to find it.

After you have finished selecting symbols, restore the Text tool by pointing to the **Symbol** tool, pressing and holding down the mouse button until the flyout appears, and then selecting the **Text** tool.

THESAURUS

CorelDRAW's Thesaurus allows you to look up the meaning of words and to find words with similar meanings, called synonyms.

Looking Up Words in Artistic and Paragraph Text

1. Use the **Text** tool to highlight a word in your drawing.
2. Select **Text ➤ Thesaurus**. The Thesaurus dialog box appears. If the word is in the CorelDRAW dictionary, the dialog box displays the word's part of speech and one or more definitions, one of which is highlighted. One or more synonyms for the highlighted definition are listed as well.
3. If necessary, click one of the definitions to see a list of appropriate synonyms.
4. If you want to replace the original word with a synonym, click the synonym, and then click **Replace**. Otherwise, click **Cancel**.

Looking Up Other Words

1. With no words selected on your drawing, select **Text ➤ Thesaurus**. The Thesaurus dialog box appears.
2. Select the **Synonym for** dialog box and delete any word in it.
3. Type the word you want to look up.
4. Click **Lookup**.
5. Follow steps 3 and 4 in the previous procedure.

TOOLBOX

The CorelDRAW toolbox, shown in Figure I.26, contains nine tools, two of which exist in alternative forms.

Pick Tool

Use the **Pick** tool to select individual objects or groups of objects. You can also use this tool to move, rotate, scale, skew, and stretch objects.

Shape Tool

Use the Shape tool to

- change the shape of lines and curves by manipulating nodes,
- edit character attributes and kern text,
- crop bitmaps,
- round the corners of rectangles,
- create arcs and wedges from ellipses.

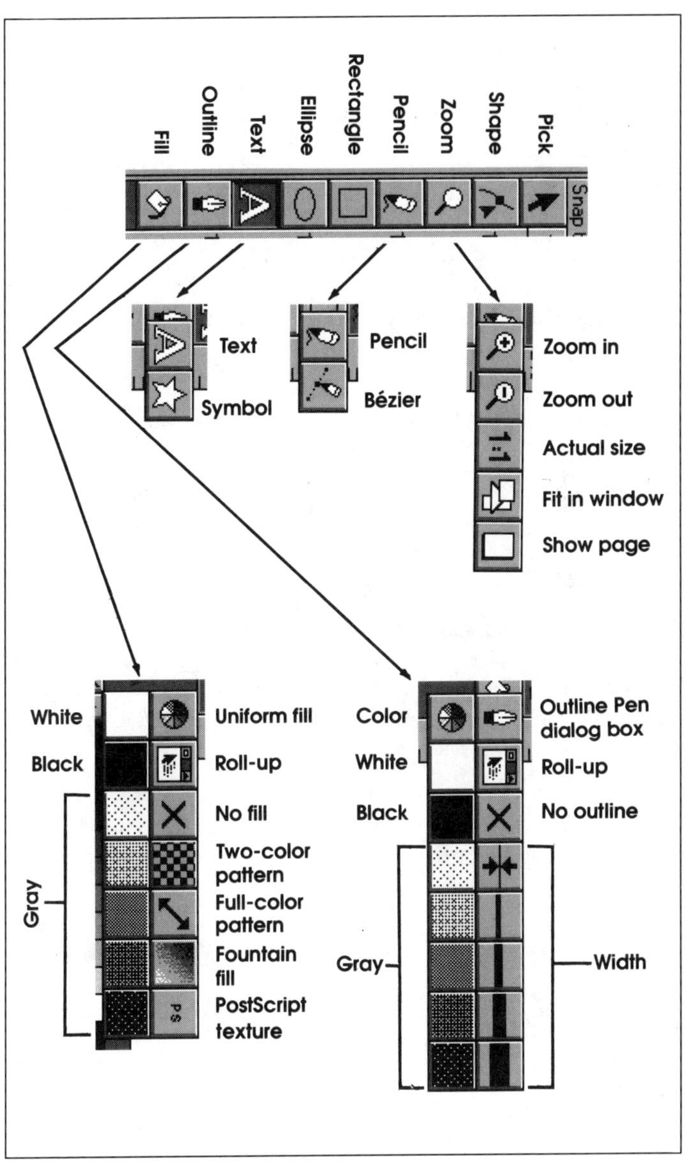

Figure I.26: The CorelDRAW toolbox (top) with flyouts from the tools

Zoom Tool

When you click the Zoom tool you get the flyout menu shown in Figure I.26. Click the icon you wish to use.

ICON	ACTION
Zoom in	magnifies part of the screen.
Zoom out	halves the magnification of what is on the screen.
Actual size	displays part of the drawing at the size it will be printed.
Fit in window	magnifies, or reduces magnification, so that all objects in the drawing are shown on the screen.
Show page	displays the entire printable page.

Pencil Tool

There are Freehand and Bézier versions of the Pencil tool. To change from one to the other, point to the Pencil tool and then press and hold down the mouse button until the flyout shown in Figure I.26 appears. Click on the left icon to select the Freehand tool, or on the right icon to select the Bézier tool. The icon in the toolbox shows which of the two is currently selected.

Use the Freehand tool to draw lines and curves by a click and drag technique. Use the Bézier tool to draw with a connect-the-dots style. See *Drawing Objects* for more information.

Rectangle Tool

Use the Rectangle tool to draw rectangles and squares.

Ellipse Tool

Use the Ellipse tool to draw ellipses and circles. You can subsequently use the Shape tool to change ellipses and circles into arcs and wedges. See *Drawing Objects*.

Text Tool and Symbol Tool

The toolbox contains either the Text tool or the Symbol tool. To change from one to the other, point to the tool and then press and hold down the mouse button until the flyout shown in Figure I.26 appears. Click on the *A* to select the Text tool or on the star to select the Symbol tool. The icon in the toolbox shows which is selected.

Use the Text tool to place artistic text and paragraph text on your drawing, and also to highlight text. Use the Symbol tool to select and place symbols.

Outline Tool

When you select the Outline tool, the flyout shown in Figure I.26 appears. Select icons in this flyout to select:

- the Outline Pen dialog box;
- the Pen roll-up;
- one of six preset line widths, including zero width;
- the Outline Color dialog box;
- one of seven shades of gray, including white and black.

Fill Tool

When you select the Fill tool, the flyout shown in Figure I.26 appears. Select icons in this flyout to select

- the Uniform Fill dialog box;
- the Fill roll-up;
- no fill;
- the Two-Color Pattern dialog box;
- the Full-Color Pattern dialog box;
- the Fountain Fill dialog box;
- the PostScript Texture dialog box;
- one of seven shades of gray, including white and black

TRACING BITMAPPED IMAGES

By tracing a bitmap image, you convert it into a vector-format CorelDRAW drawing so that you can manipulate it as you can any other object.

CorelDRAW offers two methods of tracing bitmaps: one is Auto-Trace, which is built in to CorelDRAW itself, and the other is the more powerful CorelTRACE program. The built-in method is described here. See Part V of this book for information about CorelTRACE.

Using AutoTrace to Trace a Black-And-White Bitmap

AutoTrace is intended for tracing black-and-white bitmaps. It cannot be used satisfactorily with color bitmaps. Do the following to trace an object:

1. Bring the bitmap into your drawing. See *Importing Objects.*
2. Use the **Zoom** tool to magnify the object so that you can see all of it clearly.
3. If necessary, select the bitmap object. Use the **Pick** tool to click on its frame. The status line tells you that you have selected a monochrome bitmap.
4. Click the **Freehand Pencil** tool. The status line shows you that AutoTrace is enabled, and the cursor changes to the AutoTrace shape.
5. Place the cursor to the left of a black area in the object and click the mouse button. CorelDRAW takes a few seconds to trace around the black area.
6. Repeat step 5 until you have traced the entire bitmapped object.
7. Select the **Pick** tool to leave AutoTrace.

• **NOTES** It is usually difficult to see which part of a bitmap object has been traced and which is still in its original bitmap form. To overcome this problem, leave the bitmap black and create the tracing in a contrasting color. After you have imported the bitmap, deselect it. Then choose an outline color. Reselect the bitmap and start tracing. Now you will be able to see clearly which parts of your object have been traced and which parts have not.

You can control how accurately AutoTrace traces bitmaps by adjusting values in the Preferences–Curves dialog box:

- **AutoTrace Tracking** controls how closely the Bézier curves produced by AutoTrace follow the edges of the bitmap; low numbers produce more accurate results.
- **Corner Threshold** determines the threshold at which Autotrace rounds corners; low numbers produce sharper corners.
- **Straight Line Threshold** sets the threshold for deciding between lines and curves; low numbers favor curves.

See *Preferences* for information about changing these settings.

UNDOING

After you have performed an operation on your drawing, you can select **Edit ➤ Undo** to make your drawing return to the state it was in before the operation. Subsequently, you can select **Edit ➤ Redo** to return your drawing to the state it was in before you selected the Undo command.

After you have applied a transformation to an object, you can select another object and then select **Edit ➤ Repeat** to apply the same transformation to the second object as well.

VIEWING OBJECTS AT DIFFERENT MAGNIFICATIONS

You can use the Zoom tool to view objects at different magnifications. See *Tools* for information about using the Zoom tool.

ZOOMING

See *Tools*.

Part II

CorelCHART

3-D VIEW TOOL

The 3-D View tool is a four-component tool that provides versatile facilities for optimizing three-dimensional charts.

Activating the 3-D View Tool

Do the following to activate the 3D View tool:

1. Display a three-dimensional chart in the Chart window.
2. Select **Chart ➤ Show 3-D View Tool**. The 3D View tool appears in one of the four forms, all of which are shown in Figure II.1.

• **NOTES** The component of the 3D View tool that you first see is the one that was displayed the last time the tool was used.

Using the 3-D Movement Tool

The 3-D Movement tool allows you to move a chart in any of the three dimensions. Do the following:

1. If necessary, use the **Pick** tool to click the 3-D Movement icon at the top-left of the 3-D View tool. The 3-D Movement icon appears in the action area of the 3-D View tool.
2. Point onto one of the red arrows on the 3-D Movement tool. Press and hold down the mouse button. A moving dashed rectangle shows the position of the chart.
3. Release the mouse button.
4. Click **Redraw** in the 3-D View tool.

• **NOTES** The Show Chart button in the 3-D View tool is normally checked. Click this button to remove the check mark and replace the chart with its outline.

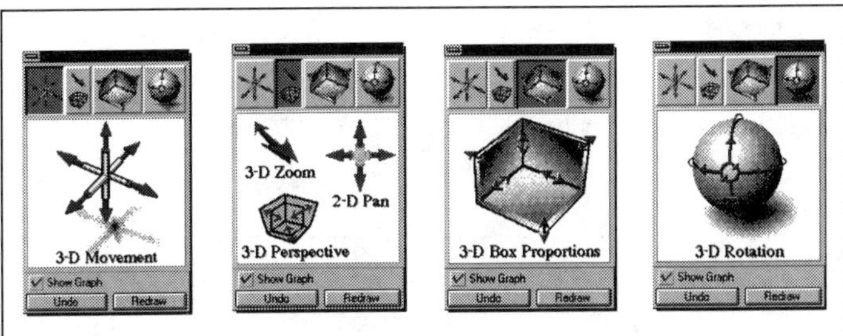

Figure II.1: The four components of the 3-D View tool

The 3-D Zoom, 3-D Perspective, and 2-D Pan Tools

These three tools, available together, allow you to increase or decrease the size of a three-dimensional chart, change its perspective, and pan it horizontally or vertically. The tools are activated and used in the same way as the 3-D Movement tool, described above.

The 3-D Box Proportions Tool

This tool allows you to change the width, height, and depth of a three-dimensional chart. Activate and use it in the same way as the 3-D Movement tool, described above.

The 3-D Rotation Tool

This tool allows you to rotate a three-dimensional chart about any of the three axes. Activate and use it in the same way as the 3-D Movement tool, described above.

Undoing 3-D View Changes

To restore a three-dimensional chart to the state it was in before you used any of the 3-D View tools, click **Undo** in the 3-D View tool.

Hiding the 3-D View Tool

To hide the 3-D View tool, either double-click the tool's **Control-menu** box, or select **Chart ➤ Show 3D View Tool**.

ADDING DATA TO A WORKSHEET

You can add data to a worksheet either by typing it in each cell, or by importing data created in another application. See *Screen* for information about the various areas of the Data Manager screen.

A typical worksheet, such as that shown in Figure II.2, has four distinct parts:

- the array of values, which are used to create charts;
- the column headers, which are used as group labels on the chart;
- the row headers, which are used as verticle axis labels on the chart;
- the text, which becomes the title, subtitle, and footnote on the chart.

Two bar charts created from this worksheet are shown in Figures II.3 and II.4. The two charts present the same data but in different ways.

The array of values in a worksheet consists of rows and columns. The values in rows are normally called "series" and those in columns are called "groups." However, if you wish, you can use rows as groups and columns as series. The charts in the preceding figures show the difference.

By default, CorelCHART uses rows as series. See the explanation of Using columns as series in the *Bar Charts* entry.

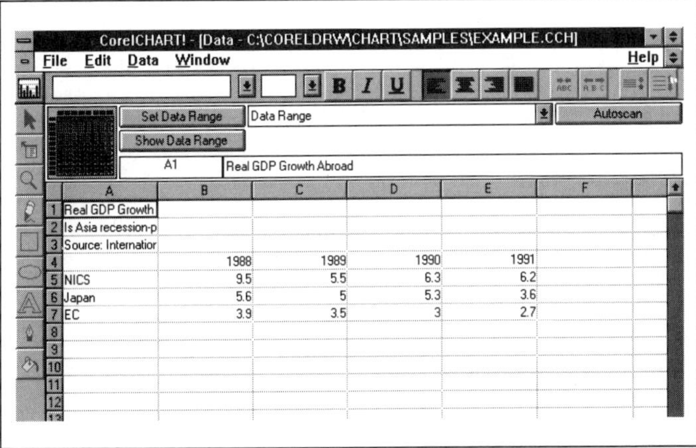

Figure II.2: A typical worksheet containing chart data

Importing Data into a Worksheet from Another Application

One way to create a chart is to import data from another application. To do this:

1. Display a blank Data Manager window, usually as part of the process of creating a new chart. See *Files*.
2. Optionally, maximize the Data Manager window.
3. Select **File ➤ Import Data**. The Import File With File Type dialog box appears.
4. Open the List Files of Type list box, and select the application in which the data you want to import was created.
5. In the Directories box, select the directory which contains the file whose data you want to import. The names of files in that directory which are of the type you selected in step 4 appear in the File Name list box.
6. Click the name of the file you want to import.
7. Click **OK**. The imported data appears in the Data Manager worksheet.

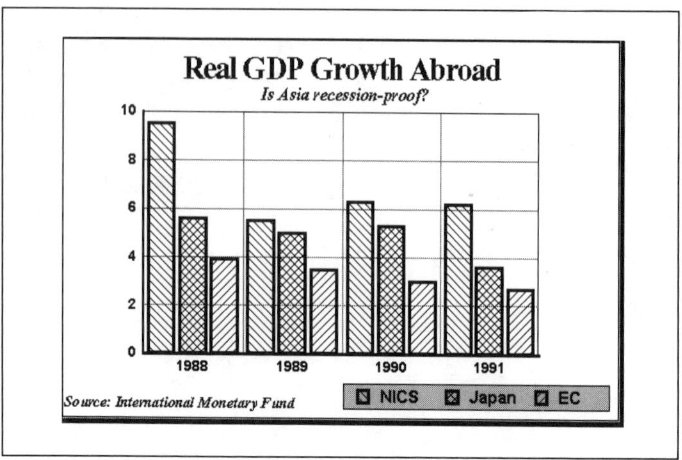

Figure II.3: A bar chart created from the worksheet in Figure II.2. Here, values in rows are used as series, and values in columns are used as groups.

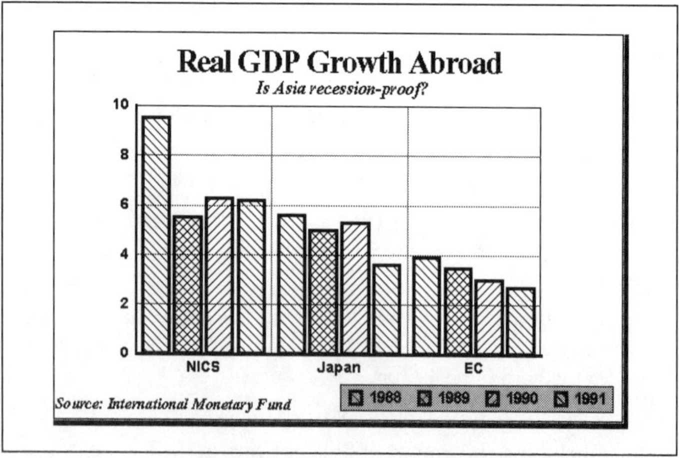

Figure II.4: A bar chart created from the worksheet in Figure II.2. Here, values in columns are used as series, and values in rows are used as groups.

• NOTES You can import data from the following formats:

- ASCII with comma-separated values (.CSV)
- ASCII with space-separated values (.TXT)
- ASCII with tab-separated values (.TXT)
- dBASE (.DBF)
- Harvard Graphics (.CHT)
- Lotus 1-2-3 (.WK1 and .WK3)
- Excel (.XLS)

Manually Placing Data into a Worksheet

You can manually place data into a worksheet the same way you would place data into a spreadsheet. You can also edit data imported from another application.

1. Display a blank Data Manager window, usually as part of the process of creating a new chart. See *Files*.
2. Optionally, maximize the Data Manager window.
3. Select the rectangular block of cells into which you want to place data. See *Selecting Cells in a Worksheet*.
4. Type the value or text for the cell at the top-left corner of the block of cells. The characters you type appear in the Contents box.
5. Press Enter. The data in the Contents box appears in the cell, and the next cell is automatically selected (see the note below).
6. Repeat steps 4 through 5 to add data into other cells.

• NOTES Each time you press Enter, the next cell in the rectangular block is automatically selected. Cells are selected beginning with the top-left cell, then the cells moving down the first column, then the cells moving down the second column, and so on. After you type data in the bottom-right cell and press Enter, the top-left cell is selected automatically.

You can use a similar technique to place data into scattered cells. In this case, data is placed into the cells in the order you originally selected them as a scattered group.

You can place data into a block of cells without first selecting the block. Select the first cell, type the data for it, and press Enter or one of the cursor keys. One of the four adjacent cells is automatically selected:

PRESS	NEXT CELL SELECTED
Enter *or* ↓	one down
↑	one up
←	one to the left
→	one to the right

Editing Worksheet Data

Editing worksheet data is similar to placing new data into the worksheet (see above). To change the contents of a cell, select the cell. Its value or text appears in the Contents box. You can use the following methods to edit the data:

- Type the first character of the new data. The old data disappears and whatever you type completely replaces the old data.
- Point anywhere into the existing data in the Contents box and click the mouse button. A flashing insertion marker appears. At this point you can press Backspace to delete one character at a time to the left of the insertion point, or Delete to delete two characters at a time to the right of the insertion point. The characters you type are inserted at the insertion point. Press the cursor keys to move the insertion point one character at a time to the left or right, press Home to move it to the beginning of the data, or press End to move it to the end of the data.
- Select **Edit ➤ Clear** to completely delete data from the selected cell or cells.

ANNOTATING A CHART

Each chart consists of two layers; one with all the data from the Data Manager, and one for annotations. Annotations can be graphics or text used to highlight specific points. You can annotate a chart using CorelCHART's text and graphics tools, or you can import annotations from a file created in another application.

Adding Text as an Annotation

Adding annotation text is similar to adding paragraph text in CorelDRAW. Do the following to add text as an annotation to a chart:

1. With a chart displayed in the Chart window, click the **Text** tool.
2. Move the cross-shaped cursor to the top-left corner of the area where you want the annotation to be.
3. Press and hold down the mouse button, and drag down and to the right. Drag until you reach the bottom-right corner of the annotation area.
4. Release the mouse button. A flashing insertion point shows the top-left corner of the annotation.
5. Type the text for the annotation. The text is wrapped automatically when it reaches the right side of the annotation area. The depth of the annotation area is automatically increased, if necessary.
6. Click the **Pick** tool. The temporary background behind the annotation disappears.

• **NOTES** To change the font, size, or other attributes of the annotation text, use the **Pick** tool to select the text, and then use the **Text Ribbon** to make your changes. To change the color of the annotation text, select the text with the **Pick** tool and click a color in the color palette.

Annotating a Chart with Rectangles and Squares

You can add rectangles and squares as annotations, often to outline text annotations.

1. With a chart displayed in a Chart window, point onto the **Rectangle** tool and click the mouse button.
2. Point to the place on the chart where you want the top-left corner of the rectangle or square to be, and press and hold down the mouse button.
3. Drag down and to the right to the where you want the bottom-right corner to be, and release the mouse button. The rectangle appears. Notice the handles at the four corners, at the mid-points of the top and bottom edges, and at the mid-points of the sides.

• **NOTES** Hold down the Ctrl or Shift keys while you drag to create a square, or to grow the rectangle from the center. See *Drawing Objects* in Part I of this book for information.

Annotating a Chart with Ellipses and Circles

To create an ellipsis or circle use the same procedure as that for creating rectangles and squares (described above), except use the Ellipse tool.

Annotating a Chart with Lines, Polygons, Curves, and Arrows

You can annotate a chart with straight lines, polygons, curves, and arrows by using the Line tool. Proceed as follows:

1. With a chart displayed in a Chart window, point onto the **Line** tool and click the mouse button. A flyout menu appears with four icons that represent straight lines, polygons, curves, and arrows.
2. Click the icon representing the type of line you want to draw.
3. With the cross-shaped cursor, point to where you want to start drawing a line, then press and hold down the cursor

button. For a straight line or an arrow, drag to extend the line in any direction (you can press and hold down the Ctrl key to create a horizontal or vertical line). For a polygon, click the mouse button at each point of the polygon, and double-click to close the polygon. For a curve, simply draw the curve with the mouse button held down.

4. Release the mouse button. The line graphic appears with selection handles.

Changing the Size and Attributes of Graphics

See *Resizing* for information about changing the size of a graphic.

To change the color or thickness of a line, or the outline of a graphic:

1. Use the **Pick** tool to select the graphic.
2. Click the **Outline** tool. The flyout menu appears.
3. To change the outline thickness, click one of the preset thickness icons in the flyout menu. When you change the thickness of an arrow, the size of the arrowhead changes in proportion.
4. To change the outline color, click the **Color** icon to display the Color dialog box, click a color, and then click **OK**.

To change the fill color, either click a color in the color palette, or proceed as follows:

1. Use the **Pick** tool to select the graphic.
2. Click the **Fill** tool. The Fill flyout menu appears.
3. In the flyout menu, click the **Color** icon. The Color dialog box appears.
4. Click a color in the Color dialog box.
5. Click **OK**.

• **NOTES** You can also select the Quick Pic tool from the dialog box and use it to fill rectangles, ellipses, and other closed shapes, or you can select fills from the Fill flyout menu. See *Fill Effects* for more information.

Annotating Charts with Imported Graphics

You can import graphics files in many different formats and use them as annotations in charts. See Appendix A for a complete list of supported files.

Do the following to import a graphic:

1. With a chart in the Chart window, select **File ➤ Place**. The Place Graphic dialog box appears.
2. In the Place Graphic dialog box, select the directory which contains the graphic file you want.
3. Open the List Files of Type list box and click the relevant type of file. A list of available files appears in the File Name list box.
4. Click the name of the file you want to use as an annotation.
5. Click **OK**. After a few seconds, the graphic appears in your chart with handles around it.
6. If necessary, resize and move the graphic.

• NOTES If the imported graphic is too large to fit on your chart, CorelCHART displays a message and offers to automatically reduce the size to make it fit.

Duplicating an Annotation

To duplicate an annotation, proceed as follows:

1. Use the **Pick** tool to select an annotation on a chart.
2. Select **Edit ➤ Duplicate**. A duplicate of the annotation appears below and to the right of the original. The duplicate is automatically selected.
3. Move the duplicate to the appropriate position.

BAR CHARTS

CorelCHART can create vertical and horizontal bar charts in unstacked and stacked forms. You can create a bar chart based on a template and then make minor or major changes to its appearance.

Creating a Bar Chart

To create a horizontal or vertical bar chart, start at the initial CorelCHART screen or else display an existing chart window. Then do the following:

1. Select **File ➤ New**. The New dialog box, as shown in Figure II.5, appears.
2. In the Gallery list box, click **Bar**.
3. In the Chart Types sample box, click the thumbnail with a format similar to the one you want to use.
4. Click **OK**. A blank worksheet within a Data Manager window appears.
5. Add data into the Data Manager window. See *Adding Data to a Worksheet*.
6. Click the **Chart** icon. The chart appears within a Chart window.

• **NOTES** A vertical bar chart is also known as a column chart.

Changing Bar Thickness

Bars always have the same thickness. You can choose from five standard thicknesses.

1. With a chart displayed, use the **Pick** tool to point onto any bar.
2. Click the right mouse button. A Bar pop-up menu appears.
3. In the pop-up menu, point to **Bar Thickness** and click the left mouse button. A flyout menu appears offering a choice of five thicknesses.

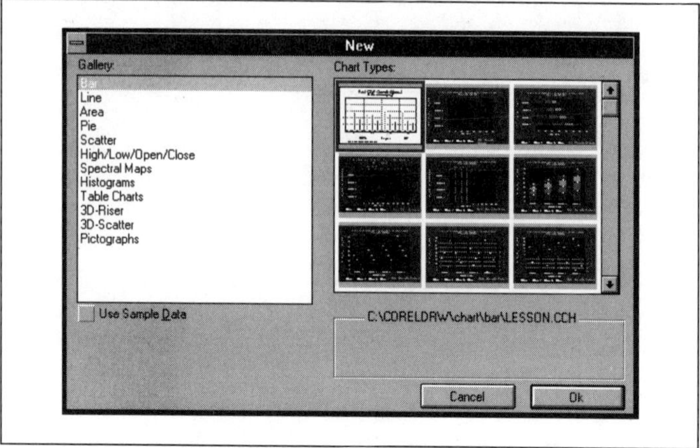

Figure II.5: The New dialog box

4. Press and hold down the left mouse button while you point to various thicknesses. As you do, the thumbnail at the top of the flyout menu shows you what the various thicknesses look like.
5. With the thickness you want displayed, release the mouse button. The bars in your chart change to the new thickness.

Changing Bar Spacing

The spacing between the bars in each series is always the same. You can choose from five standard spacings Follow the steps listed under "Changing Bar Thickness", but in step 3 click **Bar-Bar Spacing** in the pop-up menu.

Reversing Series

You can reverse the series for all types of charts except table charts.

For a bar chart, the sequence of values in one row of a worksheet is known as a series, although you can choose to use the sequence of values in a column as a series (see *Adding Data to a Worksheet*). When you display a bar chart, the series are shown in the order they occur in the worksheet—the first row, then the second, and so on. Reversing a series allows you to reverse the order in the chart so that the last row in the worksheet is the first in the chart, the next-to-last is second, and so on. To reverse the series:

1. With a chart displayed, use the **Pick** tool to point onto any bar.
2. Click the right mouse button. A Bar pop-up menu appears.
3. In the pop-up menu, point to **Data Reversal** and click the left mouse button. A flyout appears for choosing between Reverse Series and Reverse Groups.
4. Click **Reverse Series**. The chart is regenerated with the series reversed.

• **NOTES** To revert to the original series order, repeat steps 1 through 4.

Reversing Groups

You can reverse groups for all types of charts except table charts.

In a vertical bar chart, a group is the data in a column of the worksheet. When you display a bar chart, the groups are shown in the order they occur in the worksheet—the first column, then the second, and so on. Reversing groups allows you to reverse the order in the chart so that the last column in the worksheet is the first in the chart, the next-to-last is second, and so on.

To reverse the groups, follow the steps listed under "Reversing Series," but click **Reverse Groups** instead of Reverse Series in step 4.

Using Columns as Series

As explained above under "Reversing Series," a series is normally the sequence of values in one row of a worksheet. To use the sequence of values in columns as a series, do the following:

1. With a chart displayed, click the **Data Manager** icon to display the chart's worksheet.
2. Select **Data ➤ Data Orientation**. The Data Orientation dialog box appears, normally with the **Series are ROWS** button selected.

3. Click the **Series are COLUMNS** button.
4. Click **OK**.
5. Click the **Chart** icon to redisplay the chart.

Changing the Shape of Bars

By default, CorelCHART shows bars as rectangles. You can, if you wish, replace the rectangles with various shapes, with a different shape for each bar in a series. To do this:

1. With a chart displayed, use the **Pick** tool to point onto one bar of a group.
2. Click the right mouse button. The Bar pop-up menu appears.
3. In the pop-up menu, point to **Marker Shape** and click the left mouse button. A flyout menu appears with a list of various shapes you can use.
4. Click one of the shape names. The chart is regenerated, and all the bars representing the group you selected in step 1 are given the new shape.
5. Repeat steps 1 through 4 to create a chart with different shapes for other groups.

Changing the Vertical Scale

CorelCHART automatically chooses a linear vertical scale for vertical bar graphs with zero as the lowest point on the scale and a maximum value large enough for the largest data value in the worksheet. In some circumstances, you may want to change these automatic choices. To do this:

1. With a chart displayed, point to one of the numbers in the vertical axis and click the right mouse button. The Data Axis Scale pop-up menu appears with many choices, some of which are checked by default.
2. Point to the item in the pop-up menu and click the left mouse button to choose what you want to modify. The list below describes the choices.

- Display the vertical axis on the left or right of the chart.
- Display the vertical axis as a linear or logarithmic scale.
- Change the range of the vertical axis. When you choose this option, you get the Scale Range dialog box for specifying the vertical axis minimum and maximum values.
- Change the format of the numbers on the vertical axis. You can choose such things as the number of decimal places to display, whether to display the values as numbers, dollars, or percentages, whether to display values conventionally or in scientific format, and whether to display values as times or dates.
- Choose to display or not to display horizontal and vertical grid lines, and to display or not to display tick marks on the axes.
- Change the order of values on the vertical axis from ascending to descending.
- Change the display of values adjacent to the vertical axis. Instead of being one above the other, you can have a staggered layout in which alternate values are moved to the left.

CASCADING VIEWS

When the Data Manager and Chart windows are displayed together on the screen, you can return to the normal one-at-a-time display by selecting **Window ➤ Cascade**.

• NOTES In this view, one window is superimposed over the other, and just the border of the window in back shows. You can click on the back window to bring it to the front. You can click on either window's Maximize button to expand it.

CHANGING THE APPEARANCE OF A WORKSHEET

There are several ways to change the appearance of a worksheet.

Changing Column Widths

When CorelCHART creates a worksheet, all the columns are initially the same width. To change the width of individual columns:

1. Point into the row that contains the column letters at the top of the worksheet and move the cursor onto the dividing line that separates the column you want to change from the column on the right. When the cursor is in the correct position it changes to a double-headed arrow.
2. Press the mouse button and drag to the right or left. As you drag, the line separating the columns moves.
3. When you are satisfied with the column width, release the mouse button.

Changing the Number Format

When CorelCHART creates a worksheet, it makes certain assumptions about the type of data represented by numbers, and formats them accordingly. You can change the format of numbers in individual cells or groups of cells. You can choose various numeric, money, and percentage formats. You can also choose to display values as times or dates. Do the following:

1. Select the cell or cells containing number formats you want to change.
2. Select **Data ➤ Number Format**. The Number Format dialog box appears.

3. Scroll down the Format list box and click the format you want to use. An example of that format appears below the list box.
4. Click **OK** to apply that format to the selected cells.

Changing Text Alignment

When CorelCHART creates a worksheet, all cell data is given the General alignment. In this alignment, numbers are aligned on the right edge of the cell and labels (alphabetic text) are aligned on the left edge. You can select individual cells, or groups of cells, and change their alignment.

1. Select one or more cells in the worksheet.
2. Select **Data ➤ Alignment**. A flyout menu appears.
3. In the flyout menu, click **Left**, **Right**, or **Center**, according to which alignment you want.

Sorting Data

You can change the order of columns in a worksheet by sorting according to the values in one row, and you can change the order of rows by sorting according to the values in a column. To change columns in ascending order to descending order:

1. Select the cells containing the data to be sorted. You must include the row containing the data which determines the sort order.
2. Select **Data ➤ Sort**. The Sort dialog box appears.
3. Click one of the buttons under Sort Method, in this case **By Columns**.
4. Click one of the buttons under Sort Type, in this case **Descending**.
5. Replace the character in the Sort Key text box with a letter or number representing the column or row containing the data on which the sort is to be based. For example, if you were sorting that data in row 4, you would type in 4.
6. Click **OK**. The worksheet reappears with the data sorted in the new order.

Exchanging Data between Rows and between Columns

You can swap the data between two rows or between two columns.

1. Without any specific cells selected, select **Data ➤ Exchange**. The Exchange dialog box, shown in Figure II.6, appears.
2. In the Exchange dialog box, click **Rows** to exchange data between rows, or **Columns** to exchange data between columns.
3. In the First Row (or First Column) text box, type the number of a row (or letter of a column).
4. In the Second Row (or Second Column) text box, type the number of another row (or letter of another column).
5. Click **OK**. The worksheet reappears with the two rows (or two columns) exchanged.

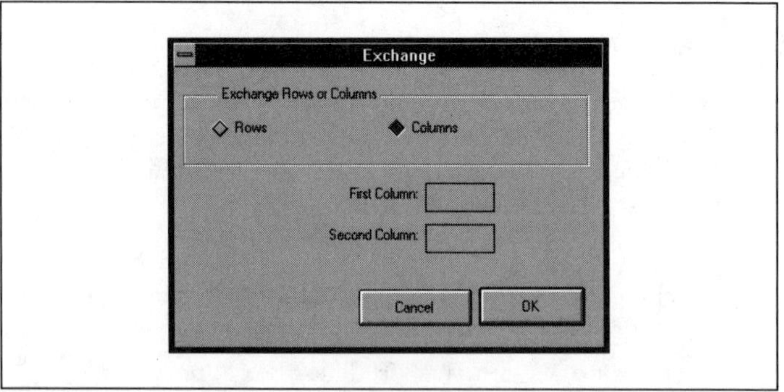

Figure II.6: The Exchange dialog box

CHART COMPONENTS

The many types of charts you can create with CorelCHART have many components in common. The components of a typical chart are described below.

COMPONENT	DESCRIPTION
Annotation	Explanatory text or graphics placed anywhere on the chart.
Category Axis	The axis on which the categories of values are represented, often the horizontal axis.
Data Axis	The axis on which the charted values are represented, often the vertical axis.
Footnote	A comment, such as a credit for the data plotted, usually at the bottom of the chart.
Legend	Definitions of colors or hatch patterns that represent data.
Subtitle	A secondary name or explanation of the chart, usually placed under the title.
Title	The name of the chart, usually placed at the top.

CHART TEMPLATES

You can use an existing chart without its data as a template for another chart. The CorelDRAW package contains several templates you can use in this way. When you create a new chart, you can choose the template you want to use from thumbnail-size previews. See *Files*.

Changing a Chart's Template

You can change the appearance of a chart by changing from one template to another, as follows:

1. With a chart displayed in the Chart Window, select **File ➤ Apply Template**. The Open Chart dialog box appears.

2. In the Open Chart dialog box, select the directory containing the chart with the template you want to use. A list of available chart templates is displayed in the File Name list box.
3. Scroll, if necessary, and click a file name. The Preview window shows a thumbnail of the selected template.
4. When you have found the template you want, click **OK**. Your chart reappears using the new template.

CHART TYPES

CorelCHART can create 18 types of charts, each with many variations. You can choose any of these chart types when you initially create a chart, and you can change an existing chart from one type to another.

The available chart types are

- high, low, open, close
- histograms
- horizontal area
- horizontal bar
- horizontal line
- pie
- scatter
- spectral maps
- tables
- three-dimensional connect group
- three-dimensional connect series
- three-dimensional floating
- three-dimensional riser
- three-dimensional scatter

- three-dimensional surface
- vertical area
- vertical bar
- vertical line

See the CorelDRAW *User's Manual* for advice on choosing the right type of chart in a particular situation.

In this book, most of the information is presented as it applies to bar graphs. Significant differences between bar graphs and other types of graphs are noted.

Changing from One Type of Chart to Another

To change a chart type:

1. With a chart displayed in the Chart window, select **Gallery**. The Gallery menu appears with the type of the displayed chart checked.
2. Click a new type name. In each case, a flyout menu appears with a list of variations of the new type.
3. Click the variation you want to use. The chart is redisplayed in the new format.

• NOTES If, in step 2, you click the current type of the chart, the flyout window allows you to choose a different variation of that type.

There are too many chart types and their variations to show in this book. You may want to choose those types and variations that interest you and print them for future reference.

CHART VARIATIONS

Templates provided with CorelCHART offer many variations of the basic chart types. You can also the use the charts you create as templates for new charts.

To display the available templates:

1. With a chart window displayed, select **File ➤ New**. The New dialog box appears.
2. In the Gallery list box, click on one of the basic chart types. The Chart Types box displays the templates available for the selected type of chart.

COLORING CHART ELEMENTS

You can apply colors or shades of gray to chart elements either by choosing from a limited range in the color palette at the bottom of the chart window or by choosing from a more extensive range in the Color dialog box. You can also fill chart elements with patterns and fountain fills. See *Fill Effects*.

Using the Color Palette

To change the color of a chart element:

1. Use the **Pick** tool to select a chart element.
2. Click a color or shade of gray in the color palette. The selected element and all like it change to the new color.

• **NOTES** When you color one bar of a bar chart, one slice in a multiple pie chart, one riser in a three-dimensional chart, or any other marker representing a part of a series, that color is automatically applied to all other markers in the same series.

Using the Color Dialog Box

To change the color of an element:

1. Use the **Pick** tool to select a chart element.

2. Click the **Fill** tool. A flyout appears.
3. In the flyout, click the **Color** icon. The Color dialog box appears, as shown in Figure II.7.
4. Click a color. The selected element and all like it change to the new color.

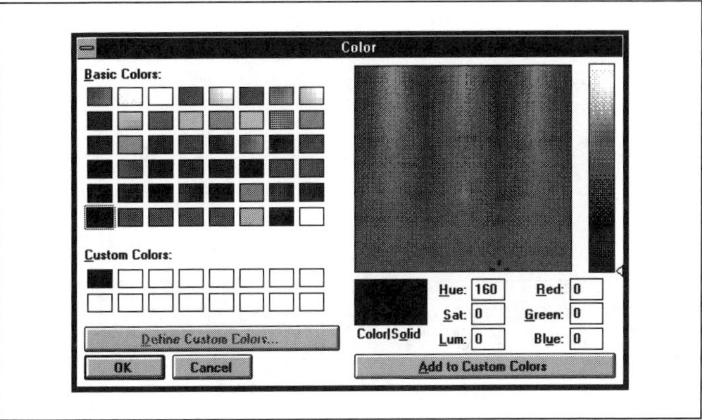

Figure II.7: The Color dialog box

COMBINATION CHARTS

You can create combination charts in which two types of chart are shown within the same chart. As an example, do the following:

1. Display a bar chart in the Chart window.
2. Select one of the bars in the series.
3. Select **Chart ➤ Display As Line** to show it as a line. The chart is redrawn with the selected series shown as a line.

DATA MANAGER

The Data Manager contains a worksheet in the form of a matrix, similar to a spreadsheet in Lotus 1-2-3 or Excel. It contains the data from which CorelCHART creates charts. You can place data into the worksheet cells manually, or you can import or link data from other applications. The only way you can change chart data is in the Data Manager, whether you make changes directly or by linking to other applications.

The Data Manager is also the place where you assign cell tags to indicate how the contents of each cell are used in a chart. See *Tagging Cells*.

DELETING CELL DATA IN A WORKSHEET

You can delete data from individual cells or from multiple cells in a worksheet.

1. Select the cells from which you want to delete data
2. Either press the Delete key or select **Edit ➤ Clear**.

DELETING, INSERTING, AND MOVING ROWS AND COLUMNS

Deleting, inserting, and moving rows and columns in a worksheet is done by cutting to the Clipboard and then pasting from the Clipboard.

Deleting a Row from a Worksheet

To delete a row:

1. With the **Pick** tool, point onto the leftmost cell of the row you want to delete.
2. Press and hold down the mouse button, and drag to the right to include all the cells in the row.
3. Release the mouse button. The row of cells is highlighted.
4. Select **Edit ➤ Cut**. The highlighted row of cells is still present, but contains no data.
5. With the **Pick** tool, point onto the leftmost cell in the row below the empty row.
6. Press and hold down the mouse button, then drag down and to the right to include all the cells below the empty row.
7. Release the mouse button. The selected cells are highlighted.
8. Select **Edit ➤ Cut**. The selected cells contain no data.
9. Point to the leftmost cell of the deleted row and click the mouse button. The cell is highlighted.
10. Select **Edit ➤ Paste**. The data you removed in step 8 is pasted back into the worksheet.

Deleting a Column from a Worksheet

Follow the steps in "Deleting a Row from a Worksheet" above, but replace "row" with "column," and "column" with "row."

Inserting a Row into a Worksheet

1. With the **Pick** tool, point onto the leftmost cell in the row above which you want to insert a row.
2. Press and hold down the mouse button, and drag down and to the right to include all the cells in and below that row.
3. Release the mouse button. The selected cells are highlighted.
4. Select **Edit ➤ Cut**. The selected cells contain no data.

5. To insert a row, point to the left cell of the row below where you want the inserted row to be. The cell is highlighted.
6. Select **Edit ➤ Paste**. The data you removed in step 8 is pasted back into the worksheet, leaving an empty row.

Inserting a Column into a Worksheet

Follow the steps in "Inserting a Row into a Worksheet" above, but replace "row" with "column," and "column" with "row."

Moving Rows and Columns in a Worksheet

To move one or more rows, or one or more columns, use the cut-and-paste technique described above. To move two columns, for example:

1. Identify the place where the columns will be moved to and insert two empty columns there.
2. Cut the two columns to be moved.
3. Paste the two columns into the empty columns you created in step 1.
4. Cut the two empty columns remaining after step 2.

DISPLAYING AND HIDING CHART ELEMENTS

You can choose which of the elements of a chart to display. To do this:

1. With a chart displayed in the Chart window, select **Chart ➤ Display Status**. The Display Status dialog box appears. Chart elements currently being displayed are checked, as shown in Figure II.8.

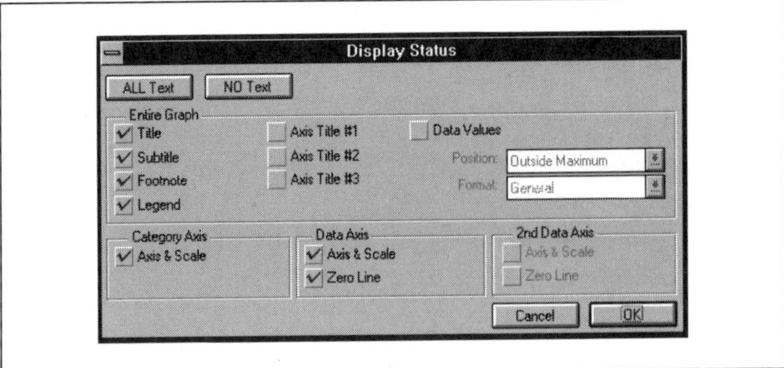

Figure II.8: The Display Status dialog box

2. Click the appropriate buttons to check or uncheck the chart elements you want to display or hide. Alternatively, click **ALL Text** to display all the text in the chart, or **NO Text** to display the graphics without any text.
3. Click **OK**.

• **NOTES** If you check the Data Values box, each data value is displayed on the chart in numbers, as well as by the size of a chart element. You can choose the position and format of these numbers.

If you are working with a three-dimensional chart, the 3D Graph Display Status dialog box appears. This allows you to select which of the three-dimensional background elements you want to include in the chart.

DYNAMIC DATA EXCHANGE

You can setup links between CorelCHART charts and another application in which the data for those charts was prepared. To do so, however, the application must support dynamic data exchange (DDE). You must establish DDE links in the original file. Subsequently, your charts are updated automatically whenever a change is made to the original data. Changes you make to the data in CorelCHART do not affect the original file.

Do the following to create a DDE link:

1. Display the CorelCHART Data Manager screen to which you want to link data.
2. Minimize, but do not close, CorelCHART.
3. Open the application, Excel for example, from which the link is to be established.
4. In that application, open the file containing the data you want or to link into CorelCHART.
5. Select the range of cells to be linked.
6. Select **Edit ➤ Copy**. The selected cells are copied into the Clipboard.
7. Click the **CorelCHART** icon at the bottom of the screen to make CorelCHART the active application.
8. In the Data Manager window, click on the cell where the linked cells should begin.
9. Select **Edit ➤ Paste Link**. The data from the other application appears in the worksheet.
10. Optionally, return to the other application, make a change to some of the linked data, and return to the Data Manager window to confirm that the change has occurred.

EMBEDDING AND LINKING CHARTS

You can embed or link a CorelCHART chart into a CorelDRAW file, CorelSHOW presentation, or other OLE-capable Windows applications. See *Embedding and Linking Objects* in Part I of this book.

EXPORTING A CHART

You can export a chart as a file, or you can export it by way of the Clipboard.

Exporting a Chart to a File

You can export a chart to a file in many different formats. See Appendix A for a complete list of available formats. Do the following to export a chart:

1. Display the chart in the Chart window.
2. Select **File ➤ Export**. The Export Chart dialog box appears.
3. In the Directories list box, select the directory into which you want to write the exported chart.
4. Open the **List Files of Type** list box.
5. Click the format in which you want to export the chart. The format name appears in the List Files of Type text box.
6. Click in the **File Name** text box to create an insertion point.
7. Click **OK**. The chart is written to disk.

Exporting a Chart by Way of the Clipboard

The easiest way to export a chart to another Windows application is by way of the Clipboard.

1. Display a chart in the Chart window.
2. Select **Edit ➤ Copy Chart**. The chart is copied into the Clipboard.
3. Make the other Windows application active.
4. Select **Edit ➤ Paste**. The entire chart is copied into that application.

FILES

This section deals with topics concerned with CorelCHART files. It explains opening charts, and saving and closing files.

Opening a New Chart

1. Select **File ➤ New**. The New dialog box appears.
2. In the Gallery list box, click the type of chart you want to create. The Chart Type sample box displays several templates for charts of the type you select.
3. Click the template you want to use. The information box below the sample box shows the file name of the template you have selected, and provides a brief description of the template.
4. If the Use Sample Data check box has a check mark in it, click the box to remove the check mark.
5. Click **OK**. A Data Manager window appears.
6. Add data into the Data Manager cells. Refer to *Adding Data to a Worksheet*.

• **NOTES** If you check the Use Sample Data button in the New dialog box and then click OK, you see a sample chart based on the template you selected. Select the template that most nearly matches the chart you want to create. You can subsequently modify the appearance of the chart.

Opening an Existing Chart

1. Select **File ➤ Open**. The Open Chart dialog box appears, as shown in Figure II.9. Depending on how it was last used, the dialog box may or may not show a chart image in the Preview box.
2. In the Directories list box, select a directory that contains CorelCHART charts. The File Name list box shows charts in the selected directory.

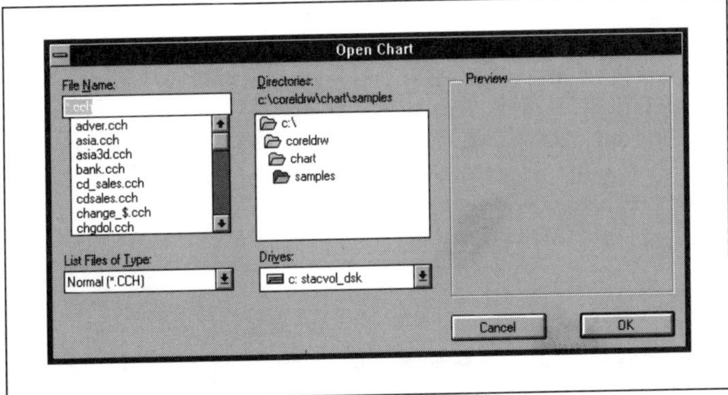

Figure II.9: The Open Chart dialog box

3. In the File Name list box, click the name of the file you want to open. The Preview box shows a miniature image of the selected chart.
4. Click **OK**. A window opens showing the chart.

Saving Files

For information about saving a file with its existing name and saving a file with a new name, see *Files* in Part I of this book. You must have a chart window displayed before you can save a file. CorelCHART automatically adds the extension .CCH to chart file names.

You can save a description with your file but, unlike CorelDRAW, you cannot list keywords.

Closing Files

To close a chart file, you must have the Chart window displayed.

1. If necessary, make the Chart window active.
2. Select **File ➤ Close**.

• **NOTES** The Chart and Data Manager windows are both part of the same file. When a file is open, the Chart window is always on the screen, although it may be partly or even entirely hidden by the Data Manager window. You can display the Chart window with or without the Data Manager window. However, you cannot remove the Chart window without closing the file and, at the same time, removing the Data Manager window.

FILL EFFECTS

You can fill chart elements with colors, hatch patterns, fountain fills, bitmap patterns, and vector graphics. See *Coloring Chart Elements*. The information that follows shows how to use the Quick Pic tool to fill chart elements. You can also select various types of fills from the Fill flyout.

Filling Chart Elements with a Preset Hatch Pattern

When you are going to print charts in black and white, as in this book, it is useful to fill bars with different hatch patterns. To do this:

1. With the chart displayed, use the **Pick** tool to click the **Fill** tool. The Fill flyout appears.
2. Click the second icon from the left in the top row of the Fill flyout. The Quick Pic tool appears, as shown in Figure II.10. The Quick Pic tool is similar to the roll-ups in CorelDRAW, with the exception that you cannot minimize it.
3. In the Quick Pic tool, click the **Hatch Pattern** button, the top button in the column at the left edge of the tool. A hatch pattern appears in the sample box.
4. Click the right-pointing or left-pointing arrow under the sample box to see which hatch patterns are available. Stop at the pattern you want to use.
5. Click the chart element to which you want to apply the hatch pattern.

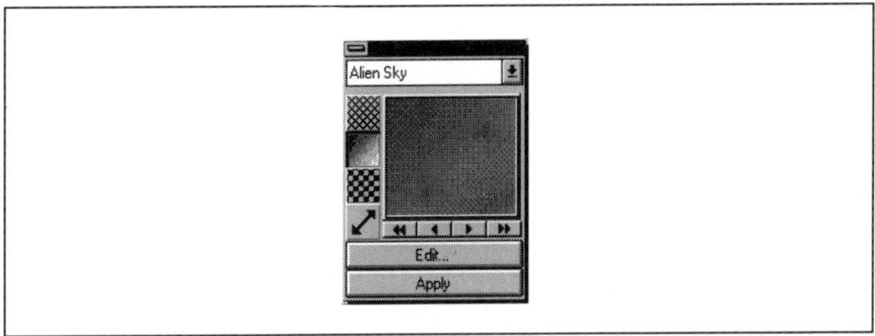

Figure II.10: The Quick Pic tool

6. Click **Apply** in the Quick Pic tool. The chart is redrawn with the new hatch pattern filling the chart element you selected and all others like it.

• **NOTES** By default, hatch patterns are black but you can change them to another color. To change the color of hatch patterns, display a pattern in the Quick Pic tool, and click **Edit**. The Color dialog box appears. Choose a color in the Color dialog box and click **OK**. Hatch patterns now appear in the new color.

Filling Chart Elements with a Preset Fountain Fill

You can choose from 24 preset fountain fills for chart elements or for the background of a chart. Do the following:

1. Follow steps 1 and 2 in "Filling Chart Elements with a Preset Hatch Pattern" above.
2. In the Quick Pic tool, click the **Fountain Fill** button, the second button in the column at the left edge of the tool. A sample fountain fill appears in the large sample window.
3. Click the right-pointing or left-pointing arrow under the sample window to find the preset fountain fill you want to use.
4. Use the **Pick** tool to click the outer border of the chart. A colored line around the chart indicates that the background is selected.

5. Click **Apply**. The chart is redrawn with the fountain fill as a background.

• **NOTES** You can use the same technique to apply fountain fills to other elements on the chart. In step 5 above, select another element you want to fill before you click Apply. If you do not select a chart element before clicking Apply, an error message appears telling you that the fill cannot be applied.

Creating a Custom Fountain Fill

You are not limited to the preset fountain fills supplied with CorelCHART. Do the following to apply a custom fountain fill:

1. Follow steps 1 and 2 in "Filling Chart Elements with a Preset Fountain Fill" above.
2. Click **Edit** in the Quick Pic tool. The Fountain Fill Effect dialog box appears.
3. Open the **Presets** list box and select a preset fountain fill similar to the one you want to create.
4. Open the **Fill Type** list box and select a fill type.
5. Open the **Fill Direction** list box and select a fill direction.
6. Click **Start**. The Color dialog box appears.
7. Choose a starting color for the fill.
8. Click **OK**.
9. Click **End**. The Color dialog box appears.
10. Choose an ending color for the fill.
11. Click **OK**.
12. Click **Save As**. The Save Effect As dialog box appears.
13. Type a name for the fill effect.
14. Click OK.
15. In the Fountain Fill Effect dialog box, click **Done**. The Quick Pic tool reappears with the new fountain fill displayed.
16. Click **Apply** to apply the fill to a selected chart element.

Filling Chart Elements with a Bitmap Pattern

Using bitmap patterns is similar to using hatch patterns. See "Filling Chart Elements with a Preset Hatch Pattern" above for information. Select the **Bitmap Patterns** button in the Quick Pic tool, the third button from the top.

Most Bitmap patterns are in Windows bitmap format and are stored as .BMP files. You can edit these files, or create new ones, in CorelPHOTO-PAINT.

Filling Chart Elements with a Vector Image

Vector images used to replace bars in bar graphs and histograms are also known as pictographs.

Using vector images is similar to using hatch patterns. See "Filling Chart Elements with a Preset Hatch Pattern" above for information. Select the **Vector Image** button, the one on the bottom-left in the Quick Pic tool. When you fill a chart element with a vector image, the height and width of the image are automatically changed to fit within the element.

Vector images are in Windows metafile format and are stored in files with a .WMF extension. You can import these files into CorelDRAW, where you can edit them. You can create your own images to use for filling CorelCHART chart elements.

Removing a Fill from a Chart Element

To remove a fill, replace it with white or any other solid color, as follows:

1. Select the chart element or elements from which you want to remove the fill.
2. Click white, or any other color, in the color palette. The color replaces the fill.

HELP

CorelCHART provides extensive online Help. To access indexed information, press **F1**, or select **Help ➤ Contents** from the Main menu.

You can choose from five categories of help:

Using Help	provides information about how to find what you want in online help.
Commands	offers lists of items in the Chart and Data Manager windows and information about each item.
Tools	provides information about the toolbox and the individual tools.
How To	gives detailed instructions about using CorelCHART to perform certain operations.
Glossary	is an indexed glossary of terms used in CorelCHART and in the charts you create with the module.

You can make a printed copy of any information in online Help.

IMPORTING DATA

You can import data into the Data Manager from ASCII text files, dBASE and compatible databases, from Excel and Lotus 1-2-3 spreadsheets, and from Harvard Graphics. To import data:

1. Display an empty worksheet in the Data Manager window.
2. Select **File ➤ Import Data**. The Import File with File Type dialog box appears.
3. In the Directories list box, select the directory that contains the file you want to import.

4. Open the **List Files of Type** list box.
5. Click the type of file you want to import. The names of files of that type in the selected directory appear in the File Name list box.
6. Click the name of the file to be imported. Its name appears in the File Name text box.
7. Click **OK**. The worksheet reappears with the text and data in place.

MAGNIFYING AND REDUCING THE SCREEN IMAGE OF A CHART

You can use the Zoom tool to magnify or reduce the screen image of a chart.

1. In the Chart window, click the **Zoom** tool. A flyout menu appears.
2. Click one of the magnification icons. The chart is redrawn at the size you chose.
3. If necessary, use the scroll bars at the right and bottom of the Chart window to see a specific part of the chart.

• **NOTES** The FIT icon in the flyout window creates a chart image that just fits in the Chart window. This is useful if you have reduced the size of the window.

MENUS

CorelCHART has standard menus as well as context-sensitive menus.

Main Menu Bar

The Main menu bar is different when the Chart window is active and when the Data Manager window is active, as shown in Figure II.11. Even menus that have the same name in the two menu bars contain different items. See the CorelCHART online Help for detailed information about menus.

1. Select **Help ➤ Contents**.
2. Click the **Commands** icon.
3. Click the name of the menu about which you need information.

Context-Sensitive Menus

Context-sensitive menus provide fast access to the attributes of chart elements. To display a context-sensitive menu, either

- point to a chart element and click the right mouse button; or
- click the **Context-Sensitive Pop-up Menu** tool, the second tool from the top in the toolbox.

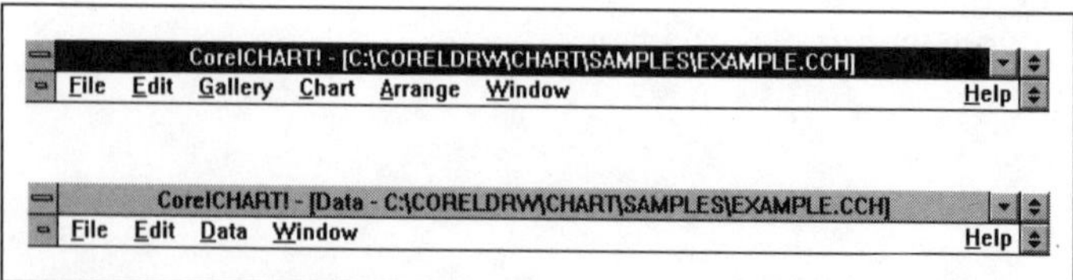

Figure II.11: Main menu bars when the Chart and Data Manager windows are active

In either case, a pop-up menu appears. Click the item on the menu you want to use.

MOVING CHART ELEMENTS

You can move a chart as well as its title, subtitle, footnote, and legend.

Moving a Chart

Do the following to move a two-dimensional chart:

1. Using the **Pick** tool, point onto a chart, but not onto a specific element within the chart.
2. Press and hold down the mouse button until the cursor changes to a four-pointed arrow.
3. Drag the mouse. A dashed rectangle shows the new position of the chart.
4. Release the mouse button. The chart is redrawn in the new position.

You use the 3D Movement tool to move a three dimensional chart. See *3D View Tool*.

Moving Elements Outside a Chart

Use the method described under "Moving a Chart" above to move the title, subtitle, footnote, or legend.

OPENING A NEW OR EXISTING CHART

See *Files*.

OUTLINING BARS

You can outline bars in a bar chart in black, a shade of gray, or another color to enhance their visibility. All the bars in a chart must have the same outline.

Outlining Bars in Black or Gray

Do the following to draw a black outline around all the bars:

1. Use the **Pick** tool to select any bar in the chart.
2. Click the **Outline** tool. A flyout appears.
3. Click one of the ten thickness icons in the top row of the flyout.
4. Repeat step 3.
5. Click the black icon, or one of the gray icons, in the bottom row of the flyout.
6. Click **OK**.

Outlining Bars in Color

Do the following to draw a colored outline around all the bars:

1. Follow steps 1 through 4 in "Outlining Bars in Black or Gray" above.
2. Click the **Color** icon in the flyout, the leftmost icon in the bottom row. The Color dialog box appears.

3. Click one of the basic colors, or a color in the Color Array box.
4. Click **OK**.

Removing Bar Outlines

To remove black, gray, or colored outlines around bars:

1. Follow steps 1 through 3 in "Outlining Bars in Black or Gray" above.
2. Click the *X* in the top row of the flyout.
3. Click **OK**.

PAGE SETUP

The Page Setup command allows you to establish your page size and orientation.

1. If the Data Manager window is displayed, switch to the Chart window or to a tiled view of both windows. You cannot access Page Setup from a Data Manager window.
2. Select **File ➤ Page Setup**.
3. Click the appropriate orientation button.
4. Click the appropriate size button.
5. If you select **Custom** size, type values for the horizontal and vertical sizes.
6. Click **OK**.

PIE CHARTS

CorelCHART allows you to create the following type of pie charts:

- basic pie charts;
- ring pie charts;
- multiple pie charts;
- multiple ring pie charts;
- multiple proportional pie charts;
- multiple proportional ring pie charts.

Creating a Pie Chart

You create a pie chart in the same way you create a bar chart. See *Bar Charts*. Figure II.12 shows a typical pie chart.

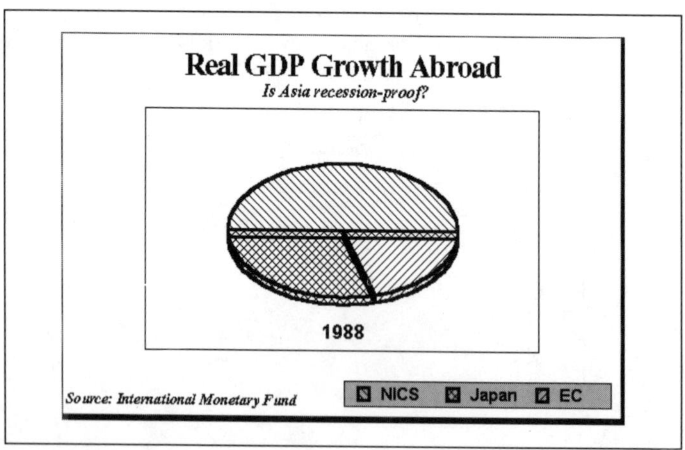

Figure II.12: A typical pie chart

Changing the Overall Appearance of a Pie Chart

Do the following to change the overall appearance of a pie chart:

1. With a pie chart displayed in the Chart window, point outside the chart and click the right mouse button. The Pie Chart Frame pop-up menu appears, as shown in Figure II.13.
2. Point onto the menu choice you want, and click the left mouse button.

Changing the Tilt of a Pie Chart

You can change the tilt of a pie chart as follows:

1. Display the Pie Chart Frame pop-up menu, as described above.
2. Click **Pie Tilt**. A flyout menu appears.
3. Click one of the five choices in the flyout menu to select the tilt you want. The pie chart is redrawn with the selected tilt.

Changing the Thickness of a Pie Chart

You can change the thickness of a pie chart as follows:

1. Display the Pie Chart Frame pop-up menu, as described above.
2. Click **Pie Thickness**. A flyout menu appears.
3. Click one of the five choices in the flyout menu to select the thickness you want. The pie chart is redrawn with the selected thickness.

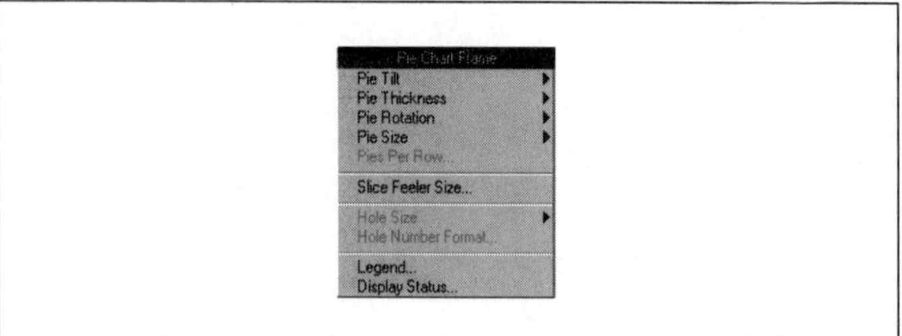

Figure II.13: The Pie Chart Frame pop-up menu

Changing the Rotation of a Pie Chart

You can change the rotation of a pie chart as follows:

1. Display the Pie Chart Frame pop-up menu, as described above.
2. Click **Pie Rotation**. A flyout menu appears.
3. Click one of the five choices in the flyout menu to select the rotation you want. The pie chart is redrawn with the selected rotation.

Changing the Size of a Pie Chart

You can change the size of a pie chart as follows:

1. Display the Pie Chart Frame pop-up menu, as described above.
2. Click **Pie Size**. A flyout menu appears.
3. Click one of the five choices in the flyout menu to select the size you want. The pie chart is redrawn to the selected size.

Changing the Number of Pies Per Row in a Multiple Pie Chart

Do the following to change the number of pies per row:

1. Display the Pie Chart Frame pop-up menu, as described above.
2. Click **Pies Per Row**. A dialog box appears.
3. In the text box, type the number of pies you want in a row.
4. Click **OK**. The chart is redrawn with the new number of pies per row.

Changing the Feeler Size

This menu item duplicates that in the Pie Slice Pop-up menu. The feeler is the line that connects the numeric value or name of a slice to a slice. See "Changing the Slice Feeler Size for Individual Slices" below for information.

Changing the Size of the Hole in a Ring Pie Chart

Do the following to change the size of the hole in a ring pie chart:

1. Display the Pie Chart Frame pop-up menu, as described above.
2. Click **Hole Size**. A flyout menu appears.
3. Click one of the five choices of hole size. The chart is redrawn with the new hole size.

Changing the Format of the Number in the Center of a Ring Pie Chart

The number in the center of a ring pie chart represents the total of the values in each slice. Do the following to change the format of the number:

1. Display the Pie Chart Frame pop-up menu, as described above.

2. Click **Hole Number Format**. The Number Format dialog box appears.
3. Click one of the choices of number formats. The chart is redrawn with the number in the new format.

Changing the Legend in a Pie Chart

The legend tells you what the colors or fill patterns in a pie chart mean. You can change the way the legend is shown as follows:

1. Display the Pie Chart Frame pop-up menu, as described above.
2. Click **Legend**. The Legend dialog box appears.
3. In the Legend dialog box, click the appropriate buttons to choose whether or not to display the legend, the position of the legend text relative to the marker, and the orientation of the legend.
4. Click **OK**. The chart is redrawn with the legend as specified.

Changing the Status of a Pie Chart

Changing the status allows you to determine which categories of text are displayed with a pie chart. To change the status:

1. Display the Pie Chart Frame pop-up menu, as described above.
2. Click **Display Status**. The Pie Chart Display Status dialog box appears.
3. Click the appropriate buttons to display or hide various categories of text.
4. Click **OK**. The chart is redrawn with the selected text categories displayed.

Changing the Appearance of a Pie Chart Slice

Do the following to change the appearance of a slice in a pie chart:

1. With a pie chart displayed in the Chart window, point onto the slice you want to change and click the right mouse button. The Pie Slice pop-up menu appears, as shown in Figure II.14.
2. Point onto the pop-up menu choice you want to use, and click the left mouse button.

Detaching a Slice from a Pie Chart

You can detach one or more slices from a pie chart as follows:

1. Display the Pie Slice pop-up menu, as described above.
2. Click **Detach Slice**. A flyout menu appears.
3. Click one of the choices in the flyout menu to select no detachment, or one of four degrees of detachment. The pie chart is redrawn with the selected detachment.

Deleting a Slice from a Pie Chart

You can delete one or more slices from a pie chart as follows:

1. Display the Pie Slice pop-up menu, as described above.
2. Click **Delete Slice**. The pie chart is redrawn with the slice deleted.

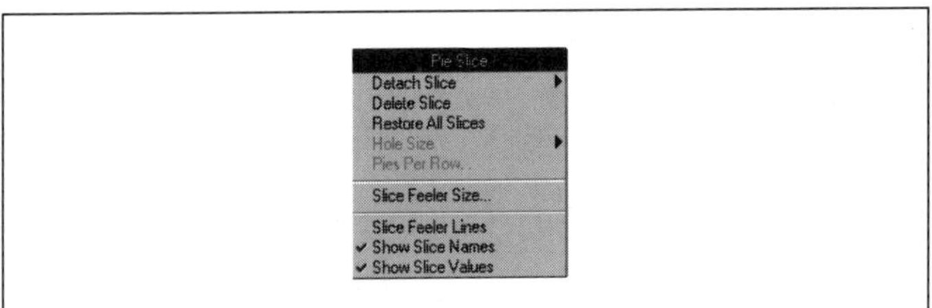

Figure II.14: The Pie Slice pop-up menu

Restoring Slices to a Pie Chart

After you have deleted one or more slices from a pie chart, you can restore them all as follows:

1. Display the Pie Slice pop-up menu, as described above.
2. Click **Restore All Slices**. The pie chart is redrawn with all slices present.

Changing the Slice Feeler Size for Individual Slices

Do the following to change the size of a feeler. A feeler is a line that connects a numeric value or a name of a slice (if shown) to a slice.

1. Display the Pie Slice pop-up menu, as described above.
2. Click **Slice Feeler Size**. The Slice Feeler Size dialog box appears.
3. In the dialog box, drag the circles on the feeler to change the feeler size.
4. Click **OK**. The chart is redrawn with the new size feeler for the selected slice.

Showing and Hiding Feelers

Feelers—the lines that connect slice names and values to slices—can be shown or hidden. When feelers are hidden, slice names and values can still be shown. If they are shown, they appear in the same position they would be in if feelers were present. Do the following to show or hide feelers:

1. Display the Pie Slice pop-up menu, as described above.
2. Click **Slice Feeler Lines** to hide feelers if they were shown, or to show them if they were hidden. The chart is redrawn.

Showing and Hiding Slice Names

The names of slices can be shown or hidden. Do the following to show slice names:

1. Display the Pie Slice pop-up menu, as described above.
2. Click **Show Slice Names**. The chart is redrawn with slice names indicated by feelers.

Showing and Hiding Slice Values

The values of slices can be shown or hidden. Do the following to show slice values:

1. Display the Pie Slice pop-up menu, as described above.
2. Click **Show Slice Values**. The chart is redrawn with slice values indicated by feelers.

PRINTING CHARTS AND WORKSHEETS

The facilities for printing charts are similar to those for printing documents in most Windows applications. See *Printing Drawings* in Part I of this book for information.

CorelCHART does not allow you to print worksheets. You can create a Table chart, which is similar to a worksheet, and print that.

REPLACING BARS WITH PICTOGRAPHS

See the explanation of filling chart elements with a vector image in *Fill Effects*.

RESIZING

You can resize a chart, and you can separately resize text in the title, subtitle, footnote, and legend.

Resizing Charts

To change the size of an entire chart, including the elements within the chart, do the following:

1. With a chart displayed in the Chart window, use the **Pick** tool to point within the chart, but not on a specific element, and then click the mouse button. Handles appear at the four corners of the chart and at the mid-points of the top, bottom, and sides.
2. Point onto a corner handle, press and hold down the mouse button, and drag diagonally to change the size of the chart but keep the height and width in proportion. Use a handle at the center of the top or bottom to change the height of the chart but keep the width unchanged. Use a handle at the center of a side to change the width but keep the height unchanged. A dashed outline shows the new size.
3. Release the mouse button. The chart is redrawn at the new size.

• **NOTES** You can use the technique described above to change the size of the entire legend.

Resizing Text

To change the size of text in the title or subtitle, do the following:

1. Use the **Text** tool to highlight all the text characters to be changed.
2. Open the Font Size list box.
3. Scroll, if necessary, to the new font size and click.

• **NOTES** You can only resize text in proportion; you cannot stretch or compress it.

SCREEN

See *Screen* in Part I of this book for information about the parts of CorelCHART screens that are similar to CorelDRAW screens. Screen components unique to CorelCHART are described below.

The Chart Screen

Figure II.15 shows a typical CorelCHART chart screen. The screen components that are different from those in CorelDRAW screens are explained below.

COMPONENT	PURPOSE
Data Manager icon	With a chart displayed, click the Data Manager icon to access the data on which the chart is based.
Text Ribbon	The Text Ribbon allows you to quickly modify the attributes of text on a chart. See *Text Ribbon*.

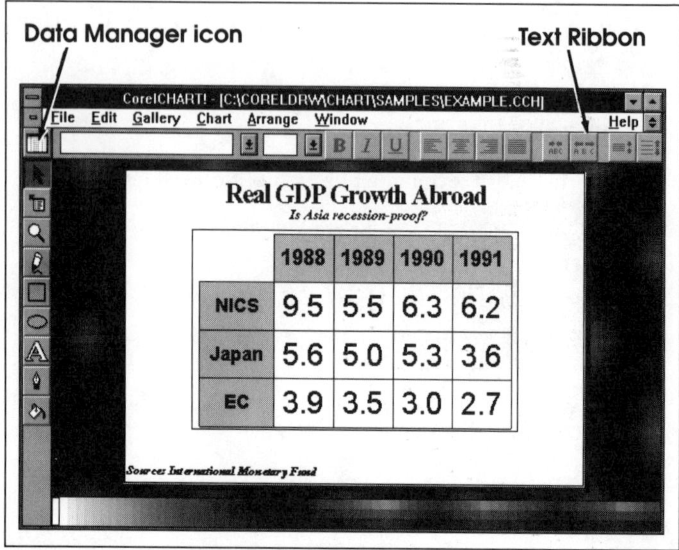

Figure II.15: A typical CorelCHART chart screen

The Data Manager Screen

Figure II.16 shows a typical CorelCHART Data Manager screen. The screen components different from those in Corel-DRAW screens are explained below.

COMPONENT	PURPOSE
Contents box	This box shows the contents of the selected cell.
Font Name box	This box shows the name of the font used in the selected area of the screen. If no area is selected, the box is blank.
Font Size box	This box shows the size of the font used in the selected area of the screen. If no area is selected, the box is blank.
Preview box	This box shows a thumbnail preview of the current chart.

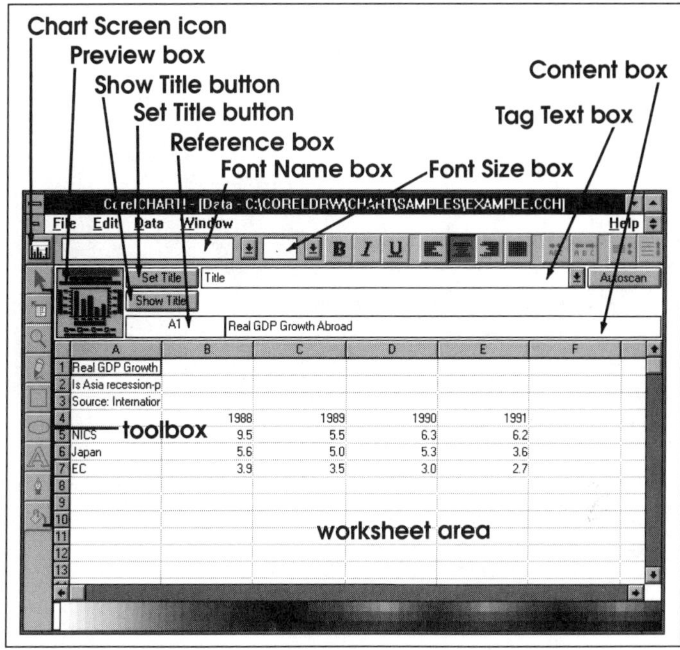

Figure II.16: A typical CorelCHART chart screen

COMPONENT	PURPOSE
Reference box	This box shows the column and row of the selected cell.
Set Title button	Click this button to assign the tag shown in the Tag Text box to selected cells.
Show Title button	Click this button to highlight cells to which the tag shown in the Tag Text box has been assigned.
Tag Text box	This box shows the currently selected tag. Click this box to drop down a list of tags.
toolbox	All toolbox icons are dimmed and not available when the Data Manager window is displayed.

COMPONENT	PURPOSE
worksheet area	This area contains the cells in which the Data Manager stores data.

SELECTING AND DESELECTING ELEMENTS ON A CHART

You select chart elements in order to make changes to them. You can select individual objects or multiple objects.

Selecting Individual Objects

To select a single object:

1. Use the **Pick** tool to point onto an object.
2. Click the mouse button. All previously selected objects are deselected and the object you are pointing onto is selected.

Selecting Multiple Objects

To select more than one object:

1. Use the **Pick** tool to point onto the first object.
2. Click the mouse button.
3. Point onto another object.
4. Hold down the Shift key while you click the mouse button.
5. Repeat steps 3 and 4 to select additional objects.

Deselecting All Selected Objects

To deselect all selected objects:

1. Use the **Pick** tool to point onto a blank area of the chart window.
2. Click the mouse button.

Deselecting One out of Many Selected Objects

When you have many objects selected, do the following to deselect them one at a time:

1. Point to the object you want to deselect.
2. Hold down the Shift key and click the mouse button.

SELECTING CELLS IN A WORKSHEET

You can select individual cells, rectangular blocks of cells, or scattered cells.

Selecting an Individual Cell

1. Point onto the cell.
2. Click the mouse. Dark lines outline the selected box, the Reference box shows the cell's column and row, and the Contents box shows the cell's contents.

Selecting a Rectangular Block of Cells

1. Point to the cell at one corner of the rectangular block and click the mouse button.

2. Point to the cell at the opposite corner of the rectangular block and hold down the Shift key while you click the mouse button. Dark lines outline the first selected cell and the other cells in the block become black with white lettering. The Reference box shows the first cell's column and row, and the Contents box shows the last cell's contents.

Selecting Scattered Cells as a Group

1. Point onto one cell and click the mouse button.
2. Point onto another cell and hold down the Ctrl key while you click the mouse button.
3. Repeat step 2 to select additional cells. Dark lines outline the last selected cell and the other selected cells become black with white lettering. The Reference box shows each cell's column and row as it is selected, and the Contents box shows the cell's contents.

SHORTCUT KEYS

Most procedures in this book are described in terms of selecting from menus, but CorelCHART provides keyboard shortcuts to speed certain actions. Many of these shortcuts appear in dialog boxes. When you find yourself using a command often, look in the dialog box to learn its shortcut.

Function Key Shortcuts

FUNCTION KEY	ACTION
F1	accesses online Help.
Shift-F4	executes the Tile Vertically command.
Shift-F5	executes the Cascade command.

Speed Key Shortcuts

KEY	ACTION
Ctrl-D	executes the Duplicate command.
Ctrl-I	opens the Import Data dialog box.
Ctrl-O	opens the Open Chart dialog box.
Ctrl-P	opens the Print Options dialog box.
Ctrl-S	saves the chart under the current file name.
Ctrl-W	executes the Redraw Window command.
Ctrl-X	exits CorelCHART.
Shift-Insert	executes the Paste command.
Ctrl-Insert	executes the Copy command.
Delete	executes the Clear command.
Shift-Delete	executes the Cut command.
Alt-Backspace	undoes the most recent action.
PageDown	executes the Backward One command.
Shift-PageDown	executes the To Back command.
PageUp	executes the Forward One command.
Shift-PageUp	executes the To Front command.

STACKING ORDER

You can use the Arrange menu to change the stacking order of objects in the annotation layer of a chart. See *Stacking Order* in Part I of this book for information.

STATISTICAL DATA

CorelCHART can calculate statistical data based on values in a series. Use the following steps:

1. Display a bar chart in the Chart window.
2. Use the **Pick** tool to point onto one member of a series.
3. Click the right mouse button. A Bar Riser pop-up menu appears.
4. With the left mouse button, click **Data Analysis**. The Data Analysis dialog box appears, as shown in Figure II.17.
5. Click one or more buttons in the dialog box to select the statistical data you want.
6. Click **OK**. The chart reappears with a line representing each of the types of statistical data you selected in step 5.

• NOTES The lines representing the statistical data are in the same color as the series data in the chart. As these lines are not labeled, it is advisable to request only one type of statistical data at a time.

You can also display the Data Analysis dialog box from the Chart menu.

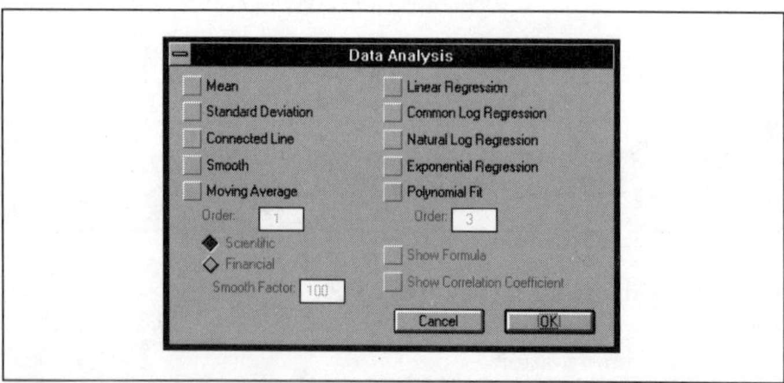

Figure II.17: The Data Analysis dialog box

SWITCHING BETWEEN DATA MANAGER AND CHART VIEWS

In a Data Manager window, click the Chart icon just above the toolbox to display the corresponding chart window.

In a chart window, click the Data Manager icon just above the toolbox to display the corresponding Data Manager window.

For information about how to display the corresponding Data Manager and Chart windows side-by-side on the screen, see *Tiling Views*.

TABLE CHARTS

CorelCHART allows you to present data in tabular form. You create a table chart in the same way you create a bar chart. See *Bar Charts*.

Automatically Coloring Rows and Columns in a Table Chart

Do the following to control how CorelCHART applies colors to a table chart:

1. With a table chart displayed in the Chart window, select **Chart ➤ Divisions**. The Table Chart Divisions dialog box appears.
2. In the top part of the dialog box, click one of the three buttons to select **No Color Divisions** (to make all data cells the same color), **Color by Rows**, or **Color by Columns**.

3. If you selected either Color by Rows or Color by Columns, click the **Include Headers** check box in the top part of the dialog box to extend, or not extend, the coloring of data cells into the header.
4. In the bottom part of the dialog box, you can change the numbers in boxes to control how many adjacent rows or columns have the same color, and how many colors are used for these rows or columns.

Manually Coloring Rows and Columns in a Table Chart

You can choose individual colors for columns or rows.

1. Follow steps 1 and 2 above, selecting either **Color by Rows**, or **Color by Columns**.
2. Click close to the edge of a cell. A colored outline appears around the cell. Make sure the entire cell is selected, not just the text or number inside it.
3. Click a color in the color palette at the bottom of the screen. The entire row (if you selected Color By Rows) or the entire column (if you selected Color by Columns) of cells changes to the new color.

• **NOTES** You can also select a color, or other fill, for cells from the Color dialog box. See *Coloring Chart Elements*.

Coloring Text and Numbers in Cells

Follow the three steps under "Manually Coloring Rows and Columns in a Table Chart" except, in step 2, click close to the center of a cell to select the text or number inside it.

Turning Grids and Borders On or Off

You can turn table borders, as well as the grid lines between cells, on or off. To do this:

1. With a table chart displayed in the Chart window, select **Chart ➤ Grids & Borders**. The Grids and Borders dialog box appears.
2. Click the individual segments of the grids and borders image in the dialog box to change them from black to white. Those segments that are black exist in the table; those that are white are not shown in the table.
3. Click **OK**.

Changing the Thickness of the Border or a Grid Line

Do the following to change the thickness of the border or a grid line:

1. Click the border or a grid line to select it.
2. Click the **Outline** tool. A flyout appears.
3. Click one of the thickness icons to select one of ten preset line thicknesses. The border or grid line changes thickness.

Changing the Color of the Border or a Grid Line

To change a line color:

1. Click the border or on a grid line to select it.
2. Click a color in the color palette. The selected line changes color.

TAGGING CELLS

You can tag cells in a worksheet so that CorelCHART will automatically use the data in those cells correctly when it creates a chart. Each cell can have one of the following tags:

- Axis title #1,
- Axis title #2,
- Axis title #3,
- Column header,
- Data,
- Footnote,
- Row header,
- Subtitle,
- Title.

Tagging allows you to place text and values anywhere in a worksheet, as long as the values in the data range are in a contiguous range of cells, and text that will appear in the chart axes are in contiguous rows or columns.

For example, if you place text and data in the following cells, CorelCHART will correctly interpret it, even if you do not tag it.

- Place the title in cell A1.
- Place the subtitle in cell A2.
- Place the footnote text in cell A3.
- Place row headers in a column of cells, with the first in cell A5, the second in cell A6, and so on.
- Place the column headers in a row of cells, with the first in cell B4, the second in cell C4, and so on.
- Place the values in a matrix of cells, starting at cell C5, and filling cells to the right and down.

If you have additional elements, such as a data axis title or a category title, you must tag them.

Displaying Existing Tags

1. With a worksheet displayed, select any cell that contains data or text.
2. Click the Tag text box to open the tag list box, which is shown in Figure II.18.
3. Click one of the tag names.
4. Click the **Show Title** button. If any cells have the tag you selected in step 3, those cells become highlighted. If there are no cells with that tag, a message box appears with the words "Item has no defined range."
5. Repeat steps 2 through 4 to identify cells with other tags.

Assigning Tags to Cells

1. With a worksheet displayed, select one or more cells to which you want to assign a tag.
2. Click the Tag text box to open the tag list box.
3. Click the tag you want to assign to the selected cell or cells.
4. Click the **Set Title** button.
5. Repeat steps 1 through 4 to assign tags to other cells.

• **NOTES** To assign the Row Header tag, select any cell in the column that contains row headers. All cells in that column are tagged

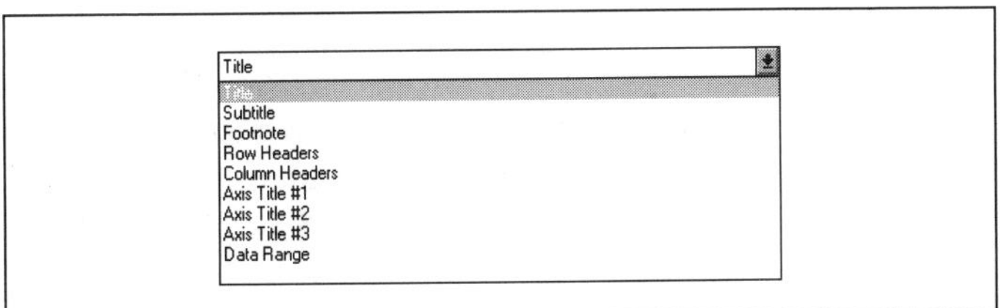

Figure II.18: The Tag list box

as row headers. To assign the Column Header tag, select any cell in the row that contains column headers. All cells in that row are tagged as column headers.

TEXT RIBBON

The Text Ribbon, shown in Figure II.19, provides a fast means of modifying the attributes of text on a chartor worksheet. The text Ribbon is available whenever you select chart text.

To change the attributes of all the characters in a chart component, select that component with the **Pick** tool and then click the appropriate button in the Text Ribbon. To change individual characters in the title or subtitle, select those characters with the **Text** tool and click **Text Ribbon** buttons.

A similar Text Ribbon is available in the Data Manager window. When you click a Text Ribbon button, the changes affect all text in the worksheet.

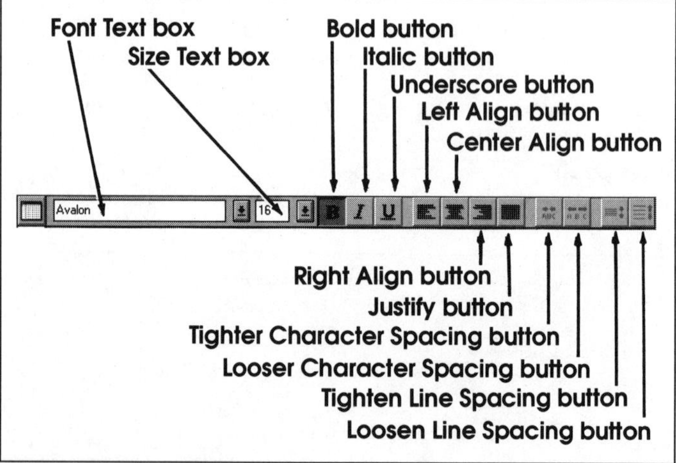

Figure II.19: The Text Ribbon

From left to right, the boxes and buttons in the Text Ribbon have the following functions:

Font Text box	This box initially shows the font name for the currently selected text. To change to another font, click the arrow to the right of the box to drop down a list of other available fonts. Then, click the name of the font you want to use. Alternatively, type the font name and press Enter.
Size Text box	This box initially shows the size of the current selected text. To change the size, click the arrow to the right of the box to drop down a list of other sizes. Then, click the size you want to use. Alternatively, type the font size and press Enter.
Bold button	Click this button to change the selected text to or from bold. Bold is not available in all fonts.
Italic button	Click this button to change the selected text to or from italic. Italic is not available in all fonts.
Underscore button	Click this button to change the selected text to or from underscored.
Left Align button	Click this button to align the selected text at the left margin.
Center Align button	Click this button to center the selected text between the margins.
Right Align button	Click this button to align the selected text at the right margin.
Justify button	Click this button to add spaces between words so that the selected text extends from the left margin to the right margin.

Tighten Character Spacing button	Click this button to reduce character spacing in the selected text.
Loosen Character Spacing button	Click this button to increase character spacing in the selected text.
Tighten Line Spacing button	Click this button to reduce line spacing in the selected text.
Loosen Line Spacing button	Click this button to increase line spacing in the selected text.

THREE-DIMENSIONAL CHARTS

CorelDRAW has extensive capabilities for creating and modifying three-dimensional charts.

Creating a Three-Dimensional Chart

To create a three-dimensional chart, use the same procedure for creating a bar chart, except such as shown in Figure II.20, click **3D-Riser**. See *Bar Charts*. Alternatively, you can change a chart of another type into a three-dimensional chart.

Changing the Appearance of a Three-Dimensional Chart

Use the techniques described in *Bar Charts* to make changes to a three-dimensional chart. In each case, use the **Pick** tool to point onto an element of the chart, and then press the right mouse button to see a pop-up menu. Choose what you want to change from the items in the pop-up menu.

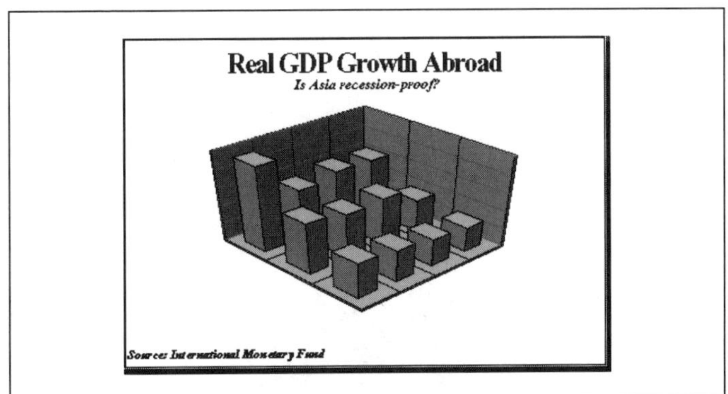

Figure II.20: A typical 3D-Riser three-dimensional chart

Changing the Viewing Angle

You can change the viewing angle to enhance the visual appeal of a chart. In some cases, you might have to change the viewing angle to make certain elements of the chart visible. You can use the steps described here to select one of 16 preset viewing angles, or you can have more detailed control by using the 3D View tool. See *3D View Tool*. Do the following to select a preset viewing angle:

1. Display a three-dimensional chart in the chart window.
2. Select **Chart ➤ Preset Viewing Angles**. A flyout menu appears with a list of 16 preset viewing angles (Standard Angle is the default).
3. Click a different viewing angle. The chart is redrawn with the new viewing angle.

TILING VIEWS

Tiling allows you to display the corresponding chart and Data Manager windows together on the screen. See *Cascading Views* for information about restoring separate windows.

- With either a Data Manager or chart window displayed, select **Window ➤ Tile Horizontally** or **Window ➤ Tile Vertically**.

• NOTES You can use normal Windows techniques to change change the size of the two windows.

TOOLS

The CorelCHART toolbar, shown in Figure II.21, consists of nine tools, most of which are similar to, but slightly different from, CorelDRAW tools. The various tools are explained below.

Pick Tool

Use the Pick tool to select, move, or modify individual chart components or groups of components.

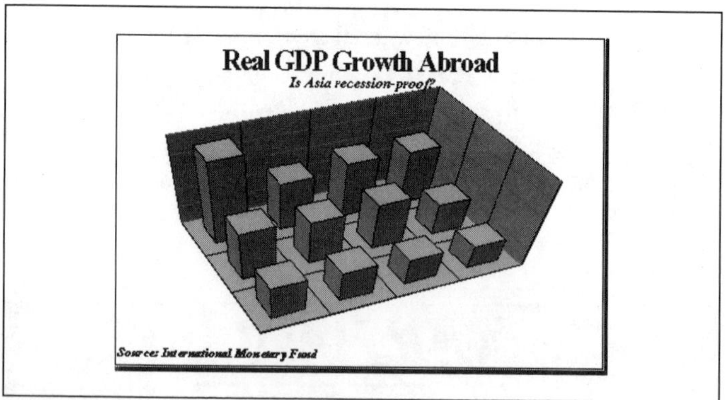

Figure II.21: The CorelCHART toolbox

Context-Sensitive Pop-Up Menu Tool

Use this tool to select a chart element and click to get direct access to the Chart menu commands you can use to modify the element's attributes.

Zoom Tool

When you click the Zoom tool you get a flyout menu. Click an icon to select the magnification you want.

Pencil Tool

When you click the Pencil tool you get a flyout menu. Click the icon representing the type of object you want to draw:

- click the first icon to draw a straight line;
- click the second icon to draw a polygon;
- click the third icon to draw a freehand curve;
- click the fourth icon to draw arrows.

Rectangle Tool

Use the Rectangle tool to draw rectangles and squares.

Ellipse Tool

Use the Ellipse tool to draw ellipses and circles.

Text Tool

Use the Text tool to create paragraph text as chart annotations, to edit existing annotations, and also to edit titles, subtitles, and footnotes.

Outline Tool

When you select the Outline tool, the flyout shown in Figure II.22 appears. Click icons in the flyout to select

- the outline width in points;
- no outline;
- one of ten pre-set outline widths;
- the outline color;
- one of 11 shades of gray, including white and black.

Fill Tool

When you select the Fill tool, the flyout shown in Figure II.23 appears. Click icons in the flyout to select

- the fill color;
- the fill Quick Pick Tool;
- no fill;
- a vector fill;

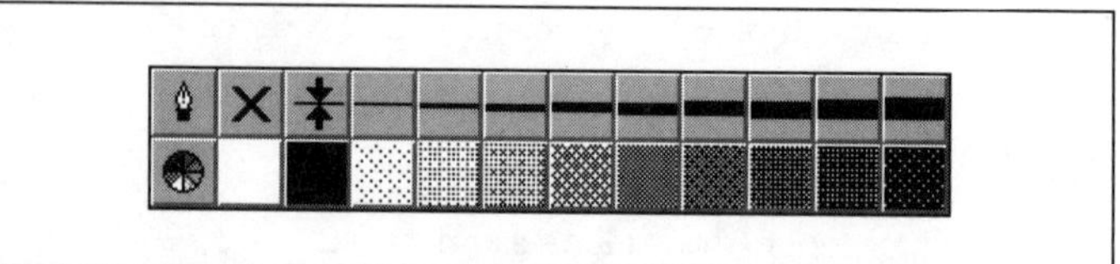

Figure II.22: The Outline flyout

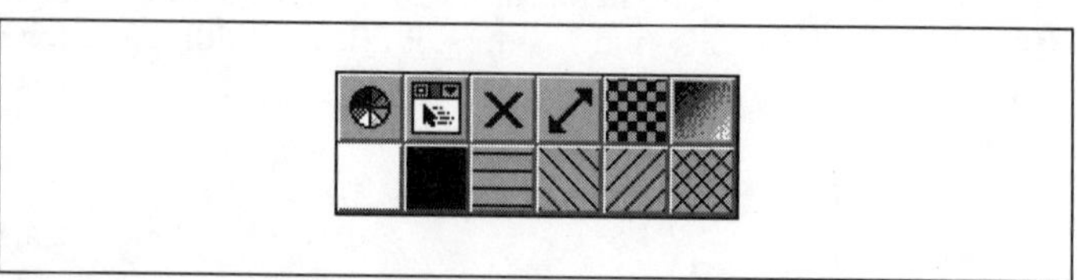

Figure II.23: The Fill flyout

- a two-color pattern bitmap editor;
- a fountain fill;
- white, black, or one of four hatch fills.

UNDOING OPERATIONS

You can cancel your most recent operation and restore your chart to its previous state. To do this:

- Select **Edit ➤ Undo**.

Part III

CorelPHOTO-PAINT

CAPTURING SCREENS

The screen capture facility, CCAPTURE, packaged with CorelDRAW is not a part of CorelPHOTO-PAINT, but it is described in the CorelPHOTO-PAINT section of the Corel *User's Manual*. This part of the book also describes CCAPTURE.

CCAPTURE is similar to the Windows screen capture facility. Both can capture an entire Windows screen or just the active window in a Windows screen. In addition, CCAPTURE can capture an active window without its title bar. Windows Capture and CCAPTURE both place the captured image in the Clipboard.

Activating and Deactivating CCAPTURE

Activate CCAPTURE from the Windows Program Manager as follows:

1. With the Windows Program Manager displayed, double-click the **Corel Graphics** icon. The Corel Graphics program group is displayed.
2. Double-click the **CCAPTURE** icon in the Corel Graphics program group. CCAPTURE is activated and the Corel Screen Capture information box is displayed.
3. Click anywhere on the screen. The information box disappears.

To deactivate CCAPTURE, repeat the procedure above, but in step 2, click **Yes** in the dialog box to confirm that you want to deactivate CCAPTURE.

Capturing a Screen

With CCAPTURE activated, do the following:

1. Display the screen you want to capture.
2. To capture the entire screen, tap the **Print Screen** key. To capture the active Windows window, hold down the Alt key while you tap the **Print Screen** key. To capture the Client Area of the active window (the active window

without its title bar), hold down Alt while you tap the **Pause** key. In each case, the cursor flashes briefly while the captured image is placed in the Clipboard.

3. Open another Windows application and use its Paste command to copy the image from the Clipboard into that application.

Copying a Captured Image into a CorelPHOTO-PAINT Drawing

When you first open CorelPHOTO-PAINT, the Edit command in the Main menu is not available, so you do not have access to the Paste command. Do the following to copy a captured image into a new picture:

1. In CorelPHOTO-PAINT, select **File ➤ Open**. The Load a Picture from Disk dialog box appears.
2. In the dialog box, click **Clipboard**. After a few seconds, the captured image appears in the CorelPHOTO-PAINT window.

CLEARING THE SCREEN

To clear the screen to the current background color:

- Select **File ➤ Clear**.

COLORS AND SHADES OF GRAY

You can work with CorelPHOTO-PAINT in four modes:

- 24-Bit Color (16,777,216 colors);

- 8-Bit Color (256 colors);
- Gray-Scale (256 shades of gray);
- Black and White.

When you open a color picture with less than 256 colors, it is automatically converted to 8-bit color. When you open a 32-bit color picture, it is automatically converted to 24-bit color. You can work with more colors than your hardware supports. CorelPHOTO-PAINT uses dithering to simulate colors not available on your monitor.

Selecting a Color Mode

You choose one of the four modes listed above when you create a new picture. See the explanation of opening a new picture under the *Files* entry.

Using the Palette

When you open a picture or start a new one, the palette shows the available colors. The box at the left end of the palette shows the currently selected primary, secondary, and background colors. The primary color is the one used to draw outlines; the secondary color is the fill color; and the background color provides a background, or paper color, for your picture. Figure III.1 shows a typical palette. See *Tools* for detailed information about how to apply these three colors.

Click the **Fold** button at the right end of the palette to reduce the palette size and display only the box showing the current colors.

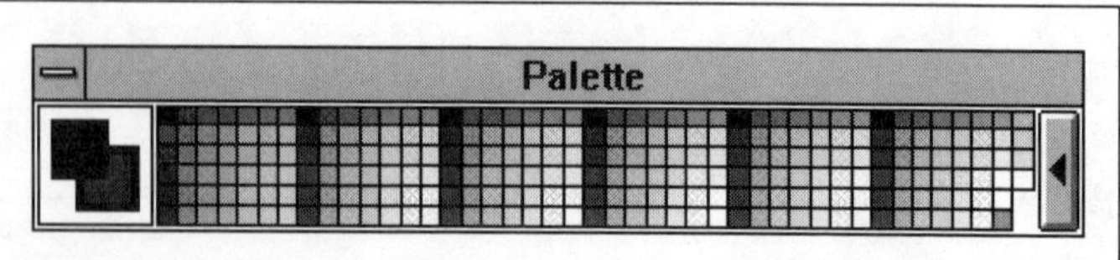

Figure III.1: A typical palette

Click the **Unfold** button at the right side of this box to display the complete palette again.

In the case of a black-and white picture, the palette shows 48 shades of gray consisting of patterns of black and white dots. For gray-scale pictures, the palette shows 256 shades of gray. For 256-color pictures, the palette shows 256 colors. For 24-bit color, the palette shows 256 of the available 16,777,216 colors. You can create and save additional palettes with 256 colors each as files, and subsequently open those palettes.

Selecting Primary, Secondary, and Background Colors

The primary, secondary, and background colors (or shades of gray) affect only the work you do after you select them, not the parts of the picture you created previously. You can change primary, secondary, and background these colors as often as you like. To select colors:

1. Display the Palette and, if necessary, unfold it.
2. Point onto the primary color you want to use and click the left mouse button. The upper-left box at the left end of the palette displays the color you selected.
3. Point onto the secondary color you want to use and click the right mouse button. The lower-right box at the left end of the palette displays the color you selected.
4. Point onto the background color you want to use and hold down the Shift key while you click the left mouse button. The background behind the two boxes at the left end of the palette displays the color selected.
5. Proceed to work on your picture using the new colors.

• **NOTES** After you have selected colors, you can fold the palette or hide it.

Selecting a background color does not affect the current background color. It only affects subsequent operations you perform that make use of the background color. Such operations include using the Eraser or Gradient Paint Roller tools, or selecting **File ➤ Clear** to erase the picture.

Changing from One Color Mode to Another

CorelPHOTO-PAINT allows you to change a picture from one color mode to another. To change modes:

1. Select **Edit ➤ Convert To**. A flyout menu appears listing the four modes. The current mode is dimmed.
2. Click on the mode you want to convert to. If you choose **24-bit Color, 256 Color**, or **Gray Scale**, another window appears to show your drawing in the new mode—provided your computer has sufficient memory. If there is not sufficient memory for the new mode, the message "Not Enough Memory for Operation" appears. If you choose **Black and White**, another flyout menu appears offering you the choice of **Line Art, Printer Halftone**, or **Screen Halftone**.
3. If you are converting to Black and White, click on the type of black-and-white picture you want (see the notes below). A black-and-white version of your picture appears in a separate window.

• **NOTES** When you convert from one color mode to another, two versions of the picture appear in separate windows on your screen. You can use the normal Windows techniques to select the one you want to work with. Be careful to select the correct one when you save your picture to a file.

To improve CorelPHOTO-PAINT's performance, consider converting to 24-Bit Color or Gray-Scale modes before applying filters or working with the retouching tools.

When you convert a picture to a mode with less colors than the original, some colors in the original are lost in the converted version. Changing the converted version back to the original mode does not restore the original colors.

When you convert a picture to black and white, choose the **Line Art** variation for a high-contrast effect, choose the **Printer Halftone** variation if you plan to print on a laser printer, or choose the **Screen Halftone** variation for the best on-screen appearance.

Changing Colors in the Entire Palette

In 24-Bit or 256-Color modes, you can change the entire color palette as follows:

1. Select **Options ➤ Palette**. A flyout menu appears.
2. In the flyout, click on **All Colors**. The Adjust the Entire Palette dialog box appears. The dialog box has four sliders for adjusting brightness, contrast, hue, and amount. There is also a sample palette which is initially the same as the current palette.
3. In the dialog box, adjust the sliders and observe the effect in the sample palette.
4. When you have achieved the range of colors you want, click the **Screen Preview** button. The new colors are temporarily transferred to the main palette and, if you are using 256-Color mode, to your picture.
5. Repeat steps 2 through 4 until you achieve the effect you want. At any time, you can click the **Restore** button to return to the initial palette.
6. When you are satisfied, click **OK**. The changes are permanently incorporated in the palette.

Changing Individual Colors in the Palette

In 24-Bit and 256-Color modes, you can change individual colors in the palette as follows:

1. Select **Options ➤ Palette**. A flyout appears.
2. In the flyout, click on **Color Picker**. The Color Picker dialog box appears, as shown in Figure III.2.
3. Click the color you want to change in the sample palette within the dialog box.

4. Change the color either visually or by choosing values for its components.

   - To change it visually, move the arrow up or down the central slider to produce a range of color in the large square at the left of the dialog box. Then drag the cross cursor within the large square to the specific color you want.
   - To choose values for the color, select a color model and choose specific values for the color components. See *Color* in Part I of this book for additional information.

   If you wish to return to the original color, click **Restore**.

5. When you are satisfied with the new color, click **OK**.

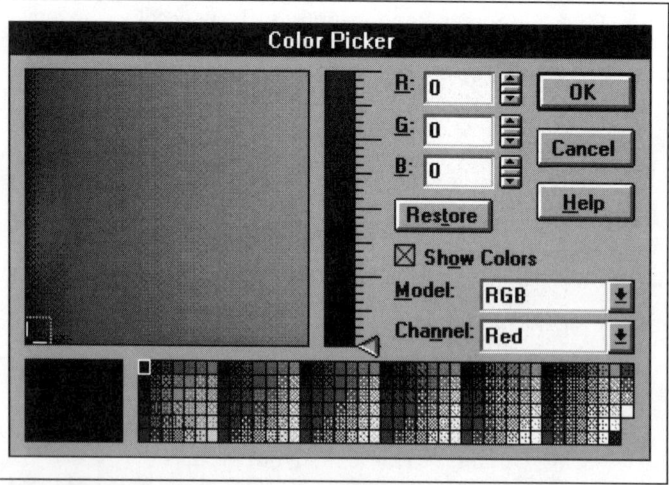

Figure III.2: The Color Picker dialog box

Changing the Range of Colors in the Palette

In 24-Bit and 256-Color modes, you can change the range of colors in the palette as follows:

1. Select **Options ➤ Palette**. A flyout appears.
2. In the flyout, click **Range of Colors**. The Adjust Palette color Range dialog box appears, as shown in Figure III.3.
3. In the dialog box, open the **Color Model** list box and choose the color model you want to use.
4. Click the left mouse button on the color in the sample palette that you want to be the beginning of the range.
5. Click the right mouse button on the color you want to be the ending of the range.
6. Optionally, modify the starting and ending colors by changing the values in the color component text boxes.

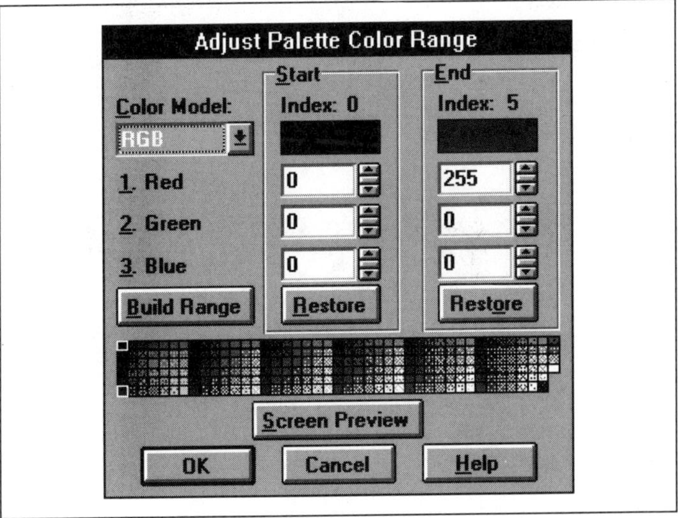

Figure III.3: The Adjust Palette Color Range dialog box

7. Click **Build Range** to replace the colors in the sample palette with a range between the two colors you selected.
8. Click **OK** to transfer these new colors to the main palette.

Adjusting Individual Colors

You can adjust individual palette colors.

1. Select **Options ➤ Palette**. A flyout appears.
2. In the flyout, click **Single Colors**. The Adjust Individual Palette Color dialog box appears.
3. Open the **Color Model** list box and select the color model you want to use.
4. In the sample palette, click on a color you want to change.
5. Change the color either by dragging the sliders or by typing color component values.
6. Click **OK**.

• **NOTES** After you have changed a palette, you can save it as a disk file. Use the **Options ➤ Palette** command to save and subsequently open palette files.

COPYING PARTS OF A PICTURE

You can copy a part of a picture to another place in the same picture, to another picture, or to another Windows application by way of the Clipboard. You can also copy a part of a picture to a file.

Copying a Part of a Picture to the Clipboard

To copy a part of a picture to the Clipboard:

1. Select the part of the picture you want to copy. See *Selection Tools.*
2. Select **Edit ➤ Copy**. The selected part of the picture is copied to the Clipboard.

Pasting from the Clipboard into a Picture

To paste the contents of the Clipboard into a picture:

1. Select **Edit ➤ Paste**. The picture in the Clipboard is pasted into the picture window. If necessary, CorelPHOTO-PAINT converts the color mode of the picture in the Clipboard to that of the picture window.
2. Move the picture in the window and change its size as necessary.

• **NOTES** The Clipboard picture is not scaled to fit into the picture window; only the part of it that will fit is shown. If necessary, you can drag on a handle to reduce the size of the image from the Clipboard so that its complete image fits into the picture window.

Copying a Part of a Picture to a File

To copy a part of a picture to a file:

1. Select the part of the picture you want to copy. See *Selection Tools.*
2. Select **Edit ➤ Copy To**. The Copy a Picture to Disk dialog box appears.
3. In the dialog box, open the **List Files of Type** list box and click on the type of file you want.
4. In the **Directories** list box, select the directory into which you want to write the file.
5. In the **File Name** text box, type the file name.
6. Click **OK**.

DELETING PART OF A PICTURE

To delete a part of a picture:

1. Select the part of the picture you want to delete. See *Selection Tools.*
2. Select **Edit ➤ Delete**. The selected part of the picture is deleted.

DISPLAY TOOLS

This section provides brief notes about using the three display tools.

The Zoom Tool

Use the Zoom tool to magnify or reduce the screen image.

1. Click the **Zoom** tool icon in the toolbox.
2. Point onto your picture.
3. Click the left mouse button to magnify the image, or the right mouse button to reduce it. The new magnification percentage is shown in the title bar.

• NOTES When you magnify an image, the magnified view is centered on the cursor position.

To return to the normal size, point onto the **Zoom** tool icon in the toolbox and double-click. Alternatively, select **Display ➤ 100%**.

You can also select **Display ➤ Zoom** to choose specific magnifications and reductions, and you can select **Display ➤ Zoom to Fit** to resize a picture to fit within the available window.

To edit individual pixels, use the Zoom tool to magnify your painting to the maximum amount of 1600 percent, and then use the Fountain Pen tool.

The Locator Tool

Use the Locator tool to point onto an image and locate the same point on a duplicate image.

1. With duplicate copies of a picture—probably with different magnifications—on your screen, click the **Locator** tool icon in the toolbox.
2. Point onto one copy of your picture.
3. Click the mouse button. The same area on the duplicate picture is displayed.

The Hand Tool

Use the Hand tool to move the picture on your screen.

1. Click the **Hand** tool icon in the toolbox.
2. Point onto your picture, then press and hold down the mouse button.
3. Drag in any direction. As you drag, the hand-shaped cursor moves and the scroll boxes also move within the scroll bars.
4. Release the mouse button. The picture is redrawn in a new position on the screen.

DISPLAYING AND HIDING WORKBOXES

CorelPHOTO-PAINT has three workboxes which can be displayed or hidden: the Palette, the Toolbox, and the Width and Shape box. To display or hide these:

1. Select **Display ➤ Workboxes**. A flyout menu appears.
2. Click on the appropriate choice in the flyout menu to display or hide workboxes.

• **NOTE** You can move the displayed workboxes to convenient places on the screen. To move a workbox, point onto its title bar, press the mouse button, drag the workbox to a new position, and release the mouse button

FILES

This section deals with topics concerned with CorelPHOTO-PAINT files.

Opening a New Picture

To begin a new picture, proceed as follows:

1. Select **File ➤ New**. The Create a New Picture dialog box appears, as shown in Figure III.4. The dialog box shows the size and mode of the last file used. It also shows the amount of memory you have available and the memory required for the displayed size and mode.
2. If necessary, open the **Units** list box and select the measurement units in which you want to define the width and height of the new picture.

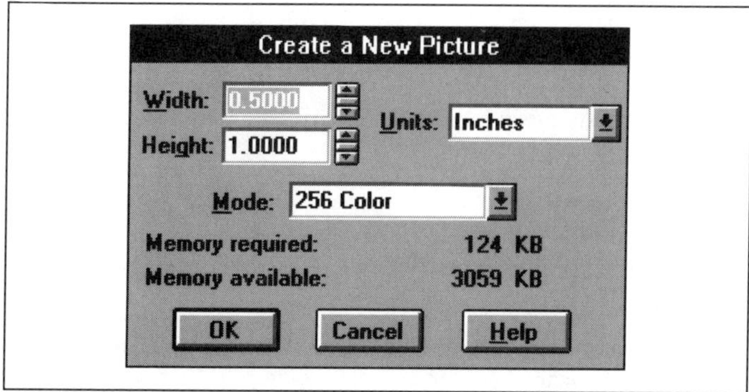

Figure III.4: The Create a New Picture dialog box

3. Select or type the **Width** of the new picture.
4. Select or type the **Height** of the new picture.
5. Open the **Mode** list box and click the mode you want to use.
6. Compare the Memory required shown in the dialog box with the Memory available. See the notes below for information about what to do if insufficient memory is available.
7. If sufficient memory is available, click **OK**. A new window appears in which you can create your picture. The new picture is given the provisional name New-1.PCX (another number is used instead of 1 if new pictures have already been opened).

• NOTES If insufficient memory is available, try the following;

- make more memory available by closing other pictures that may be open, by closing other Windows applications (including any that are minimized) that may be running, and by removing terminate-and-stay-resident (TSR) programs that may be occupying memory;
- reduce the size of the picture;
- change to a mode that uses less memory.

If these suggestions are not possible or acceptable, you will have to install more memory in your computer.

While you have the Create a New Picture dialog box open, select various picture sizes and modes to gain an understanding of their memory requirements. This will show you whether your computer has sufficient memory for the types of picture you intend to create.

Opening a Picture

To open a picture previously stored as a file on disk or one copied to the Clipboard, do the following:

1. Select **File ➤ Open**. The Load a Picture from Disk dialog box appears.
2. If a picture has previously been copied to the Clipboard, you can click **Clipboard** to open that picture. Whether or not a picture has been copied to the Clipboard, you can select a directory and then click on a file name to select the picture in that file.
3. Optionally, if you select a file name, click **Info** to see an information box with information about that file. If **Show Thumbnail** in this box is selected, you see a thumbnail image of the picture (provided a thumbnail file is available). Click **OK** in this window to return to the Load a Picture from Disk dialog box.
4. Click **OK**. A window opens showing the picture from the file. The title bar above the window shows the file name and the magnification in which the picture is shown.

Inserting a Cutout from a File

Do the following to paste a cutout from a file into your picture:

1. Select **Edit ➤ Paste From**. The Paste a Picture from Disk dialog box appears.
2. In the **Directories** list box, select the directory which contains the file you want to paste.
3. Open the **List Files of Type** list box and select the type of file you want to paste. The names of files of that type appear in the File Name list box.

4. Click the name of the file you want to paste.
5. Click **OK**. The pasted cutout appears in the upper-left corner of your picture.
6. Click outside the cutout, or click on a tool in the toolbox.

• NOTES If the cutout contains colors that are not in your picture's palette, the cutout's colors change when you paste it. To avoid this, change the colors in your palette, or convert your picture to 24-Bit mode before you paste the cutout.

Saving a Picture

See the explanation of saving a file with its existing name and saving a file with a new name under *Files* in Part I of this book.

CorelPHOTO-PAINT normally saves files in the PCX format. If you wish, you can choose an alternative format by selecting **File ➤ Save As**, opening the List Files of Type list box, and clicking on a different format. See Appendix A for a list of available file formats.

• NOTES If you have opened the same file two or more times to simultaneously display it in different versions, be careful to save the correct version.

FILTERING PICTURES

Filters allow you to enhance images and create special effects in a complete picture or a selected part of a picture. When you select a part of a picture before you apply the filter, the filter operates on only the selected area. When no part of a picture is selected before you apply the filter, the filter operates on the entire picture.

You can use all the filters, and get the best results with filters, in 24-Bit color and Gray-Scale modes. Only certain filters are available in 256-Color and Black-and-White modes.

Adding a Granular Effect to Pictures

Use the Add Noise filter in 24-Bit color and Gray-Scale modes to add a granular effect to your picture.

1. Select **Edit ➤ Filter**. The Filter flyout, shown in Figure III.5, appears.
2. Click **Add Noise**. The Add Noise dialog box, which is shown in Figure III.6, appears.
3. Select or type a number between 0 and 255 in the **Variance** text box. Higher numbers give a more pronounced granular effect.
4. Open the **Distribution** list box and click on **Bell Curve** or **Flat**. Flat gives more noticeable changes than Bell Curve.
5. Open the **Channels** list box and click the color component you want the filter to affect.
6. Click **Screen Preview** to see how the filter affects your picture.
7. Repeat steps 3 through 6 until you get the effect you want.
8. Click **OK** to make the effect permanent.

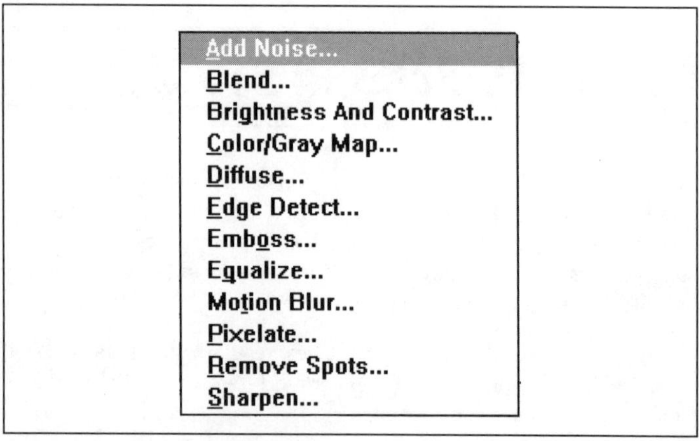

Figure III.5: The Filter flyout menu

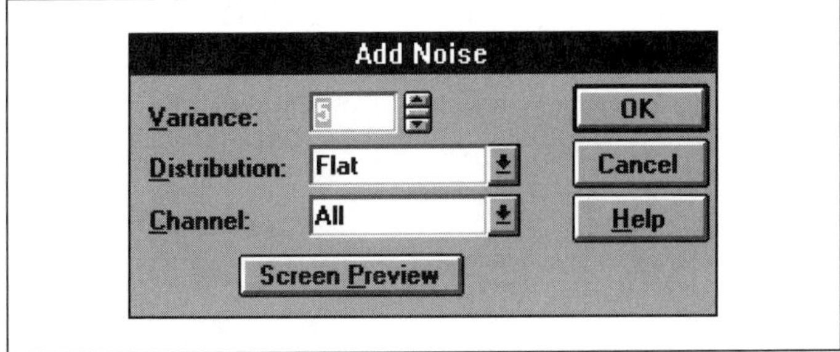

Figure III.6: The Add Noise dialog box

Smoothing and Softening Colors

Use the Blend filter in 24-Bit Color and Gray-Scale modes to smooth and soften colors in your picture.

1. Select **Edit ➤ Filter**. The Filter flyout appears.
2. Click **Blend**. The Blend dialog box, which is shown in Figure III.7, appears.
3. Select or type a number between 0 and 100 in the **Blending Amount** text box. Higher numbers give a more pronounced effect.
4. Click the **Wide Aperture** button if you want to create a smoother blend.
5. Click **Screen Preview** to see how the filter affects your picture.
6. Repeat steps 3 through 5 until you get the effect you want.
7. Click **OK** to make the effect permanent.

Adjusting Brightness and Contrast

Use the Brightness and Contrast filter to adjust the brightness and contrast of your picture.

1. Select **Edit ➤ Filter**. The Filter flyout appears.

2. Click **Brightness and Contrast**. The Brightness and Contrast dialog box, shown in Figure III.8, appears.
3. Select or type a number between –100 and 100 in the **Brightness** text box.
4. Select or type a number between –100 and 100 in the **Contrast** text box.
5. Click **Screen Preview** to see how the filter affects your picture.
6. Repeat steps 3 through 5 until you get the effect you want.
7. Click **OK** to make the effect permanent.

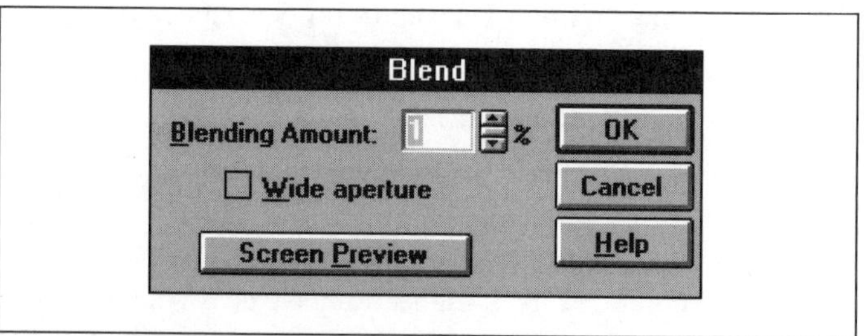

Figure III.7: The Blend dialog box

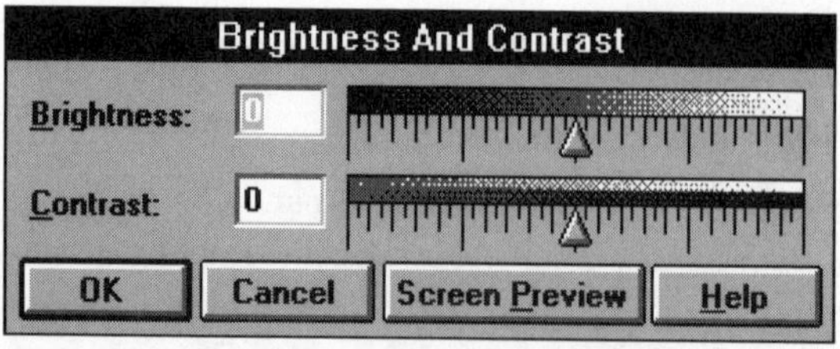

Figure III.8: The Brightness and Contrast dialog box

Lighting and Special Effects

Use the Color/Gray Map filter to adjust for lighting inaccuracies and to create special effects in your picture.

1. Select **Edit ➤ Filter**. The Filter flyout appears.
2. Click **Color/Gray Map**. The Change the Image/Cutout Response Curve dialog box, shown in Figure III.9, appears.
3. Open the **Channel** list box and select the color you want the filter to affect.
4. If you want CorelPHOTO-PAINT to automatically adjust your picture, open the Preset list box and choose the option you want to use. The response curve on the left side of the dialog box graphically shows the effect.
5. If you want to adjust the response curve yourself, open the **Style** list box and choose **Curve**. The response curve on the left side of the dialog box has five handles you can drag to alter the response curve. Alternatively, you can choose **Linear** (for a linear response curve) or **Freehand** (for the response curve selected in the Preset list box).

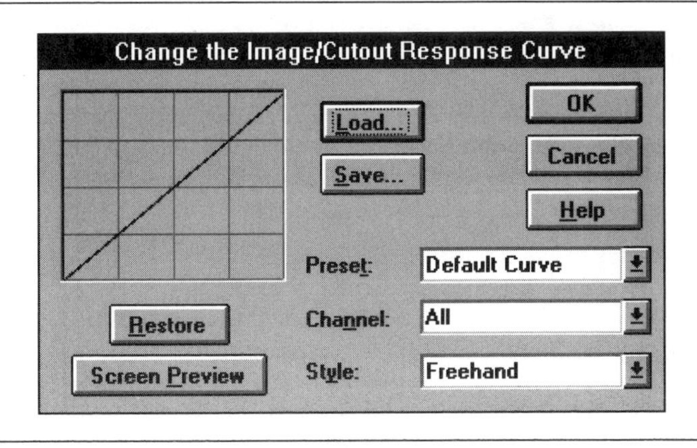

Figure III.9: The Change the Image/Cutout Response Curve dialog box

6. Click **Screen Preview** to see how the filter affects your picture.
7. Repeat steps 4 through 7 until you get the effect you want.
8. Click **OK** to make the effect permanent.

• NOTES The horizontal axis of the response curve represents tones in the original picture, with dark tones to the left and light tones to the right. The vertical axis represents tones in the filtered picture, with dark tones at the bottom and light tones at the top.

Click **Save** in the dialog box to save a compensation map to disk. Click **Load** to load a previously saved compensation map from disk.

Scattering Colors

Use the Diffuse filter in 24-Bit Color and Gray-Scale modes to scatter colors in your picture.

1. Select **Edit ➤ Filter**. The Filter flyout appears.
2. Click **Diffuse**. The Diffuse dialog box, shown in Figure III.10, appears.
3. Select or type a number between 1 and 6 in the **Width** text box to specify the width of the diffused colors.
4. Select or type a number between 1 and 6 in the **Height** text box to specify the height of the diffused colors.
5. Click the **Allow Color Shift** button to allow the filter to introduce new colors, if that is what you want.
6. Click **Screen Preview** to see how the filter affects your picture.
7. Repeat steps 3 through 6 until you get the effect you want.
8. Click **OK** to make the effect permanent.

• NOTES Enable **Identical Values** if you want the changes you make to either the Width or Height value applied to both.

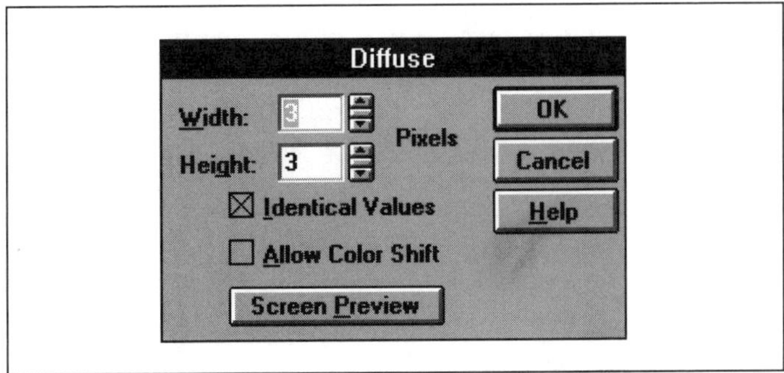

Figure III.10: The Diffuse dialog box

Creating an Outline Effect

Use the Edge Detect filter in 24-Bit Color and Gray-Scale modes to create an outline effect in your picture.

1. Select **Edit ➤ Filter**. The Filter flyout appears.
2. Click **Edge Detect**. The Edge Detect dialog box, shown in Figure III.11, appears.
3. Select or type a number between 1 and 10 in the Sensitivity text box to specify how much difference there has to be between one pixel and the next to recognize an edge. With a low number, an edge is recognized only when there is a large difference between adjoining pixels. With a high number, an edge is recognized when there is a slight difference between adjoining pixels.
4. Open the Color list box and choose the color you want for the non-outlined areas of the filtered picture.
5. Open the Auto list box. Choose **Auto** if you want Corel-PHOTO-PAINT to automatically adjust the outline. Choose **Light** for light-colored outlines, or **Dark** for dark-colored outlines.
6. Click **Screen Preview** to see how the filter affects your picture. Depending on the nature of the picture, it may take a considerable time for the filter to take effect.

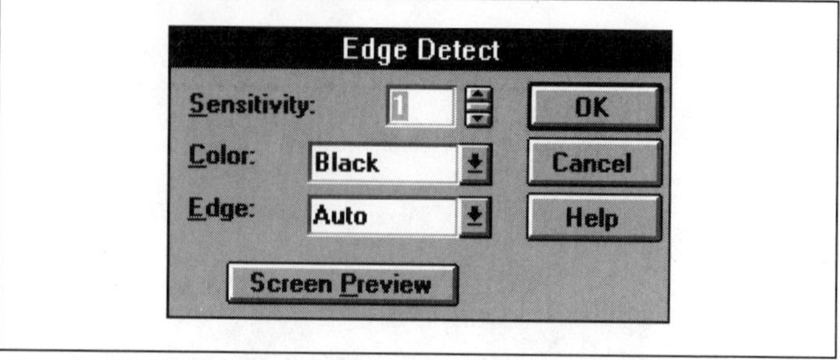

Figure III.11: The Edge Detect dialog box

7. Repeat steps 3 through 6 until you get the effect you want.
8. Click **OK** to make the effect permanent.

Creating a Raised-Relief Effect

Use the Emboss filter in 24-Bit Color and Gray-Scale modes to create a three-dimensional, raised-relief effect in your picture.

1. Select **Edit ➤ Filter**. The Filter flyout appears.
2. Click **Emboss**. The Emboss dialog box, shown in Figure III.12, appears.
3. Click one of the eight directional buttons to control the position of the light source and the direction of shadows.
4. Open the **Emboss Color** list box to set the overall color of the embossed picture.
5. Click **Screen Preview** to see how the filter affects your picture.
6. Repeat steps 3 through 5 until you get the effect you want.
7. Click **OK** to make the effect permanent.

Redistributing Color Shades

Use the Equalize filter to redistribute shades of colors in your picture.

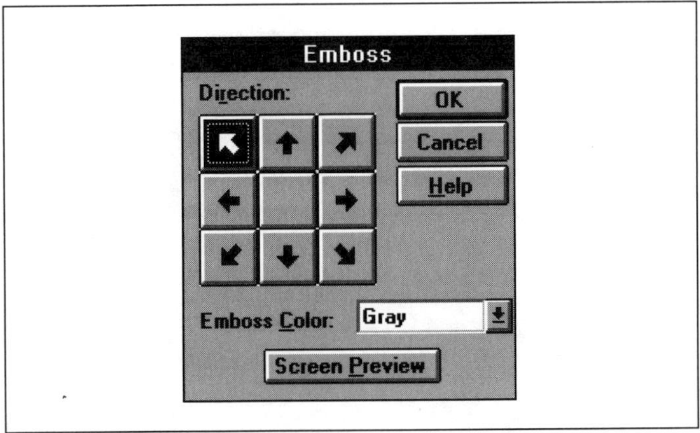

Figure III.12: The Emboss dialog box

1. Select **Edit ➤ Filter**. The Filter flyout appears.
2. Click **Equalize**. The Histogram Equalization dialog box, shown in Figure III.13, appears. In the top part of the dialog box is a histogram. Its horizontal axis represents the range of tones in your picture, or the selected part of it, with the darkest tone at the left and the lightest at the right. The vertical axis represents the number of pixels for each tone.
3. Drag the three arrows under the histogram to alter the appearance of the picture. All tones in the original picture to the left of the left arrow become black; as you move this arrow to the right, you lose details in shadows. All tones in the original picture to the right of the right arrow become white; as you move this arrow to the left, you lose details in highlights. You can move the middle arrow to redistribute tones between the low and high points.
4. Click **Screen Preview** to see how the filter affects your picture.
5. Repeat steps 3 and 4 until you get the effect you want.
6. Click **OK** to make the effect permanent.

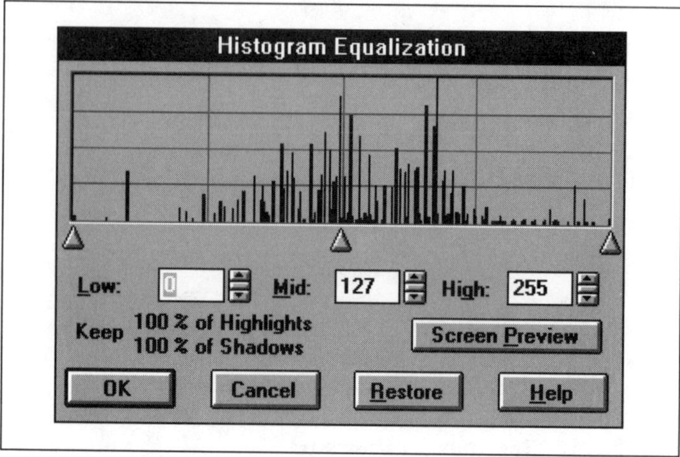

Figure III.13: The Histogram Equalization dialog box

Creating a Motion Effect

Use the Motion Blur filter in 24-Bit Color and Gray-Scale modes to create an effect of motion in your picture.

1. Select **Edit ➤ Filter**. The Filter flyout appears.
2. Click **Motion Blur**. The Motion Blur dialog box, shown in Figure III.14, appears.
3. Click one of the eight directional buttons to control the direction of motion.
4. Select or type a number in the range 1 through 50 in the **Speed** text box.
5. Click **Screen Preview** to see how the filter affects your picture.
6. Repeat steps 3 through 5 until you get the effect you want.
7. Click **OK** to make the effect permanent.

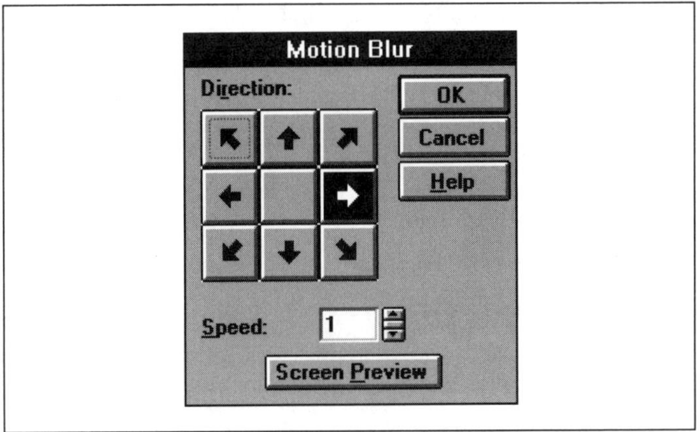

Figure III.14: The Motion Blur dialog box

Creating a Posterized Effect

Use the Pixelate filter in 24-Bit Color and Gray-Scale modes to create a posterized effect in your picture.

1. Select **Edit ➤ Filter**. The Filter flyout appears.
2. Click **Pixelate**. The Pixelate dialog box, shown in Figure III.15, appears.
3. Select or type a number in the range 1 through 16 in the **Width** text box to set the width of the effect.
4. Select or type a number in the range 1 through 16 in the **Height** text box to set the height of the effect.
5. Click **Screen Preview** to see how the filter affects your picture.
6. Repeat steps 3 through 5 until you get the effect you want.
7. Click **OK** to make the effect permanent.

• **NOTES** Enable **Identical Values** if you want the changes you make to either the Width or Height value applied to both values.

Removing Spots from a Picture

Use the Remove Spots filter to remove spots from your picture. This is the only filter available in Black-and-White mode.

1. Select **Edit ➤ Filter**. The Filter flyout appears.
2. Click **Remove Spots**. The Remove Spot dialog box, shown in Figure III.16, appears.
3. Click the **Small**, **Medium**, or **Large** button.
4. Click **Screen Preview** to see how the filter affects your picture.
5. Repeat steps 3 and 4 until you get the effect you want.
6. Click **OK** to make the effect permanent.

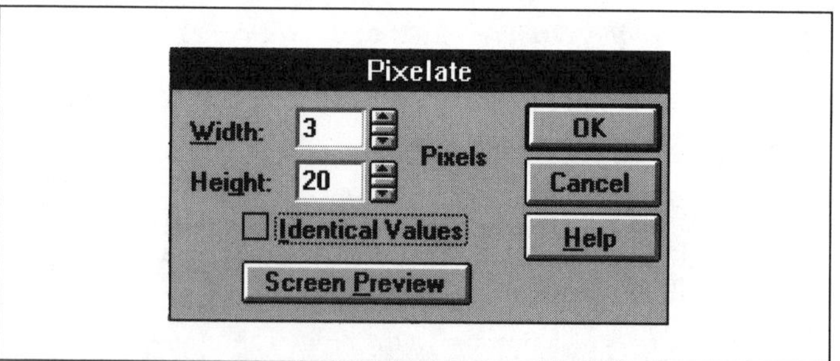

Figure III.15: The Pixelate dialog box

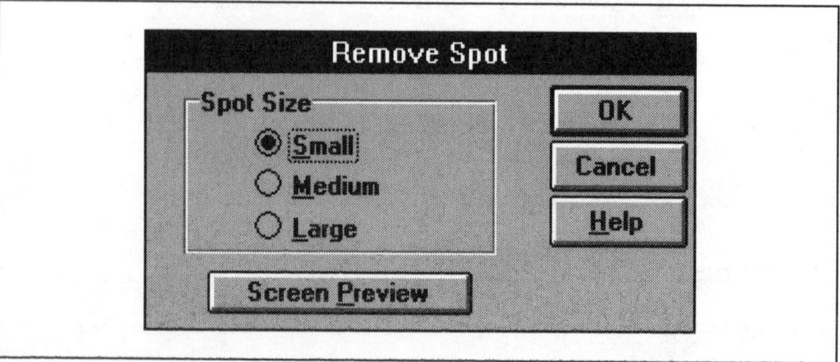

Figure III.16: The Remove Spot dialog box

Bringing Out the Details in a Picture

Use the Sharpen filter in the 24-Bit Color and Gray-Scale modes to enhance edges and bring out detail in your picture.

1. Select **Edit ➤ Filter**. The Filter flyout appears.
2. Click **Sharpen**. The Sharpen dialog box, shown in Figure III.17, appears.
3. Select or type a percentage in the range 1 through 100 in the **Sharpen Amount** text box. Higher numbers produce greater sharpness.
4. Click the **Wide aperture** button if you want to enlarge the area the filter operates on.
5. Click **Screen Preview** to see how the filter affects your picture.
6. Repeat steps 3 through 5 until you get the effect you want.
7. Click **OK** to make the effect permanent.

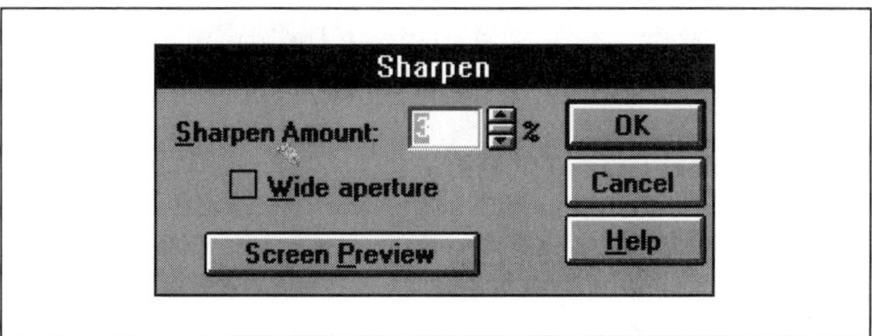

Figure III.17: The Sharpen dialog box

FONTS

CorelPHOTO-PAINT allows you to add text to your picture using any font supported by Windows that is available on your computer. You can make four fonts immediately available for use.

Selecting Fonts for Immediate Use

Do the following to select fonts:

1. Select **Font ➤ Select**. A Font dialog box appears with a list of available fonts.
2. Scroll in the **Font** list box and click on the font you want to select. A sample of that font appears in the sample box.
3. Click on the style you want to use in the **Font Style** list box.
4. Scroll in the **Size** box and click on the size you want.
5. Click on any effects you need in the **Effects** box.
6. Click OK.
7. Repeat steps 1 through 6 to select up to three additional fonts.

Adding Text to Your Picture

When you want to add text to your picture, do the following:

1. Select **Font** from the Main menu. The Font menu appears with the names of the last four fonts you selected.
2. Click on the name of the font you want to use. The Font menu disappears. If the font you want to use is not in the list, click **Select** to add another font to the list, as described above. When you select another font, the new one replaces the first of the four that are available for immediate use.
3. Click the **Text** tool in the toolbox and proceed to add text. See the explanation of using the text tool under *Painting Tools*.

HELP

CorelPHOTO-PAINT provides help in several ways.

Using the Help Bar

The Help bar at the bottom of the work area provides information about the currently selected tool and operation. You can choose to display or hide the Help bar. See *Preferences*.

Using the Help Menu

To access all the information available in online Help, click **Help** in the menu bar. A menu allows you to access these topics:

> Index, For Beginners, Commands, Procedures, Shortcuts, Tools, System Info, About PHOTO-PAINT.

Click any topic to find the information you need.

Directly Accessing the Help Index

As long as no dialog boxes are open, you can press F1 to directly access the so-called Help Index (it is really a table of contents) at any time you are using CorelPHOTO-PAINT. Then you can choose to look at these topics:

> Beginners, Commands, Tools, How to, Shortcuts, Glossary.

Accessing Help from Dialog Boxes

CorelPHOTO-PAINT dialog boxes contain a **Help** button. Click on this button to directly access help relevant to a dialog box.

MAIN MENU

See "Commands" in online **Help** for a summary of information about the Main menu.

OPTIONS

The Options menu allows you to modify the operation of various aspects of CorelPHOTO-PAINT.

Changing the Brush Style

You can change the shape of many painting and retouching tools, although usually it is more convenient to use the Width and Shape Box for this purpose. See *Width and Shape Box*. Do the following to change tool shapes from the Options menu:

1. Select **Options ➤ Brush Style**. The Select a Brush Style dialog box appears.
2. Click the tool shape you want to use.
3. Click **OK**.

Changing the Color Tolerance

You can specify a range of colors which, in some circumstances, CorelPHOTO-PAINT recognizes as a single color. Suppose, for example, you are working in 24-Bit Color mode and you want to change a shade of red in an area to a shade of blue. What your eyes see as a single shade of red is probably a range of slightly different reds. By controlling the color tolerance, you can tell CorelPHOTO-PAINT to recognize one specific shade of red together with all other colors that differ from the specific shade by certain amounts of red, green, and blue. After you have specified a color tolerance, you can change a color and colors like it to another color. To specify a color tolerance:

1. Select **Options ➤ Color Tolerance**. The Color Comparison Tolerance dialog box appears.
2. Change the Red, Green, and Blue tolerance values as necessary. Larger numbers define a wider range of colors.
3. Click **OK**.

Changing the Color Gradient

You can change the fountain fill produced by the Gradient Paint Roller tool. See *Painting Tools* for information.

Changing Soft Brush Settings

You can adjust the settings of the Airbrush, Paintbrush, Smear Paintbrush, and Clone tools. For example, to change the paintbrush soft settings, select the paintbrush, and then:

1. Select **Options ➤ Soft Brush Settings**. The Change Soft Brush Settings dialog box appears, as shown in Figure III.18.
2. Adjust the settings in the dialog box according to the effect you want.
3. Click **OK**.

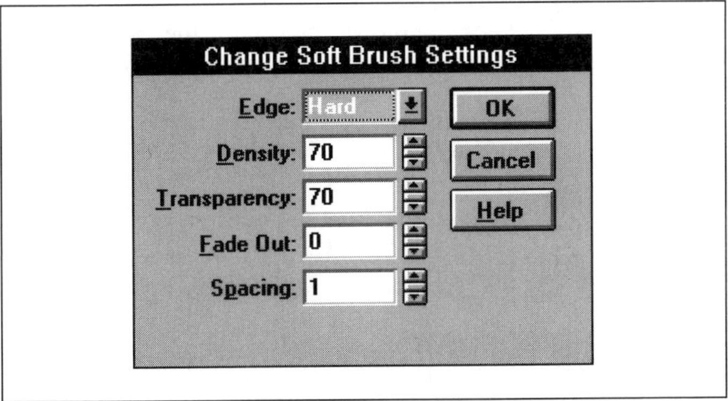

Figure III.18: The Change Soft Brush Settings dialog box

PAINTING TOOLS

This section provides brief information about using the painting tools. Use these tools to draw lines, curves, textures, and to add text to your pictures. You can also use these tools to make erasures, to replace one color with another, and to fill an area.

You can set the size and shape of most painting tools with the Width and Shape box. You cannot do this for the Text tool, the Paint Roller tools, or the Eyedropper tool.

Some painting tools are soft tools. You can adjust the effect of these tools by selecting **Options ➤ Soft Brush Settings.**

• **NOTES** Some painting tools cannot be used in certain color modes. If you try to use a painting tool that is not available in your current mode, CorelPHOTO-PAINT displays a warning message.

The Text Tool

Use this tool to add text to your picture in any font supported by Windows. Text is painted in the current secondary color.

Proceed as follows to add text to your picture:

1. Select **Font** in the Main menu and then click on the font you want to use.
2. Click the **Text** tool icon in the toolbox. The Enter Text dialog box appears.
3. Type the text you want to have in your picture.
4. Click **OK**. The text appears in your picture within a text frame.
5. Drag the handles on the text frame to change its size.
6. Point inside the text frame, press the mouse button, and drag to move the text frame.
7. Click outside the text frame or select another tool to paste the text into the picture.

• **NOTES** If the font you want to use is not immediately available in the **Font** menu, click **Select** and proceed as described in the *Fonts* entry.

Text can consists of up to approximately 400 characters. Use Ctrl-Insert to paste text from the Clipboard.

Wordwrap occurs automatically at the end of each line. Press Ctrl-Enter to start a new line.

Use the normal Windows methods to edit text in the Enter Text dialog box.

To edit existing text, use one of the selection tools to select it, and then select the **Text** tool. The Enter Text dialog box appears with the text available for editing.

The Eyedropper Tool

Use the Eyedropper tool to select a color in your picture and make it the current primary, secondary, or background color.

1. Click the **Eyedropper** tool icon in the toolbox.
2. Point onto the color you want to select in your picture.
3. Click the left mouse button to make the color the primary color, the right mouse button to make the color the secondary color, or hold down the Shift key while you click the left mouse button to make the color the background color.

The Eraser Tool

Use the Eraser tool to replace areas of your picture with the current background color.

1. Click the **Eraser** tool icon in the toolbox. Be careful not to double-click. See the notes below.
2. If necessary, adjust the size and shape of the tool in the Width and Shape box.
3. If necessary, choose the background color.

4. Point to the area you want to erase, press the mouse button, and drag over the area to be erased. As you drag, the area changes to the background color.

• **NOTES** By double-clicking the Eraser icon in the toolbox, you can erase the entire picture and replace it with the background color. If this occurs by accident, you can select **Edit ➤ Undo** to restore your picture.

The Color Replacer Tool

Use the Color Replacer tool to replace the current primary color in an area of your picture with the secondary color.

1. Click the **Color Replacer** tool icon in the toolbox. Be careful not to double-click. See the notes below.
2. If necessary, adjust the size and shape of the tool in the Width and Shape box.
3. If necessary, choose the primary color you want to replace and the secondary color with which you want to replace it .
4. If necessary, select **Options ➤ Color Tolerance** and, in the Color Comparison Tolerance dialog box, specify the range of colors you want to replace.
5. Point to the area in which you want to replace colors, press the mouse button, and drag over the area to be changed. As you drag, the area which has the current primary color (or a color within the range specified) changes to the secondary color.

• **NOTES** Hold down the Shift key while you drag to constrain the movement to horizontal or vertical. Press the spacebar to change direction.

Double-clicking the Color Replacer tool icon in the toolbox changes all occurrences of the primary color in your picture to the secondary color.

The Local Undo Tool

Use the Local Undo tool to restore parts of your picture to the state they were in before you last selected a command or tool.

1. Click the **Local Undo** tool icon in the toolbox. Be careful not to double-click. See the notes below.
2. If necessary, adjust the size and shape of the tool in the Width and Shape box.
3. Press the mouse button and drag over the parts of the picture you wish to restore.

• **NOTES** Hold down the Shift key while you drag to constrain the movement to horizontal or vertical. Press the spacebar to change direction.

Double-clicking the Local Undo tool icon in the toolbox restores the entire picture to the state it was in before you last selected a command or tool.

The Airbrush Tool

Use the Airbrush tool to spray the primary color when you are working in 24-Bit Color or Gray-Scale modes.

1. Click the **Airbrush** tool icon in the toolbox.
2. Select the primary color you want to use.
3. If necessary, adjust the size and shape of the spray in the Width and Shape box.
4. If necessary, select **Options ➤ Soft Brush Settings** and adjust the settings in the Change Airbrush Settings dialog box.
5. Point to the place on your drawing where you want to start spraying, press the mouse button, and drag to cover an area.
6. Release the mouse button.

The Spraycan Tool

Use the Spraycan tool to splatter part of a picture with the primary color. Unlike the Airbrush tool, the Spraycan tool is not limited to use in the 24-Bit Color and Gray-Scale modes.

1. Click the **Spraycan** tool icon in the toolbox.
2. Choose the primary color you want to use.
3. If necessary, adjust the size and shape of the spray in the Width and Shape box. The minimum width of the spray is three pixels.
4. Point to the place on your drawing where you want to start spraying, press the mouse button, and drag to cover an area.
5. Release the mouse button.

The Paint Roller Tool

Use the Paint Roller tool to fill an enclosed area with the primary color.

1. Click the **Paint Roller** tool icon in the toolbox.
2. Choose the primary color you want to use.
3. If necessary, select **Options ➤ Color Tolerance** and use the Color Comparison Tolerance dialog box to specify the range of colors to be considered an enclosed area.
4. Place the tip of the line extending down from the left end of the Paint Roller icon inside the area to be filled, and click the mouse button. The color spreads from the initial point and fills the area.

• **NOTES** If the area is not completely enclosed, the fill color will leak into other parts of your picture. However, you can select **Edit ➤ Undo** to remove the fill. To correct the problem, either use the Fountain Pen tool to close the gaps through which the leak occurred, or adjust the values in the Color Comparison Tolerance box to change the range of colors considered to be an enclosed area.

The Tile Pattern Paint Roller Tool

Use the Tile Pattern Paint Roller tool to fill an enclosed area with a repeating pattern.

1. Click the **Tile Pattern Paint Roller** tool icon in the toolbox.
2. Select **Options ➤ Tile Pattern**. The Load a Tile Pattern from Disk dialog box appears.
3. In the dialog box, select the directory that contains the tile pattern you want, click on the file name, and click **OK**.
4. Follow steps 3 and 4 in "The Paint Roller Tool" above.

• **NOTES** See the notes under "The Paint Roller Tool" above.

The Gradient Paint Roller Tool

Use the Gradient Paint Roller tool to fill an enclosed area with a fountain fill in which the color shades from the secondary to the background color.

1. Click the **Gradient Paint Roller** tool icon in the toolbox.
2. Select the secondary color to begin the fountain fill and the background color to end it.
4. Select **Options ➤ Gradient Type**. The Select a Gradient Effect dialog box appears.
5. Click on the gradient style you want.
6. Select or type a brightness value.
7. Click **OK**.
8. Follow steps 3 and 4 in "The Paint Roller Tool" above.

• **NOTES** See the notes under "The Paint Roller Tool."

The Paintbrush Tool

Use the Paintbrush tool to draw freehand shapes in the primary color. You can use this tool in the 24-Bit Color and Gray-Scale modes.

1. Click the **Paintbrush** tool icon in the toolbox.
2. Select the primary color you want to use.
3. If necessary, adjust the size and shape of the brush in the Width and Shape box.
4. If necessary, select Options ➤ Soft Brush Settings and adjust the settings in the Change Soft Brush Settings dialog box.
5. Point onto your drawing to where you want to start painting, press the mouse button, and drag to paint an area.
6. Release the mouse button.

The Fountain Pen Tool

Use the Fountain Pen tool to draw smooth shapes in the primary color, and also for pixel-by-pixel editing.

1. Click the **Fountain Pen** tool icon in the toolbox.
2. If necessary, adjust the size and shape of the pen in the Width and Shape box.
3. Select the primary color you want to use. You can choose the color from the palette, or you can point onto a color in your picture and click the right mouse button to select it as your drawing color.
4. Point on your drawing to where you want to start painting, press the mouse button, and drag to draw a freehand line.
5. Release the mouse button.

The Line Tool

Use the Line tool to draw straight lines in the primary color.

1. Click the **Line** tool icon in the toolbox.
2. If necessary, adjust the size and shape of the line in the Width and Shape box.
3. Select the primary color you want to use.

4. Point to where you want the line to start, then press the mouse button and hold it down.
5. Drag to where you want the line to end, and then release the mouse button.
6. If you want to add another line, joined to the first, point to where you want that line to end and press the right mouse button.
7. Repeat step 6 to create additional joined lines.

• **NOTES** Hold down the Shift key while you drag to constrain the line to horizontal, vertical, or diagonal directions.

To draw several lines all radiating from the first point, follow steps 1 through 7, with the difference that you hold down the Ctrl key while pressing the right mouse button in step 6.

The Curve Tool

Use the Curve tool to draw curved lines in the primary color.

1. Click the **Curve** tool icon in the toolbox.
2. If necessary, adjust the width of the curve in the Width and Shape box.
3. Select the primary color you want to use.
4. Point to where you want the curve to start, then press the mouse button and hold it down.
5. Drag to where you want to end the line, and then release the mouse button. A straight line appears between the two points with square handles at the ends and two circular handles on the line.
6. To shape the line into a curve, point onto one of the circular handles, and press the mouse button and hold it down while you drag in any direction. The curve changes shape as you drag.
7. If necessary, repeat step 6 to drag the other circular handle.
8. Drag the square handles to move the end-points of the curve.

9. If you want to add another curve, joined to the first, point to where you want that curve to end and press the right mouse button.
10. Repeat step 9 to create additional joined curves.
11. Paste the curve onto your drawing by clicking outside the curve. The curve is redrawn in the primary color.

• **NOTES** To draw several curves all radiating from the first point, follow steps 1 through 11, but hold down the Ctrl key while pressing the right mouse button in step 9.

The Hollow Box Tool

Use the Hollow Box tool to draw unfilled rectangles and squares in the primary color.

1. Click the **Hollow Box** tool icon in the toolbox.
2. If necessary, adjust the width of the outline in the Width and Shape box.
3. Select the primary color you want to use.
4. Point to where you want to place one corner of the rectangle, then press the mouse button and hold it down.
5. Drag to where you want to place the opposite corner of the rectangle, and then release the mouse button.

• **NOTES** Hold down the Shift key while you drag to constrain the box to a square.

Using the Hollow Rounded Box Tool

Use the Hollow Rounded Box tool to draw unfilled rectangles and squares with rounded corners in the primary color.

1. Click the **Hollow Rounded Box** tool icon in the toolbox.
2. Follow steps 3 through 5 under "The Hollow Box Tool" above.

• **NOTES** See the notes under "The Hollow Box Tool."

The Hollow Ellipse Tool

Use the Hollow Ellipse tool to draw unfilled ellipses and circles in the primary color.

1. Click the **Hollow Ellipse** tool icon in the toolbox.
2. If necessary, adjust the width of the outline in the Width and Shape box.
3. Select the primary color you want to use.
4. Point to where you want to have the center of the ellipse, then press the mouse button and hold it down.
5. Drag away from the center in any direction to create the ellipse, and then release the mouse button.
6. To draw another ellipse with the same center point, press and hold down the right mouse button while you drag to create the ellipse.

• **NOTES** Hold down the Shift key while you drag to constrain the ellipse to a circle.

The Hollow Polygon Tool

Use the Hollow Polygon tool to create hollow, many-sided shapes in the primary color.

1. Click the **Hollow Polygon** tool icon in the toolbox.
2. If necessary, adjust the width of the outline in the Width and Shape box.
3. Select the primary color you want to use.
4. Point to where you want the polygon to start, and then click the mouse button.
5. Point to where you want the first side to end, and then click the mouse button.
6. Point to where you want the next side to end, and then click the mouse button.
7. Repeat step 6 to draw the remaining sides, but double-click the end-point of the next-to-last side. Double-clicking

completes that side and also closes the polygon by joining that point to the polygon's starting point.

• NOTES You can also drag to define the sides of a polygon. Hold down the Shift key while you drag to constrain the lines to vertical, horizontal, or diagonal directions.

A polygon can have up to 200 sides.

The Filled Box Tool

Use the Filled Box tool to draw filled rectangles and squares with the outline in the primary color and the fill in the secondary color.

1. Click the **Filled Box** tool icon in the toolbox.
2. If necessary, adjust the width of the outline in the Width and Shape box.
3. Select the primary and secondary colors you want to use.
4. Point to where you want to have one corner of the rectangle, then press the mouse button and hold it down.
5. Drag to where you want to place the opposite corner of the rectangle, and then release the mouse button.

• NOTES Hold down the Shift key while you drag to constrain the box to a square.

The Filled Rounded Box Tool

Use the Filled Rounded Box tool to draw filled rectangles and squares with rounded corners using the primary color for the outline and the secondary color for the fill.

1. Click the **Filled Rounded Box** tool icon in the toolbox.
2. Follow steps 3 through 5 under "The Filled Box Tool" above.

• NOTES See the notes under "The Filled Box Tool."

The Filled Ellipse Tool

Use the Filled Ellipse tool to draw filled ellipses and circles using the primary color for the outline and the secondary color for the fill.

1. Click the **Filled Ellipse** tool icon in the toolbox.
2. If necessary, adjust the width of the outline in the Width and Shape box.
3. Select the primary and secondary colors you want to use.
4. Point to where you want to place the center of the ellipse, and then press the mouse button and hold it down.
5. Drag away from the center in any direction to create the ellipse, and then release the mouse button.
6. To draw another ellipse with the same center point, press and hold down the right mouse button while you drag to create the ellipse.

• **NOTES** Hold down the Shift key while you drag to constrain the ellipse to a circle.

The Filled Polygon Tool

Use the Filled Polygon tool to create filled, many-sided shapes using the primary color for the outline and the secondary color for the fill.

1. Click the **Filled Polygon** tool icon in the toolbox.
2. If necessary, adjust the width of the outline in the Width and Shape box.
3. Select the primary and secondary colors you want to use.
4. Point to where you want the polygon to start, then click the left mouse button.
5. Point to where you want the first side to end, and then click the left mouse button.
6. Point to where you want the next side to end, and then click the left mouse button.

7. Repeat step 6 to draw the remaining sides, but double-click the end-point of the next-to-last side. Double-clicking completes that side and also closes the polygon by joining that point to the polygon's starting point.

• **NOTES** You can also drag to define the sides of a polygon. Hold down the Shift key while you drag to constrain the lines in vertical, horizontal, or diagonal directions.

A polygon can have up to 200 sides.

The Clone Tool

Use the Clone tool to selectively copy an area of a picture into the same picture or into another picture.

1. Click the **Clone** tool icon in the toolbox.
2. If necessary, adjust the size and shape of the cloning brush in the Width and Shape box.
3. If necessary, select **Options ➤ Soft Brush Settings** and adjust the cloning brush settings in the Change Soft Brush Settings dialog box.
4. Point to the center of the source area you want to clone and click the right mouse button. A cross appears at that point.
5. Point to where you want the clone to appear, then press and hold down the left mouse button.
6. Drag to paint a clone of the first area. As you drag, the cross in the source area moves to show what you are cloning.
7. Release the mouse button when you have finished cloning.

• **NOTES** Hold down the Shift key while you drag to constrain the lines in vertical and horizontal directions. Press the spacebar to change directions.

PREFERENCES

You can make changes in the way CorelPHOTO-PAINT works to suit your preferences and computer configuration.

Choosing What Is Displayed When You Start the Program

1. Select **Options ➤ Preferences**. The Preferences dialog box appears.
2. Open the **At Startup** list box.
3. Click one of the four options.
4. Click **OK**.

• NOTES By clicking one of the four options, you can choose what is displayed when you start the program. The choices are:

- displaying the About information screen for a few seconds;
- displaying the Create a New Picture dialog box;
- displaying the Load a Picture from Disk dialog box;
- displaying the Main menu with nothing selected.

Choosing the Measurement Units in which You Want to Work

1. Select **Options ➤ Preferences**. The Preferences dialog box appears.
2. Open the **Units** list box.
3. Click one of the five measurement units.
4. Click **OK**.

• NOTES You can choose inches, centimeters, points, picas, or pixels as measurement units. A point is 1⁄72 of an inch; a pica is 1⁄6 of an inch. A pixel is one dot on your computer screen.

Displaying or Hiding the Help Bar

1. Select **Options ➤ Preferences**. The Preferences dialog box appears.
2. Click the **Display Help Bar** button to change between displaying and hiding the Help bar.
3. Click **OK**.

• NOTES The optional Help bar at the bottom of the screen displays context-sensitive information about the current picture and operation.

Keeping Thumbnail Files

1. Select **Options ➤ Preferences**. The Preferences dialog box appears.
2. Click the **Keep Thumbnail Files** button to change between keeping and not keeping thumbnail files.
3. Click **OK**.

• NOTES If you choose to keep thumbnail files, the program stores a miniature image as a .THB file whenever you save a drawing. Subsequently, you can preview pictures before you open them.

Increasing the Number of Shades of Gray on Your Monitor

This Preferences option is available if your monitor is only capable of showing less than 16 shades of gray. Click **Help** in the dialog box for information.

Adjusting the Contrast of Your Monitor

You can adjust the contrast of your monitor to optimize the way pictures appear on the screen. **Help** in the dialog box for information.

Selecting Memory Options

The performance of paint programs such as CorelPHOTO-PAINT is highly dependent on RAM size and configuration. The Corel installation procedure attempts to optimize the way CorelPHOTO-PAINT uses the available memory. You can change the way the program uses memory, but you should only do this if you completely understand memory usage in Windows applications.

PRINTING A PICTURE

CorelPHOTO-PRINT can print a picture to any printer installed under Windows. Refer to *Printing Drawings* in Part I of this book for information about setting up the printer and printing.

RETOUCHING TOOLS

This section provides brief information about using the retouching tools. You can also use filters to retouch your pictures. See *Filtering Pictures*.

The Contrast Paintbrush Tool

Use the Contrast Paintbrush tool to change the contrast of a picture.

1. Click the **Contrast Paintbrush** tool icon in the toolbox. The Palette changes to show the range of contrasts available, as in Figure III.19.
2. If necessary, adjust the size and shape of the brush in the Width and Shape box.
3. Select or type a contrast value in the Palette. The sample box at the left illustrates the selected contrast.

4. Point onto the area of the picture that you want to change, then press and hold down the mouse button.
5. Drag to cover the area to be changed. The contrast changes as you drag.
6. Release the mouse button.

• NOTES Hold down the Shift key while you drag to constrain the lines to horizontal or vertical directions. Press the spacebar to change direction.

The Brighten Paintbrush Tool

Use the Brighten Paintbrush tool to change the intensity of colors.

1. Click the **Brighten Paintbrush** tool icon in the toolbox. The Palette changes to show the range of brightnesses available, as in Figure III.20.
2. If necessary, adjust the size and shape of the brush in the Width and Shape box.
3. Select or type a brightness value in the Palette. The sample box at the left illustrates the selected brightness.

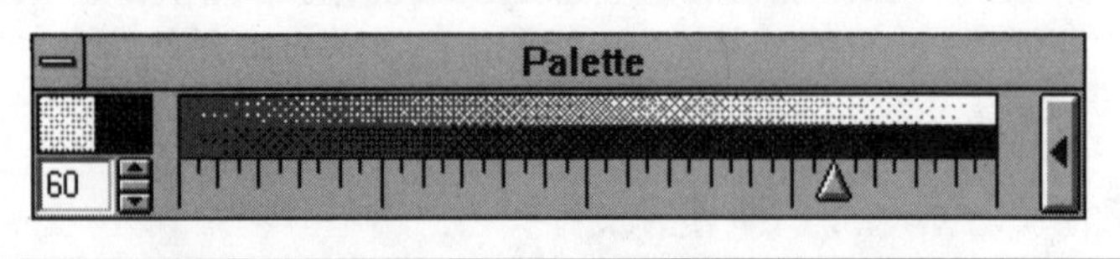

Figure III.19: The Palette showing the range of available contrasts

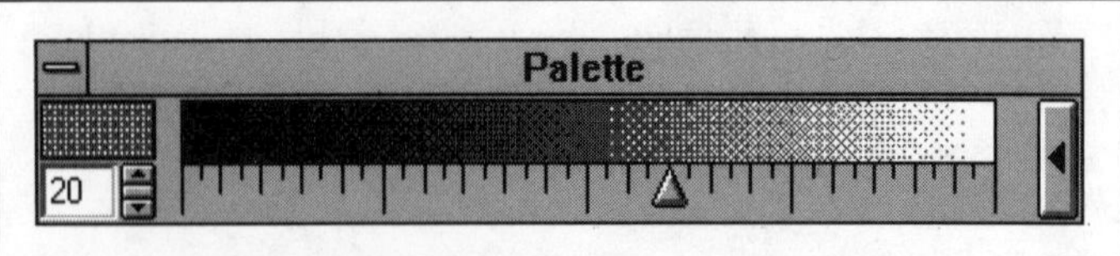

Figure III.20: The Palette showing the range of available brightnesses

4. Point onto the area of the picture that you want to change, then press and hold down the mouse button.
5. Drag to cover the area to be changed. The brightness changes as you drag.
6. Release the mouse button.

• **NOTES** Hold down the Shift key while you drag to constrain the movement to horizontal or vertical. Press the spacebar to change direction.

The Tint Paintbrush Tool

Use the Tint Paintbrush tool to tint the colors in an area of a picture.

1. Click the **Tint Paintbrush** tool icon in the toolbox. The Palette changes to show the currently selected tint, as in Figure III.21.
2. If necessary, adjust the size and shape of the brush in the Width and Shape box.
3. Select a tint in the Palette. The sample box at the left shows the selected tint.
4. Point onto the area of the picture that you want to tint, then press and hold down the mouse button.
5. Drag to cover the area to be changed. The area becomes tinted as you drag.
6. Release the mouse button.

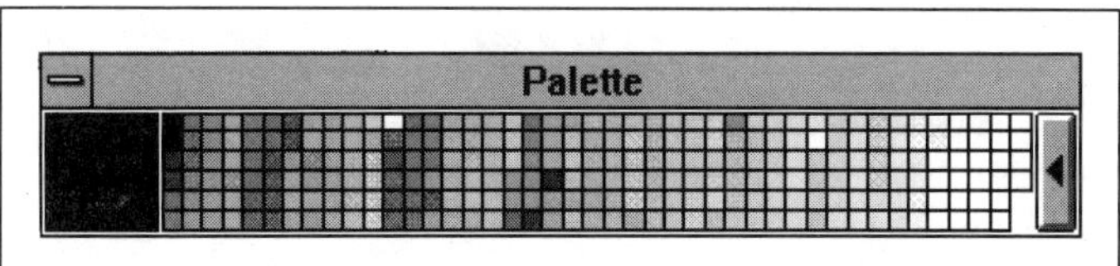

Figure III.21: The Palette showing the currently selected tint in the box on the left

• **NOTES** Hold down the Shift key while you drag to constrain the lines to horizontal or vertical directions. Press the spacebar to change direction.

The Blend Paintbrush Tool

Use the Blend Paintbrush tool to smooth and soften areas of a picture. You can only use this tool in 24-Bit Color and Gray-Scale modes.

1. Click the **Blend Paintbrush** tool icon in the toolbox. The Palette changes to show the range of available blends, as shown in Figure III.22.
2. If necessary, adjust the size and shape of the brush in the Width and Shape box.
3. Select a blend value in the Palette.
4. Point onto the area of the picture that you want to blend, then press and hold down the mouse button.
5. Drag to cover the area to be changed. Colors become progressively more blended as you drag.
6. Release the mouse button.

• **NOTES** Hold down the Shift key while you drag to constrain the lines to horizontal or vertical directions. Press the spacebar to change direction.

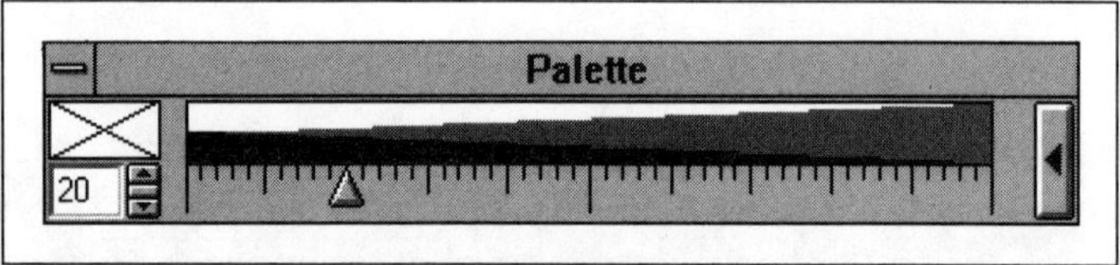

Figure III.22: The Palette showing the range of available blends

The Smear Paintbrush Tool

Use the Smear Paintbrush tool to spread colors in areas of a picture. You can only use this tool in 24-Bit Color and Gray-Scale modes.

1. Click the **Smear Paintbrush** tool icon in the toolbox.
2. If necessary, adjust the size and shape of the brush in the Width and Shape box.
3. If necessary, select **Options ➤ Soft Brush Settings** and adjust the settings in the Change Smear Settings dialog box.
4. Point onto the area of the picture that you want to smear, then press and hold down the mouse button.
5. Drag in the direction you want to smear.
6. Release the mouse button.

• NOTES Hold down the Shift key while you drag to constrain the lines to horizontal or vertical directions. Press the spacebar to change direction.

The Smudge Spraycan Tool

Use the Smudge Spraycan tool to randomly mix dots within an area of a picture.

1. Click the **Smudge Spraycan** tool icon in the toolbox.
2. If necessary, adjust the width of the smudge in the Width and Shape box.
3. Point onto the area you want to smudge, then press and hold down the mouse button.
4. Drag in the direction you want to smudge.
5. Release the mouse button.

The Sharpen Paintbrush Tool

Use the Sharpen Paintbrush tool to sharpen areas of a picture. You can only use this tool in 24-Bit Color and Gray-Scale modes.

1. Click the **Sharpen Paintbrush** tool icon in the toolbox. The Palette changes to display the range of sharpness available, as shown in Figure III.23.
2. If necessary, adjust the size and shape of the brush in the Width and Shape box.
3. Select a sharpen value in the Palette.
4. Point onto the area of the picture that you want to sharpen, then press and hold down the mouse button.
5. Drag to cover the area to be changed.
6. Release the mouse button.

• **NOTES** Hold down the Shift key while you drag to constrain the lines to horizontal or vertical directions. Press the spacebar to change direction.

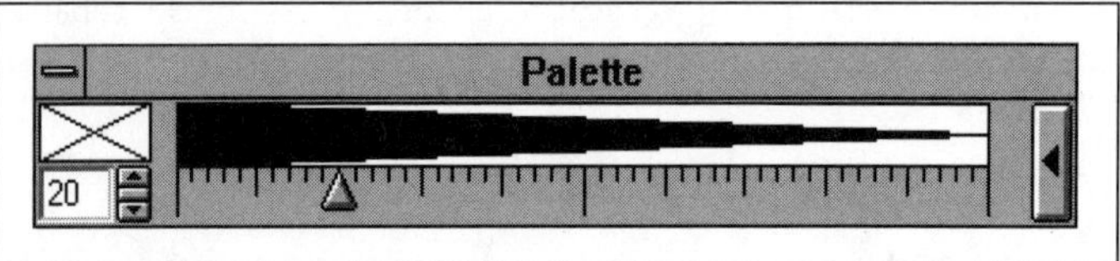

Figure III.23: The Palette showing the range of sharpness available

SCREEN

You can show the CorelPHOTO-PAINT screen in several forms. The normal screen is shown in Figure III.24. The screen has the following components:

- the active picture window
- one or more inactive picture windows
- title bars

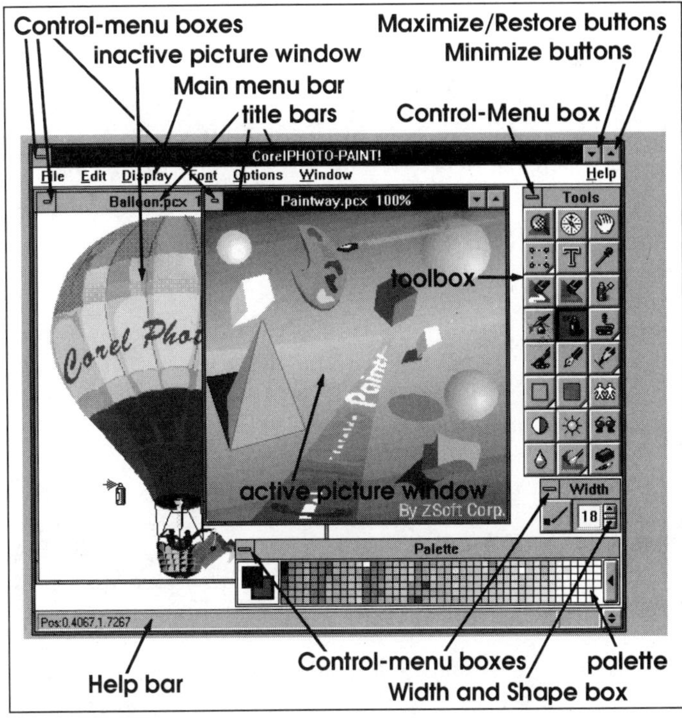

Figure III.24: The normal CorelPHOTO-PAINT screen

- Main menu bar
- Control-menu boxes
- Minimize button
- Maximize/restore button
- scroll bars (if required)
- Help bar (can be displayed or hidden)
- Toolbox (can be displayed or hidden, and can be reformatted)
- Palette (can be displayed or hidden, and can also be folded)
- Width and Shape box (can be displayed or hidden)

Displaying a Full Screen Desktop

You can display the CorelPHOTO-PAINT screen without the title bar and Main menu bar. To do this, select **Display ➤ Full Screen** or press Ctrl-F. To return to the normal display, press Ctrl-F again.

Displaying Only the Active Picture

To display only the active picture:

1. Select **Display ➤ Show Screen**.
2. Click **OK** in the Show Screen dialog box.

Press Esc to return to the previous display.

SELECTION TOOLS

This section provides brief information about using the four selection tools to select an area of a picture.

The selected area is known as a Cutout. You can stretch, shrink, move, copy, cut, delete, tilt, rotate, flip, invert, and outline a cutout, and you can paste in into another picture. You can also apply filters to it.

The Box Selection Tool

Use the Box Selection tool to select a rectangular area of a picture.

1. Click the **Box Selection** tool icon in the toolbox.
2. Point to the top-right corner of the area you want to select, then press and hold down the mouse button.
3. Drag to the bottom-left corner of the area, then release the mouse button. The cutout is marked by a dashed rectangle, and the cursor turns into a hand. Handles at the

four corners of the rectangle indicate the presence of the Gadget Box, which is superimposed on the cutout. See "The Gadget Box" below.

The Magic Wand Tool

Use the Magic Wand tool to select areas of a picture with similar colors.

1. Click the **Magic Wand** tool icon in the toolbox. The cursor changes to a magic wand shape.
2. Select **Options ➤ Color Tolerance**. The Color Comparison Tolerance dialog box appears, as shown in Figure III.25.
3. In the Color Comparison Tolerance dialog box, select or type red, green, and blue deviation values.
4. Click **OK**.
5. Point to a place on your picture that has a color value at the center of the range of colors you want to select, and click the mouse button. A dashed outline shows the cutout area with the selected range of colors, and the cursor turns into a hand. An outer rectangle marks the Gadget Box. See "The Gadget Box" below.

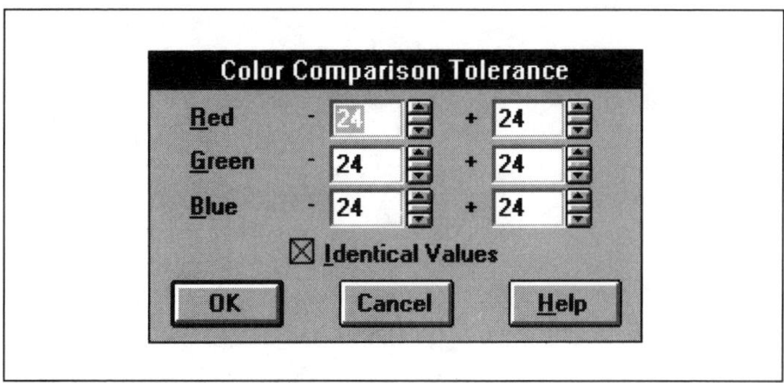

Figure III.25: The Color Comparison Tolerance dialog box

The Lasso Tool

Use the Lasso tool to select an irregularly shaped area of a picture.

1. Click the **Lasso** tool icon in the toolbox. The cursor becomes a lasso.
2. Point where you want to start the irregular cutout, then press and hold down the mouse button.
3. Drag to outline the shape of the cutout, then release the mouse button. A dashed outline shows the cutout area, and the cursor turns into a hand. An outer rectangle marks the Gadget Box. See "The Gadget Box" below.

The Scissors Tool

Use the Scissors tool to select a polygon-shaped shaped area of a picture.

1. Click the **Scissors** tool icon in the toolbox. The cursor changes into a pair of scissors.
2. Point where you want to start the polygon-shaped cutout, then click the mouse button.
3. Point to the end of the first line of the polygon and click the mouse button.
4. Repeat step 3 to add more lines.
5. Double-click to close the polygon. A dashed outline shows the cutout area, and the cursor turns into a hand. An outer rectangle marks the Gadget Box. See "The Gadget Box" below.

• **NOTES** You can also drag to define the sides of the polygon. In this case, hold down the Shift key while you drag to constrain the sides to a vertical, horizontal, or diagonal direction.

The Gadget Box

After you have created a cutout, you can

- Stretch or shrink the cutout by dragging one of the Gadget Box handles. Hold down the Shift key to maintain the width and height in proportion.
- Move the cutout by pointing inside the Gadget Box and dragging. Drag with the left mouse button to make the cutout opaque. Drag with the right mouse button to make the background of the cutout transparent. Hold down the Shift key while you drag to leave a copy of the cutout in its original place. Hold down the Ctrl key while you drag to leave a trail of copies. You can move the cutout one pixel at a time by pressing the cursor keys.
- Filter or transform the cutout. See *Filtering Pictures* and *Transforming Pictures*.
- Delete the cutout.
- Copy the cutout to the Clipboard.

After you have completed the operation, click outside the Gadget Box or choose another tool to make the change permanent.

SHORTCUT KEYS

Most procedures in this book are described in terms of selecting from menus. However, CorelPHOTO-PAINT provides shortcuts to speed certain actions. These shortcuts are shown in Table III.1 and III.2.

Table III.1: Function Key Shortcuts

FUNCTION KEY	ACTION
F1	accesses online Help.
Shift-F4	tiles windows.
Ctrl-F4	closes the current picture.
Alt-F4	exits CorelPHOTO-PAINT.
Shift-F5	cascades windows.
Ctrl-F6	switches to the next picture.

TOOLBOX

CorelPHOTO-PAINT has four categories of tools: display tools, selection tools, painting tools, and retouching tools. Select a tool by clicking on its icon in the toolbox.

Some tools are not available when you are using certain color modes. If you try to select an unavailable tool, you'll see a message telling you the tool is unavailable and a suggestion telling you which color mode you can choose if you want to use that tool.

The toolbox normally appears on the screen whenever you start CorelPHOTO-PAINT. If it is not displayed, refer to *Displaying and Hiding Workboxes* for information about displaying it.

You can get information from online **Help** about any tool by pointing onto its icon in the toolbox and clicking the right mouse button.

Table III.2: Speed Key Shortcuts

KEY	ACTION
Ctrl-1	displays 100% view.
Ctrl-A	shows or hides all workboxes.
Ctrl-D	duplicates the current picture.
Ctrl-F	switches to and from full-screen view.
Ctrl-P	shows or hides the palette workbox.
Ctrl-S	saves the picture under the current file name.
Ctrl-T	shows or hides the toolbox.
Ctrl-W	shows or hides the Width and Shape workbox.
Shift-Insert	executes the Paste command.
Ctrl-Insert	executes the Copy command.
Delete	executes the Delete command.
Shift-Delete	executes the Cut command.
Alt-Backspace	undoes the most recent action.
Esc	erases some tools' effects before you release the mouse button.
←, →, ↑ *or* ↓	move a cutout one pixel at a time.

Changing the Appearance of the Toolbox

You can change the shape of the toolbox and you can change the number of tools displayed. To change the shape of the toolbox, do the following:

1. Click the **Control-menu** box at the top-left corner of the toolbox. The Control menu appears.
2. Click **Layout**. A flyout appears.

3. In the flyout, click the number of columns or the number of rows you want the toolbox to have. The Toolbox reappears with the new shape.

The toolbox can be displayed with grouped or ungrouped tools. The toolbox is smaller when tools are grouped than when they are ungrouped. A grouped tool has a small white triangle in the lower-right corner of its icon. The toolbox in Figure III.26 is shown ungrouped with the tools arranged in two rows.

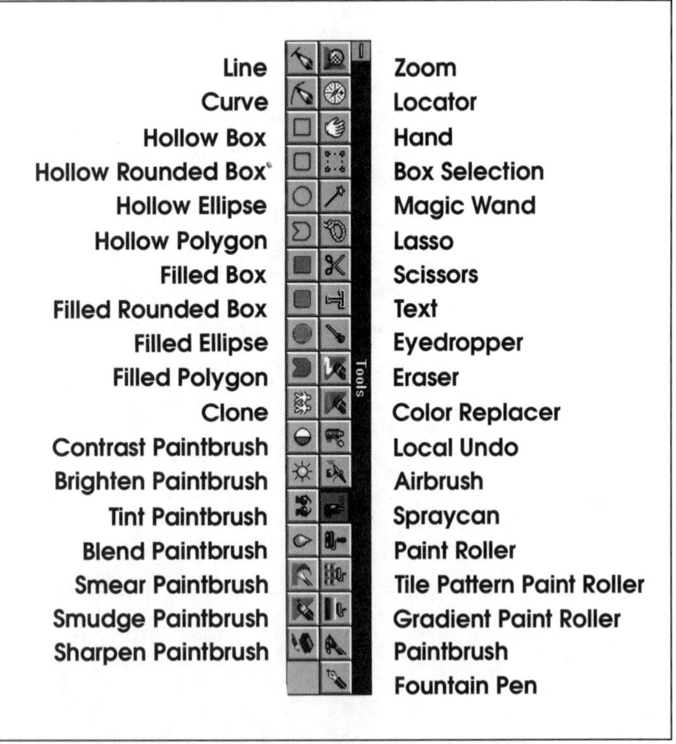

Figure III.26: An ungrouped toolbox with two rows of tool icons

To change from a grouped to an ungrouped toolbox, or vice-versa, do the following:

1. Click the **Control-menu** box at the top-left corner of the toolbox. The Control Menu appears.
2. Click **Layout**. A flyout appears.
3. Click **Ungroup** or **Group**. The toolbox reappears.

Selecting a Tool from the Toolbox

To select a tool that appears in the toolbox, point onto its icon. The name of the tool appears in the Help bar at the bottom of the work area. Click the mouse button to select the tool and its icon becomes darker than the other icons to show that it is selected.

To select a tool within group:

1. Point onto the white triangle at the lower-right corner of a group tool icon.
2. Press the mouse button and hold it down until a flyout group of icons appears.
3. Drag onto the icon of the tool you want to use, and then release the mouse button. The tool is selected and its darkened icon replaces the original icon in the toolbox.

• NOTES After you have selected a tool, point into the work area. The cursor changes shape to indicate which tool you are using.

Some tools are modified when you double-click on their icons. The actions of certain tools are constrained if you hold down the Shift key while you drag the mouse. These modifications and constraints, if they are available with a tool, are described in the tables below.

Display Tools

The Display tools, described in Table III.3, change the way pictures are displayed. See *Display Tools* for additional information about these tools.

Table III.3: Display Tools

TOOL	USE
Zoom	Changes the magnification of a picture. Returns to 100% view when double-clicked.
Locator	Displays selected areas in duplicated pictures.
Hand	Moves the picture on the screen.

Selection Tools

The Selection tools, described in Table III.4, select areas of a picture. See *Selection Tools* for additional information about these tools.

Table III.4: Selection Tools

TOOL	USE
Box Selection	Selects a rectangular area. Selects the displayed area when double-clicked. When Shift is pressed, selects a square area.
Magic Wand	Selects an area with similar colors. Displays the Color Comparison Tolerance dialog box when double-clicked.
Lasso	Selects an irregular area.
Scissors	Selects an area defined by a polygon. When shift is pressed, the polygon edges are horizontal, vertical, or diagonal only.

Painting Tools

The Painting tools, described in Table III.5, are used to draw pictures. See *Painting Tools* for additional information about these tools.

Table III.5: Selection Tools

TOOL	USE
Text	Adds text to a picture using the primary color for the outline and the secondary color for the fill.
Eyedropper	Picks up a color from the screen.
Eraser	Replaces an area with the background color. When double-clicked, clears the entire work area to the background color. When shift is pressed, constrains to vertical or horizontal movement only; press the spacebar to change direction.
Color Replacer	Replaces the primary color with the secondary color. When double-clicked, changes the primary to the secondary color in the area displayed. When shift is pressed, constrains to vertical or horizontal only; press the spacebar to change direction.
Local Undo	Replaces some or all of the erased part of picture. When double-clicked, undoes all changes made since the last time you chose a tool or command. When shift is pressed, constrains to vertical or horizontal movement only; press the spacebar to change direction.
Airbrush	Sprays the primary color with a soft brush. When double-clicked, displays the Change Airbrush Settings dialog box. When shift is pressed, contrains to vertical or horizontal movement only; press the spacebar to change direction.

Table III.5: Painting Tools (continued)

TOOL	USE
Spraycan	Sprays with a pattern of dots in the primary color. When double-clicked, displays the Select a Brush Style dialog box.
Paint Roller	Fills an area with the primary color. When double-clicked, displays the Color Comparison Tolerance dialog box.
Tile Pattern Paint Roller	Fills an area with a repeating tile pattern. When double-clicked, displays the Color Comparison Tolerance dialog box.
Gradient Paint Roller	Fills an area with a color gradient (fountain fill) from the secondary to the background color. When double-clicked, displays the Color Comparison Tolerance dialog box.
Paintbrush	Draws with a soft brush using the primary color. When double-clicked, displays the Change Soft Brush Settings dialog box. When shift is pressed, contrains to vertical or horizontal movement only; press the spacebar to change direction.
Fountain Pen	Draws freehand shapes in the primary color. When double-clicked, displays the Select a Brush Style dialog box. When shift is pressed, contrains to vertical or horizontal movement only; press the spacebar to change direction.
Line	Draws single or joined straight lines using the primary color. When double-clicked, displays the Set the Drawing Width dialog box. When shift is pressed, draws vertical, horizontal, or diagonal lines only.
Curve	Draws single or joined B~alezier curves using the primary color.

Table III.5: Painting Tools (continued)

TOOL	USE
Hollow Box	Draws outlined rectangles and squares using the primary color. When shift is pressed, draws a square.
Hollow Rounded Box	Draws outlined rectangles and squares with rounded corners using the primary color. When shift is pressed, draws a square with rounded corners.
Hollow Ellipse	Draws outlined ellipses and circles using the primary color. When shift is pressed, draws a circle.
Hollow Polygon	Draws outlined polygons using the primary color. When shift is pressed, draws vertical, horizontal, or diagonal lines only.
Filled Box	Draws filled rectangles and squares using the primary color for the outline and the secondary color for the fill. When shift is pressed, draws a box.
Filled Rounded Box	Draws filled rectangles and squares with rounded corners using the primary color for the outline and the secondary color for the fill. When shift is pressed, draws a square with rounded corners.
Filled Ellipse	Draws filled ellipses and circles using the primary color for the outline and the secondary color for the fill. When shift is pressed, draws a circle.
Filled Polygon	Draws filled polygons using the primary color for the outline and the secondary color for the fill. When shift is pressed, draws vertical, horizontal, or diagonal lines only.

Table III.5: Painting Tools (continued)

TOOL	USE
Clone	Copies one area to another. When double-clicked, displays the Change Clone Settings dialog box. When shift is pressed, contrains to vertical or horizontal only; press the spacebar to change direction.

Retouching Tools

The Retouching tools, described in Table III.6, are used to modify pictures. See *Retouching Tools* for additional information about these tools.

Table III.6: Retouching Tools

TOOL	USE
Contrast Paintbrush	Changes the contrast of areas of a picture. When double-clicked, displays the Select a Brush Style dialog box.
Brighten Paintbrush	Brightens areas of a picture. When double-clicked, displays the Select a Brush Style dialog box.
Tint Paintbrush	Tints areas of a picture. When double-clicked, displays the Select a Brush Style dialog box.
Blend Paintbrush	Blends one area of a picture into another. When double-clicked, displays the Select a Brush Style dialog box.
Smear Paintbrush	Smears one area into another with a soft brush. When double-clicked, displays the Change Smear Settings dialog box.

Table III.6: Retouching Tools (continued)

TOOL	USE
Smudge Spraycan	Smudges colors. When double-clicked, displays the Select a Brush Style dialog box.
Sharpen Paintbrush	Sharpens areas of a picture. When double-clicked, displays the Select a Brush Style dialog box.

TRANSFORMING PICTURES

You can transform an entire picture, or a part of it, in several ways. For example, you can flip, invert, or rotate a picture. If you select a part of a picture and then apply a transformation, only the selected part is transformed. To transform an entire picture, apply a transformation without selecting a part of the picture.

Flipping Horizontally or Vertically

You can flip a picture horizontally about its vertical axis or vertically about its horizontal axis.

1. Select **Edit ➤ Transform**. The Transform flyout appears.
2. Click **Flip Horizontal** or **Flip Vertical**. The picture is flipped and redrawn.

Inverting a Picture

You can reverse the colors in a picture by inverting it. Colors are reversed as they are on a photographic negative.

1. Select **Edit ➤ Transform**. The Transform flyout appears.
2. Click **Invert**. The picture is inverted and redrawn.

Outlining a Picture

You can redraw a picture so that only outlines show. All fills are shown in the background color.

1. Select **Edit ➤ Transform**. The Transform flyout appears.
2. Click **Outline**. The picture is redrawn in outline form.

Rotating a Picture

You can rotate a picture in 90-degree increments.

1. Select **Edit ➤ Transform**. The Transform flyout appears.
2. Click **Rotate 90°**. The picture is rotated 90 degrees in a clockwise direction and redrawn.

Making Multiple Transformations on a Picture

The Transform Area command allows you to flip and rotate a picture, or a selected area of it, at one time, as well as resize it.

1. Select **Edit ➤ Transform**. The Transform flyout appears.
2. Click **Area**. The Change the Selected Area dialog box appears, as shown in Figure III.27.
3. Click the **Horizontal** and **Vertical** buttons if you want to flip the picture.
4. Click one of the **Rotate** buttons if you want to rotate the picture.
5. Change the percentages in the **Resize** box if you want to change the size of the picture.
6. Click **OK**.

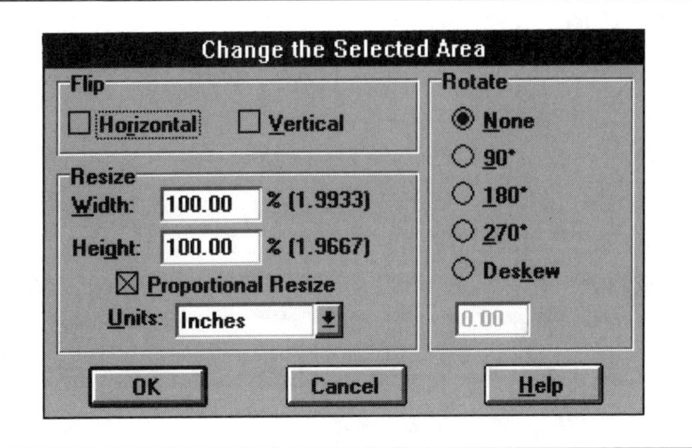

Figure III.27: The Change the Selected Area dialog box

UNDOING OPERATIONS

To cancel all changes you made to a picture since you last chose a tool or a command:

- Select **Edit ➤ Undo**.

WIDTH AND SHAPE BOX

By using the Width and Shape box, you can change the width and shape of all the painting tools except the paint roller tools, and of all the retouching tools. You cannot change the width and shape of the Eyedropper tool or of text. The width and shape you select applies to all affected tools.

Changing Tool Width

Do the following to change the width of the painting and retouching tools:

1. If necessary, display the **Width and Shape** box.
2. Use the arrows in the Width and Shape box to select a new width, or type the width value.

• **NOTES** The width shown in the Width and Shape box is always expressed in pixels, even if you have selected other measurement units as a preference. You can specify the width in other measurement units, as described below, but width is still displayed as pixels in the Width and Shape box.

Changing Tool Shape

Do the following to change the shape of the painting and retouching tools:

1. If necessary, display the **Width and Shape** box.
2. Click the large button in the Width and Shape box. The Select a Brush Style dialog box appears, as shown in Figure III.28.
3. Click on one of the seven available shapes. Proceed to step 8 unless you want to set the tool width here.
4. Optionally, click **Set Size**. The Set the Drawing Width dialog box appears.

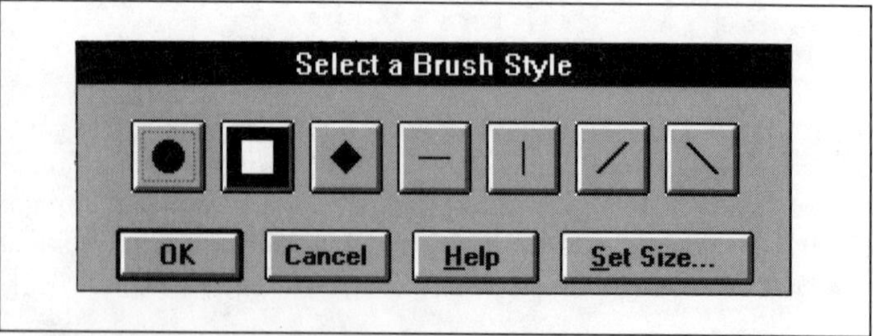

Figure III.28: The Select a Brush Style dialog box

5. In the Set the Drawing Width dialog box, open the Units list box and click on the measurement units you want to use.
6. Select or type the desired drawing width.
7. Click **OK** to return to the Select a Brush Style dialog box.
8. Click **OK**.

Part IV

CorelSHOW

ARRANGING OBJECTS

The Arrange menu gives you the ability to alter the stacking order of objects on a slide or on a slide background. See *Stacking Order* in Part I of this book for information.

BACKGROUND

You can create a slide background in an OLE server application such as CorelDRAW and then embed it in, or link it to, your slideshow. See *Embedding and Linking Objects* in Part I of this book for additional information.

Embedding a Background

Proceed as follows to embed a background:

1. Click the **Background view** button.
2. In the toolbox, click the tool which represents the server application you want to use. For example, to embed a background created in CorelDRAW, click the CorelDRAW tool.
3. Move the cursor into the presentation window and it becomes a cross. Press the mouse button and drag to create a rectangle of any size, and then release the mouse button. After a few seconds, the server application opens.
4. In the server application, create the object you want to use as a background.
5. Select **File ➤ Exit & Return** to exit from the server application and return to CorelSHOW. If your server application does not have this command, consult its documentation. After a few seconds, the CorelSHOW screen reappears with the background object on it.

6. Use the handles around the background object to size and position it. Alternatively, if you want the object to fill the whole slide, select **Arrange ➤ Fit Object To Page**.
7. Repeat steps 2 through 6 to place additional objects on the background.
8. Select **File ➤ Save Background**. The Save Background dialog box appears.
9. If you want the new background to become part of the library, click **Insert in Library**.
10. Type any keywords or notes you want to attach to the background.
11. Click **OK**.

• **NOTES** After you have embedded an object, you can select it and then edit it by selecting **Edit ➤ Edit** *Object*. The word "Object" here is replaced on screen by the full file name of the object.

Linking a Background

Proceed as follows to link an object to the background:

1. Start a server application, such as CorelDRAW, in which you want to create background objects.
2. Create the object you wish to use as a background.
3. Select the object.
4. Select **Edit ➤ Copy** to copy the object to the Clipboard.
5. Open CorelSHOW.
6. Open the presentation for which you are creating a background.
7. Click the **Background view** button.
8. Select **Edit ➤ Paste Special**. The Paste Special dialog box appears.
9. In the dialog box, click the type of graphic you are linking.
10. Click **Paste Link**. The background object appears in the presentation window.

11. Follow steps 6 through 11 in "Embedding a Background" above.

• **NOTES** Select **Edit ➤ Links** to examine and modify links between objects in slides and files in other applications.

CREATING A NEW PRESENTATION

There are five main steps in creating a new presentation:

1. Specify the format.
2. Choose or create a background.
3. Assemble individual slides.
4. Assign time on screen and transition effects to slides.
5. Place the slides in order.

Each of these steps is explained below.

Specifying the Format

To specify the slide format:

1. Select **File ➤ New**. A new presentation window appears.
2. Select **File ➤ Page Setup**. The Page Setup dialog box appears.
3. Click either **Portrait** or **Landscape**.
4. Click one of the **Page Size** buttons. For an on-screen presentation, select **Screen**.
5. If you clicked **Custom** in step 4, select or type the horizontal and vertical sizes.
6. Click **OK**.

Choosing a Background from a Library

The background, which is common to all slides in a presentation, is on a separate layer from the contents of individual slides. You can select a background from an existing library, or create a new background. See *Background*. Proceed as follows to select an existing background:

1. Click the **Background view** button to select the background layer.
2. Click the **Background Library** tool. A dialog box opens showing the available backgrounds. When you first use CorelSHOW, you see the main library of backgrounds supplied with the package.
3. If you want to select a background in another directory, click **Change Library** and then select another directory in the Select Background dialog box.
4. Click the background you want to use. The background appears within the slide outline in the presentation window.
5. Click **Done**.

Assembling Individual Slides

You assemble individual slides from components created in OLE server applications such as CorelDRAW, CorelCHART, and CorelPHOTO-PAINT. You can embed objects into slides, or link objects into slides.

The methods you use to embed and link objects is the same as that for creating a background. See *Background* for details. Each slide can contain embedded objects and linked objects. To assemble slides:

1. Click the **Slide view** button.
2. Click one of the **Page** icons at the bottom of the screen to select the slide you want to assemble.
3. Embed or link objects into that slide.
4. Size and move the objects as necessary.
5. Repeat steps 2 through 4 to assemble more slides.

• **NOTES** When you start a new slideshow, you specify the number of slides in the show. Subsequently, if you want to add more slides, select **Insert ➤ New Page**. A dialog box appears in which you can specify the number of new slides you want to add, and whether the new slides are to be inserted before or after the currently selected slide. You can insert slides in the Slide or Slide Sorter views.

To delete one or more slides, go to the Slide Sorter view, select the slides you want to delete, and press Delete.

When you resize and move objects on a slide, use the Shift and Ctrl keys to constrain the operation as you do in CorelDRAW. See *Constraining Objects* in Part I of this book.

Using Animation in Slides

Your slideshow can include Autodesk animation sequences. However, the CorelDRAW Graphics package does not provide any way to create or edit animation. To insert an animation slide:

1. Select the slide before which you want to place the animation slide.
2. Select **Insert ➤ Animation**. The Insert Animation dialog box appears.
3. In the dialog box, select the directory that contains the animation file.
4. Click the file name. The Preview box shows the beginning of the animation.
5. Click **Options**. The dialog box expands to show optional parameters.
6. Specify the optional parameters.
7. Click **OK**. The animation slide is inserted into the presentation.

• **NOTES** Animation file names have a .FLI extension.

Assigning Time on Screen and Transition Effects to Slides

You can assign a time on screen and a transition effect individually to each slide in the Slide or Slide Sorter views. Proceed as follows:

1. In Slide or Slide Sorter view, select a slide.
2. Open the **Transition Effect** list box.
3. Scroll if necessary and then click on the transition effect you want.
4. Open the **Time On Screen** list box. Select or type the time on screen for that slide.
5. Repeat steps 2 through 4 for the remaining slides.

• **NOTES** The transition effect determines how a slide first appears on the screen.

Placing Slides in Order

Use the Slide Sorter view to change the order of slides, either by dragging slides from one position to another or by numbering them. To drag slides:

1. Select the **Slide Sorter** view.
2. Point onto a slide, then press and hold down the mouse button.
3. Drag the slide to a new position.
4. Release the mouse button.

To renumber slides:

1. Select the **Slide Sorter** view. The Numbering tool appears in the Ribbon.
2. Click the **Numbering** tool. The slides in the Presentation window are redrawn with a number panel below each one.
3. Click the slide which is to be number 1. The number panel under that slide changes to show that slide number.

4. Click the slide which should be next in order. The number panel under that slide changes to show the slide number.
5. Repeat step 4 to number the remaining slides.
6. After you have numbered the last slide, the slides are automatically rearranged in the correct order and the number panels disappear.

• NOTES If you want to stop numbering slides before you have numbered them all, click the Numbering tool. The slides you have numbered are placed in order at the beginning of the presentation with the unnumbered slides following. You can move through the presentation by using the scroll bar, or by pressing the arrow (cursor control) keys.

DISPLAY SETTINGS

Background and Slide views allow you to use rulers and guidelines to help align objects, as you can in CorelDRAW.

Displaying and Hiding Rulers

To display or hide the rulers:

1. Select the **Display** menu. Show Rulers is checked if rulers are displayed, or unchecked if rulers are hidden.
2. Click on **Show Rulers** to change from displaying rulers to hiding them, or vice-versa.

Changing Ruler Origins

There are two ways to change the zero points on the rulers. You can drag or type values. To drag the zero points:

1. Point onto the square at the top-left corner of the presentation window, where the two rulers meet.

2. Press and hold the mouse button while you drag down and to the right. A horizontal and a vertical dotted line show the current zero position as you drag.
3. Release the mouse button. The rulers are redrawn with new zero points.

To type zero-point values:

1. Select **Display ➤ Ruler Setup**. The Rulers dialog box appears.
2. Select or type the distances you want the zero points to be from the bottom-left corner of the slide.
3. Click **OK**.

Using Guidelines

If you have rulers displayed, you can pull Guidelines out of the rulers just as you can in CorelDRAW. You can also specify the position of Guidelines by selecting **Display ➤ Guidelines**. See *Alignment and Placing Aids* in Part I of this book for information.

Saving Settings

After you have made changes in the Display menu, you can save these settings as defaults by selecting **Display ➤ Save Settings**.

FILES

Most commands in the File menu are similar to those in CorelDRAW. See *Files* in Part I of this book for information.

• **NOTES** The **Save Background** command allows you to save a file in the format CorelSHOW uses for backgrounds.

The **Page Setup** command allows you to choose several formats other than Screen. Use this if you want to make overhead transparencies or printed copies of your slides.

When you print black-and-white transparencies or copies of your slide, you can usually improve them by omitting the background. To do this, select **Edit ➤ Omit Background** for each slide.

HELP

CorelSHOW has a Help facility similar to that in other Windows applications. There are four ways to access Help:

- Select **Help** in the Main menu bar. The Help menu appears. Click the item you want to access.
- Press **F1**. The online Help Table of Contents appears. Click the type of information you want.
- Press **Shift-F1**. The cursor changes to an arrow with a question mark. Point to the item on the screen about which you want help and click the mouse button.
- Press **Ctrl-F1**. The Search dialog box appears with a list of Help topics. Click on the topic about which you want information.

MAIN MENU

See "Menu Commands" in online **Help** for information about each of the menus and commands.

PLAYING A SLIDESHOW

You can play a slide show from CorelSHOW, or you can use the independent Run-Time Player.

Using CorelSHOW to Play a Slideshow

To play a slideshow:

1. Open the slideshow in CorelSHOW.
2. Select **Display ➤ Presentation Options**. The Presentation Options dialog box appears.
3. In the dialog box, choose whether you want automatic or manual advance.
4. Check the **Run show continuously** button if you want the slideshow to repeat automatically.
5. Check the **Display pointer onscreen** button if that is what you want.
6. Leave the **Generate slide show in advance** button checked to minimize pauses between slides.
7. Click **OK**.
8. Click the **Screen Show** button to start the show.

• **NOTES** If you chose manual advance in step 3, double-click the left mouse button to advance from one slide to the next. Double-click the right mouse button to go back to the previous slide.

If you chose continuous running in step 4, press Esc to terminate the show.

Using Run-Time Player to Play a Slideshow

The CorelSHOW Run-time Player is an independent Windows application you can use to present a slideshow on a computer screen without installing CorelSHOW itself. The Run-time Player is a shareware program which Corel invites you to distribute freely.

You can install this program on any personal computer that has Windows 3.1 or higher without violating any software copyrights.

Double-click the **CorelSHOW Run-time Player** icon in the Program Manager to start Run-time.

Run-time's screen is a simplified version of the CorelSHOW screen. The Main Menu contains only a File and Window option. The Ribbon contains the Screen Show button and also the Transition Effect and Time On Screen Text boxes. Use these buttons and text boxes the same way you do in CorelSHOW.

Follow the steps described above in "Using CorelSHOW to Play a Slideshow" above.

SCREEN

Figure IV.1 shows the CorelSHOW Slide View screen. The Background and Slide Sorter views are slightly different. The screen components are:

COMPONENT	PURPOSE
Control-menu boxes	Provide commands for sizing and positioning windows.
cursor	Selects a specific point on the screen.
Maximize button	Expands a window to fill the entire screen.
Minimize/Restore button	Shrinks a window to an icon at the bottom of the screen. Also expands an icon at the bottom of the size screen to the size of the original window.
menu bar	Provides access to pull-down menus.
Page icons	In Slide View and Slide Sorter views, used to select individual slides.

COMPONENT	PURPOSE
presentation windows	In Background View and Slide View, areas in which individual slides are assembled. In Slide Sorter view, areas in which slideshows are assembled. There can be one active presentation window and several inactive presentation windows.
rulers	Used for sizing and positioning objects. Not available in the Slide Sorter view.
Screen Showbutton	Used to start a slideshow.
scroll bar	Used in Slide Sorter view to view slides not on the current screen.
show clocks	Show the total length of the slideshow and the time up to the current slide.
slide area	In Background and Slide view, shows the image of one slide. In Slide Sorter view, shows images of several slides.
Slide Numbering tool	In Slide Sorter view, used to put slides in order.
Time On Screen box	In Slide and Slide Sorter views, controls how long individual slides are shown on screen.
title bars	At the top of the CorelSHOW window, shows the program name. At the top of each presentation window, shows the file name of the slide show.
toolbox	Contains the tools used to create slideshows.

COMPONENT	PURPOSE
Transition Effects box	In Slide and Slide Sorter views, provides control over how a slide first appears on the screen.
View Selection buttons	Used to select Background, Slide, and Slide Sorter views.
window borders	Shows window outlines and is used to resize windows.

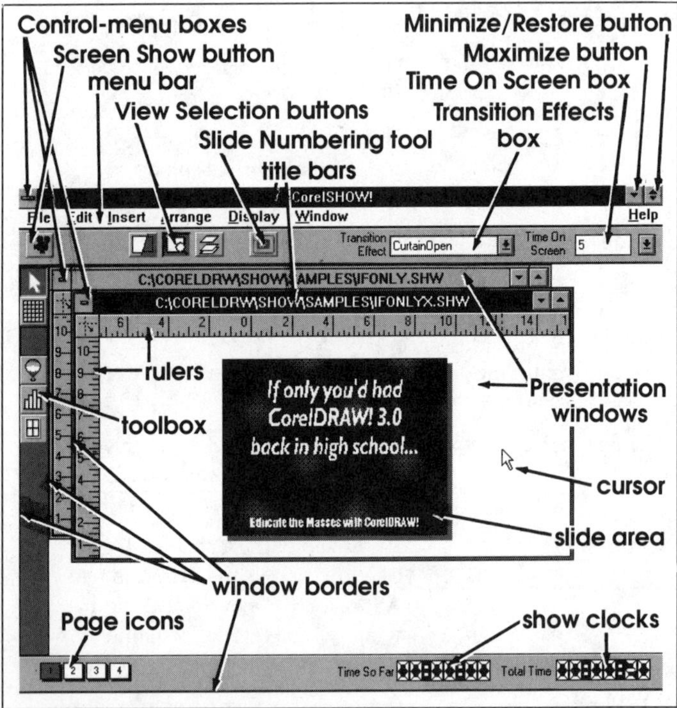

Figure IV.1: The CorelSHOW Slide View screen

SELECTING A VIEW MODE

There are three view modes:

- Background view, which is used to select or create a background for all the slides in a presentation;
- Slide view, which is used to assemble the components of individual slides; and
- Slide Sorter view, which is used to change the order of slides in a presentation.

To select a slide view:

- Click the appropriate **View** button in the ribbon.

SHORTCUT KEYS

CorelSHOW provides shortcuts to speed certain actions and, in some cases, to provide extra functions. The shortcut keys are described in Table IV.1 and Table IV.2.

TOOLBOX

The CorelSHOW toolbox, shown in Figure IV.2, contains five tools. Each is explained below.

Pick tool	Selects, moves, and resizes objects in background and Slide views. In the Slide Sorter view, it is used to change the order of slides.

Background Library tool	Selects backgrounds for slide presentations. See *Background*.
CorelDRAW Gateway tool	Embeds an object from CorelDRAW.
CorelCHART Gateway tool	Embeds an object from CorelCHART.
Gateway to Other OLE Applications tool	Embeds an object from any Windows application that supports Object Linking and Embedding.

Table IV.1: Function Key Shortcuts

FUNCTION KEY	PURPOSE
F1	Opens the online **Help** Table of Contents.
Shift-F1	Enables the question-mark cursor, which you can use to access help.
Ctrl-F1	Opens the online **Help** list of topics.
F2	In automatic slideshows, pauses the slideshow. Press F2 a second time to continue the slideshow.
F3	During slideshow, plays the show backwards.
F4	During slideshow, plays the show forwards.
Alt-F4	While show is playing, terminates the slideshow. If the show is not playing, exits CorelSHOW.
F9	During a slideshow, goes to the first slide.
F10	During a slideshow, goes to the last slide.

Table IV.2: Speed Key Shortcuts

KEY	PURPOSE
Ctrl-A	Opens the Insert Animation dialog box.
Ctrl-N	Opens the Insert New Page dialog box.
Ctrl-O	Opens the Open Presentation dialog box.
Ctrl-P	Opens the Print dialog box.
Ctrl-R	Opens the Show dialog box.
Ctrl-S	Saves the presentation under the current file name.
Ctrl-W	Executes the Refresh Window command.
Ctrl-X	Exits CorelSHOW
Insert	Inserts a new slide after the current slide (in Slide view).
Alt-Backspace	Undoes the most recent action.
PageDown	Scrolls toward the end of the presentation.
Shift-PageDown	Executes the To Back command.
Ctrl-PageDown	Executes the Forward One command.
PageUp	Scrolls toward the beginning of the presentation.
Shift-PageUp	Executes the To Front command.
Ctrl-PageDown	Executes the Backward One command.
Esc	Terminates a running slideshow.

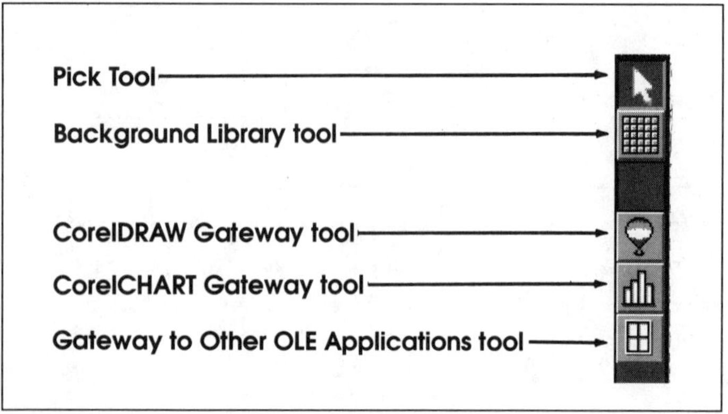

Figure IV.2: The toolbox

UNDOING OPERATIONS

To undo the most recent operation, select **Edit ➤ Undo**.

Part V

CorelTRACE

CONVERTING A BITMAP IMAGE TO A VECTOR IMAGE

There are three stages in converting a bitmap image to a usable vector image:

1. Optimizing the bitmap image.
2. Tracing the bitmap image.
3. Optimizing the vector image.

The more effort you put into optimizing the bitmap image, the less you will have to put into optimizing the vector image. Only experience can teach you how best to split your time between these two activities.

Optimizing the Bitmap Image

Before you can successfully trace most bitmap images, you should optimize them. If you are using a scanner to create bitmap images, you need to experiment with the scanner controls to create an image with good contrast between brightness levels and colors, and with a minimum number of random pixels.

If you are using an existing bitmap image, you will probably have to use your paint program's pixel-editing capabilities to improve the brightness- and color-contrast in the image, and to make sure that straight lines and corners are well defined.

Tracing the Image

CorelTRACE provides several controls for affecting the way a bitmap image is converted into a vector image. These controls affect the entire image. Set these controls in such a way that CorelTRACE converts your optimized bitmap image into a vector image that needs the least manipulation. See *Tracing an Image* for more information.

Optimizing the Vector Image

Depending on the way you optimized the bitmap image, and the controls you chose for the tracing process, the vector image needs more or less attention. In many cases, you need to convert lines to curves or curves to lines. You might need to combine several objects into one object. The more work you put into providing contrast and continuity in the original bitmap image, the less work you need to put into optimizing the bitmap image.

CREATING AN IMAGE TO BE TRACED

CorelTRACE converts bitmap images into vector images. It can accept bitmap black-and-white, gray-scale, and color images in the following formats:

- TIFF 5.0 (.TIF)
- PC Paintbrush (.PCX and .PCC)
- Windows (.BMP)
- CompuServe (.GIF)
- Targa (.TGA)

You can create bitmap images in these formats by scanning or by working in a paint program such as PC Paintbrush, Windows Paintbrush, and CorelPHOTO-PAINT. You can also purchase clip art in these formats, capture screen images, and convert bitmaps in other formats to these formats with utilities such as HiJaak and Hotshot.

In order to convert a bitmap image into a vector image, CorelTRACE has to detect definite boundaries in the bitmap image. Bitmap images that have distinct changes in brightness or color produce good results. Those that have gradual changes in brightness or color cannot be traced effectively.

HELP

There are three ways to access online Help:

- Select **Help** in the Main menu bar. The Help menu appears.
- Press **F1.** If a dialog box is open, Help for that dialog is displayed. If no dialog box is open, the Help Table of Contents appears.

PREFERENCES

CorelTRACE allows you to set certain preferences before you start to trace a bitmap. Remember that the preferences you set when you use CorelTRACE will be in effect when you next use it. You should check the preference settings before you start to trace a bitmap.

Tracing a Partial Area

You should trace only the part of the bitmap that you want to use in vector form. To trace only part of an image:

1. Select **Preferences**. The Preferences menu appears.
2. The **Trace Partial Area** item in the menu may be checked, indicating that Trace Partial Area is enabled, or not checked, indicating that Trace Partial area is not enabled. Click to change from enabled to not enabled, or vice-versa. The menu disappears when you click. To leave the Preferences menu without making any changes, click outside the menu.
3. Follow the steps described in *Tracing an Image*. After you click **Trace All**, the bitmap image appears with handles around it. There is also an **OK** button at the bottom-right of the image.

4. Drag the handles to enclose the part of the image you want to trace.
5. Click **OK** to proceed with tracing.

Viewing Dithered Colors

The **Dithered Colors** preference gives you the option of displaying colors and shades of gray on your screen as dithered or pure colors.

Enable or disable this option in the same way you enable or disable Trace Partial Area, which is described above.

Selecting Color Reduction

The **Color Reduction** preference allows you to control the number of colors or levels of gray that appear in the traced image. It also allows you to convert color bitmaps to monochrome vector images. Use this preference to reduce the complexity to what you want to have in the vector image. To set this preference:

1. Select **Preferences ➤ Color Reduction**. The Color Reduction Scheme dialog box appears, as shown in Figure V.1.
2. To reduce the number of colors, open the **Reduce Colors to** list box and click on the number of colors you want.
3. To reduce the number of levels of gray, open the **Reduce Grays to** list box and click on the number of levels of gray you want.
4. To convert the bitmap to monochrome, click the **Convert to Monochrome** button.
5. Click **OK**.

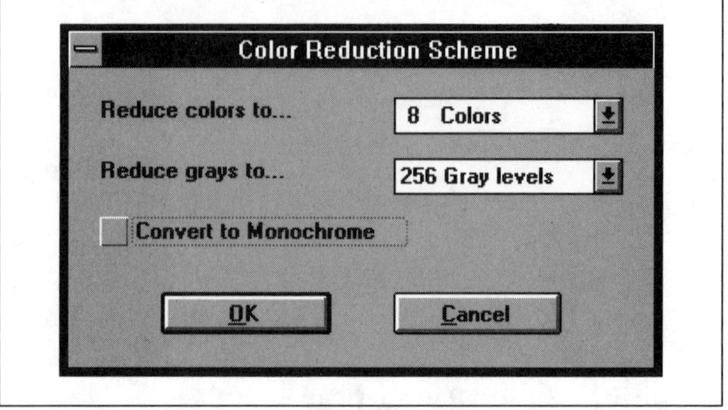

Figure V.1: The Color Reduction Scheme dialog box

SAVING TRACED IMAGES

CorelTRACE saves vector images as files in Encapsulated PostScript (EPS) format without an image header. You can import these files into CorelDRAW and other vector graphics programs. If you want to use a traced image in a graphics program that does not accept EPS format, import the file into CorelDRAW and then export it in the format the other program can accept. You can also use CorelDRAW to export the file in EPS format with an image header.

When you import a traced image into CorelDRAW, all the objects are grouped. You must ungroup them before you can edit individual objects.

You can choose the directory into which the vector image file is written, and you can also decide how to handle file name conflicts, as follows:

1. Select **File ➤ Output Options**. The Output Options dialog box appears.

2. In the dialog box, select the disk drive and directory into which the output file is to be written.
3. Check either **Always prompt** or **Always replace**. If you check Always prompt, you will be prompted if you are about to save a file with the same name as a file already in the selected directory. If you check Always replace, all files will be saved even if doing so overwrites files already in the directory.
4. Click **Make File Read Only** if you want to do that.
5. Click **OK**.

SCANNING ARTWORK

If you are using a scanner to create bitmaps that you are going to trace, there are several points you should be aware of

- Before you scan, make the artwork as clean as possible. If you are scanning a black-and-white original, use white paint to eliminate any unwanted black or gray before you scan.
- Choose the scanning mode that best suits the original and the way you want to use the scanned image.
- Scan images at the highest resolution possible for best results. Be aware, though, that high resolution scans can create very large files.
- Use the magnification and reduction capabilities of your scanner to scan the original artwork at the size you intend to use it.
- Scan only the part of the original you intend to use.
- If the original artwork has distinct horizontal or vertical lines, make sure the artwork is positioned exactly on the scanner. This usually requires some experimentation.

- When you are scanning black-and-white originals, experiment with the scanner's intensity and contrast controls to get the sharpest possible image.
- When you are scanning gray-scale or color images, the settings of the scanner's contrast and intensity controls have a significant effect on the vector image CorelTRACE produces. Be prepared to experiment.

The more effort you put into getting the best possible scanned image, the less time you will have to spend preparing the bitmap for tracing and cleaning up the vector image.

TRACING AN IMAGE

You can accept the default method of tracing an image, or you can modify the way images are traced in many ways.

The Default Method of Tracing

The steps here assume that Trace Partial Area is not enabled. See *Preferences* for the differences when Trace Partial Area is enabled. Do the following to trace an image:

1. In the Program Manager window, double-click on **Corel Graphics**.
2. In the Corel Graphics window, double-click **CorelTRACE**.
3. In the CorelTRACE dialog box, click **Open**. The Open One Or More Files To Trace dialog box appears.
4. Click the **Auto View** button so that it is checked.
5. In the **Directories** list box, select the directory which contains the file you want to trace.
6. Open the **List Files of Type** list box and select the type of file you want to trace. The available file names appear in the File Name list box.

7. Click the name of the file you want to trace. The file name appears in the File Name text box and an image of the bitmap appears in the Preview box, as shown in Figure V.2.
8. If you want to see information about the bitmap you have selected, click **Header** to see the Bitmap Header Information box. Click **Display Image** to return to the previous dialog box.
9. Click OK. The dialog box changes to that shown in Figure V.3.
10. Click **Trace All**. Tracing begins. The screen shows the progress of tracing in terms of the percentage completed and by the progression along the bar at the bottom of the left side of the dialog box. The traced image appears in the large box on the right.

• NOTES In many cases, you will not be satisfied with a tracing made with the default conditions, so you will need to repeat the tracing with different options and, perhaps, with different preferences selected.

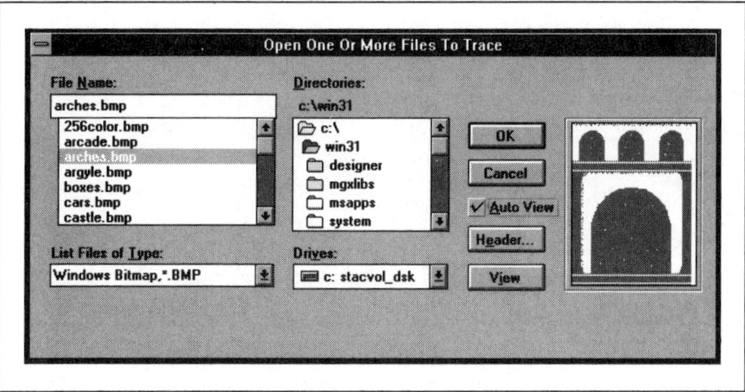

Figure V.2: The Open One or More Files to Trace dialog box with Bitmap selected

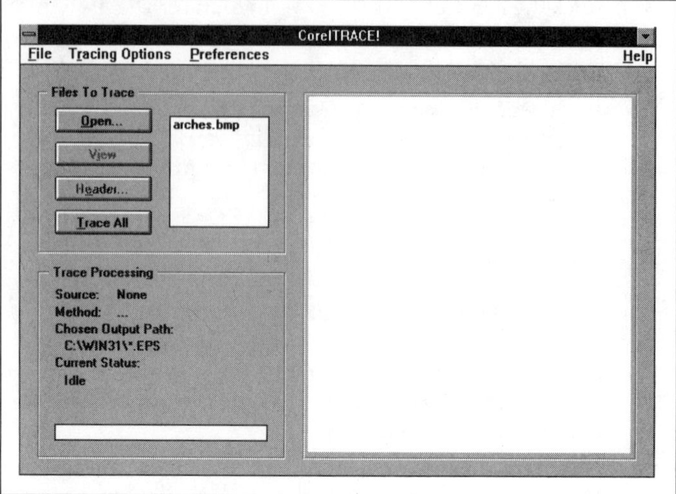

Figure V.3: The CorelTRACE dialog box ready for tracing to start

Tracing Multiple Bitmaps

You can trace several bitmaps consecutively, provided you want to use the same options and preferences for all of them. To do this:

1. Follow steps 1 through 7 in "The Default Method of Tracing" above.
2. Hold down the Ctrl key while you repeat step 7 to select additional bitmaps.
3. Follow steps 9 and 10 in "The Default Method of Tracing."

TRACING METHODS

You can choose between two tracing methods, Centerline and Outline, to control how CorelTRACE deals with thin lines.

- The Centerline method converts a thin line in the bitmap image to a single line with a specific thickness in the traced image.
- The Outline method converts a thin line in the bitmap image to a filled outline in the traced image.

In general, the Centerline method is best for tracing images that contain many thin lines, whereas the Outline method works best for images containing many thick, filled objects.

Choosing between Centerline and Outline Tracing

To choose a tracing method:

1. Select **Tracing Options**. The Tracing Options menu appears, as shown in Figure V.4.
2. Click either **Normal_Outline** or **Normal_Centerline**.

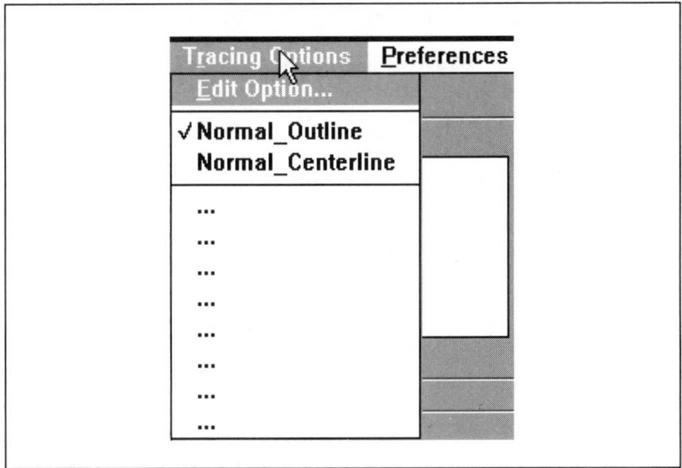

Figure V.4: The Tracing Options menu

Modifying Tracing Methods

Whenever you start CorelTRACE, the default settings for Centerline and Outline tracing are in effect. You can modify these default settings, in which case the modified settings stay in effect until you exit from CorelTRACE. You can store modified tracing methods for future use.

You can control the following aspects of a tracing method:

- **Tracing Method**. Select either **Follow Outline** or **Follow Center Line**. If you select Follow Center Line, you can choose the maximum line width. Use a low setting if you want the traced image to closely follow the bitmap; use a high setting to get smooth lines in the traced image. If you select Follow Center Line, you can also select **Use Uniform Lines** to assign a uniform line thickness to all lines in the traced image.
- **Invert Bitmap First**. Enable this option to produce negative vector images of black-and-white bitmaps or of color bitmaps which are reduced to black and white.
- **Remove Noise**. The tracing process automatically removes objects in the bitmap that are smaller than a certain number of pixels clustered together. You can select a setting of from 2 to 999 pixels.
- **Curve Length**. Choose from five curve lengths. Shorter curve lengths reproduce more detail than longer curve lengths. You must tighten the Fit Curve option and make the Sample Rate option fine for Short Curve Length to take effect.
- **Convert Long Lines**. Choose whether you want the tracing process to favor converting long lines to straight lines or curves.
- **Outline Filtering**. Choose how much you want to smooth outlined objects.
- **Fit Curve and Sample Rate**. These factors determine to what extent details in the bitmap appear in the traced

image. Choose **Very Tight** for Fit Curve and **Fine** for Sample Rate to get the most detail.

To get satisfactory results, you may have to trace various parts of a bitmap with different tracing options. You may even have to trace the same part with different options and subsequently combine the vector images.

To modify the Centerline or Outline tracing method:

1. Select **Tracing Options**. The Tracing Options menu appears.
2. Click whichever of the tracing methods you wish to modify.
3. Click **Edit Option**. The Tracing Options dialog box, shown in Figure V.5, appears.
4. Select whichever options you need.
5. If you want to keep the modified tracing method for future use, type a file name in the Option Name text box.
6. Click **OK**.

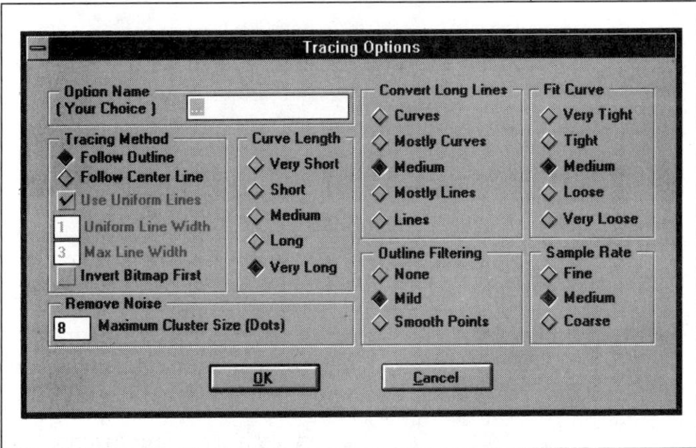

Figure V.5: The Tracing Options dialog box

• NOTES If you gave the modified tracing method a name, that name will subsequently appear in the Tracing Options menu so that you can select it.

If you want to create a new tracing method without basing it on the Centerline or Outline method, double-click on one of the lines in the Tracing Options menu that contains only three dots.

Appendix A

CorelDRAW File Formats

Table A.1: File Formats Supported by CorelDRAW

FORMAT	SOURCE	READ	WRITE
ABK	CorelDRAW Auto Backup	✓	✓
AI	Adobe Illustrator	✓	
BAK	CorelDRAW Backup	✓	✓
BMP	Windows Bitmap	✓	✓
CDR	CorelDRAW Drawing	✓	✓
CGM	Computer Graphics Metafile	✓	✓
DXF	AutoCAD	✓	✓
EPS	Encapsulated PostScript	✓	✓
GEM	Graphic Environment Manager	✓	✓
GIF	CompuServe	✓	✓
IPL	CorelDRAW Color Palette	✓	✓
PAL	CorelDRAW Color Palette	✓	✓
PAT	CorelDRAW Pattern	✓	✓
PCT	Macintosh	✓	✓
PCX	CorelPHOTO-PAINT, etc.	✓	✓
PFB	Adobe Type 1 Font	✓	✓
PIC	Lotus 1-2-3 Graphic	✓	
PIF	IBM Graphics	✓	✓
PLT	Hewlett-Packard Plotter	✓	✓
PRN	Print File		✓
SCD	Matrix/Imapro SCODL		✓
TGA	Targa	✓	✓
TIF	Tag Image File Format	✓	✓
TTF	TrueType Font	✓	✓
TXT	Text	✓	

Table A.1: File Formats Supported by CorelDRAW (continued)

FORMAT	SOURCE	READ	WRITE
WFN	CorelDRAW Symbols	✓	✓
WMF	Windows Metafile	✓	✓
WPG	WordPerfect Graphic		✓

Table A.2: File Formats Supported by CorelCHART

FORMAT	SOURCE	READ DATA	READ GRAPHICS	WRITE
AI	Adobe Illustrator		✓	
BMP	Windows Bitmap		✓	✓
CCH	CorelCHART	✓	✓	✓
CGM	Computer Graphics Metafile		✓	✓
CHT	Harvard Graphics	✓		
CSV	ASCII (comma separated)	✓		
DBF	dBASE	✓		
DXF	AutoCAD		✓	✓
EPS	Encapsulated PostScript		✓	✓
GEM	Graphical Environment Manager		✓	✓
GIF	CompuServe		✓	✓
PCC	PC Paintbrush		✓	✓

Table A.2: File Formats Supported by CorelCHART (continued)

FORMAT	SOURCE	READ DATA	READ GRAPHICS	WRITE
PCT	Macintosh		✓	✓
PCX	CorelPHOTO-PAINT, etc.		✓	✓
PIC	Lotus 1-2-3 Graphics		✓	
PIF	IBM Graphics		✓	✓
PLT	Hewlett-Packard Plotter		✓	✓
PRN	Print File			✓
SCD	Matrix/Imapro SCODL			✓
TGA	Targa		✓	✓
TIF	Tag Image File Format		✓	✓
TXT	Text (comma or tab separated)	✓		
WK1	Lotus 1-2-3 Spreadsheet	✓		
WK3	Lotus 1-2-3 Spreadsheet	✓		
WMF	Windows Metafile		✓	✓
WPG	WordPerfect Graphics			✓

Table A.3: File Formats Supported by CorelPHOTO-PAINT

FORMAT	SOURCE	READ	WRITE
BMP	Windows Bitmap	✓	✓
EPS	Encapsulated PostScript		✓
GIF	CompuServe	✓	✓
MSP	Microsoft Paint	✓	
PCX	CorelPHOTO-PAINT, etc.	✓	✓
PRN	Print File		✓
TGA	Targa	✓	✓
THB	CorelPHOTO-PAINT Thumbnail	✓	✓
TIF	Tag Image File Format	✓	✓

Table A.4: File Formats Supported by CorelSHOW

FORMAT	SOURCE	READ	WRITE
FLI	Autodesk Animation	✓	
SHB	CorelSHOW Background	✓	✓
SHW	CorelSHOW Presentation	✓	✓

Table A.5: File Formats Supported by CorelTRACE

FORMAT	SOURCE	READ	WRITE
BMP	Windows Bitmap	✓	
EPS	Encapsulated PostScript		✓
GIF	CompuServe	✓	
PCC	PC Paintbrush	✓	
PCX	CorelPHOTO-PAINT, etc.	✓	
PRN	Print File		✓
TGA	Targa	✓	
TIF	Tag Image File Format	✓	

Table A.6: File Formats Supported by CorelMOSAIC

FORMAT	SOURCE	READ	WRITE
AI	Adobe Illustrator	✓	
BMP	Windows Bitmap	✓	✓
CCH	CorelCHART	✓	
CDR	CorelDRAW	✓	
DIB	Windows Bitmap	✓	
EPS	Encapsulated PostScript	✓	✓
GIF	CompuServe	✓	

Table A.6: File Formats Supported by CorelMOSAIC (continued)

FORMAT	SOURCE	READ	WRITE
PCC	CorelPHOTO-PAINT, etc.	✓	
PCD	Kodak Photo CD	✓	
PCX	CorelPHOTO-PAINT, etc.	✓	✓
SHB	CorelSHOW Background	✓	
SHW	CorelSHOW Presentation	✓	
TGA	Targa	✓	
TIF	Tag Image File Format	✓	✓

A

B

C

D

E

F

G

H

I

J

K

L

M

N

P

R

S

T

U

V

W

Z

Selections from The SYBEX Library

DESKTOP PRESENTATION

Harvard Graphics Instant Reference

Gerald E. Jones

154pp. Ref. 726-6

This handy reference is a quick, non-technical answer manual to questions about Harvard's onscreen menus and help displays. Provides specific information on each of the program's major features, including Draw Partner. A must for business professionals and graphic artists who create charts and graphs for presentation.

Harvard Graphics 3 Instant Reference (Second Edition)

Gerald E. Jones

200pp; ref. 871-8

This handy, compact volume is the single complete source for quick answers on all of Harvard's menu options and features. It's small enough to keep on hand while you work—and fast enough to let you keep working while you look up concise explanations and exact instructions for using Harvard commands.

Mastering Animator

Mitch Gould

300pp. Ref.688-X

A hands-on guide to creating dynamic multimedia presentations. From simple animation to Hollywood-style special effects, from planning a presentation to bringing it all to life—it's all you need to know, in straightforward, easy-to-follow terms.

Mastering Harvard Graphics (Second Edition)

Glenn H. Larsen

375pp, Ref. 673-1

"The clearest course to begin mastering Harvard Graphics," according to *Computer Currents*. Readers master essential principles of effective graphic communication, as they follow step-by-step instructions to create dozens of charts and graphs; automate and customize the charting process; create slide shows, and more.

Mastering Harvard Graphics 3

Glenn Larsen
with Kristopher Larsen

525pp; Ref. 870-X

This highly praised hands-on guide uses engaging tutorials and colorful examples to show exactly how to create effective charts, graphs, presentations, and slide shows. Readers create virtually every kind of chart, including many not covered in Harvard's manual. Companion diskette features over $40 worth of clipart—absolutely free.

Teach Yourself Harvard Graphics 3

Jeff Woodward

450pp; Ref. 801-7

A graphical introduction to the hottest-selling presentation graphics program! This illustrated guide leads newcomers through the exact steps needed to create all kinds of effective charts and graphs. There are no surprises: what you see in the book is what you will see on your screen.

Up & Running with Harvard Graphics

Rebecca Bridges Altman

148pp. Ref. 736-3

Desktop presentation in 20 steps—the perfect way to evaluate Harvard Graphics for purchase, or to get a fast, hands-on overview of the software's capabilities. The book's 20 concise lessons are time-coded (each takes no more than an hour to complete), and cover everything from installation and startup, to creating specific types of charts, graphs, and slide shows.

Up & Running with Harvard Graphics 3

Rebecca Bridges Altman

140pp; Ref. 884-X

Come up to speed with Harvard Graphics 3—fast. If you're a computer-literate user who needs to start producing professional-looking presentation graphics now, this book is for you. In only 20 lessons (each taking just 15 minutes to an hour), you can cover all the essentials of this perennially popular progam.

DESKTOP PUBLISHING

The ABC's of the New Print Shop

Vivian Dubrovin

340pp. Ref. 640-4

This beginner's guide stresses fun, practicality and original ideas. Hands-on tutorials show how to create greeting cards, invitations, signs, flyers, letterheads, banners, and calendars.

The ABC's of Ventura

Robert Cowart
Steve Cummings

390pp. Ref. 537-9

Created especially for new desktop publishers, this is an easy introduction to a complex program. Cowart provides details on using the mouse, the Ventura side bar, and page layout, with careful explanations of publishing terminology. The new Ventura menus are all carefully explained. For Version 2.

Desktop Publishing with WordPerfect 5.1

Rita Belserene

418pp. Ref. 481-X

A practical guide to using the desktop publishing capabilities of versions 5.0 and 5.1. Topics include graphic design concepts, hardware necessities, installing and using fonts, columns, lines, and boxes, illustrations, multi-page layouts, Style Sheets, and integrating with other software.

Mastering CorelDRAW 2

Steve Rimmer

500pp. Ref. 814-9

This comprehensive tutorial and design guide features complete instruction in creating spectacular graphic effects with CorelDRAW 2. The book also offers a primer on commercial image and page design, including how to use printers and print-house facilities for optimum results.

Mastering Micrografx Designer

Peter Kent

400pp. Ref. 694-4

A complete guide to using this sophisticated illustration package. Readers begin by importing and modifying clip art, and progress to creating original drawings, working with text, printing and plotting, creating slide shows, producing color separations, and exporting art.

Mastering PageMaker 4 on the IBM PC

Rebecca Bridges Altman, with Rick Altman

509pp. Ref. 773-8

A step-by-step guide to the essentials of desktop publishing and graphic design. Tutorials and hands-on examples explore every aspect of working with text, graphics, styles, templates, and more, to design and produce a wide range of publications. Includes a publication "cookbook" and notes on using Windows 3.0.

Mastering Ventura for Windows *(For Version 3.0)*

Rick Altman

600pp, Ref. 758-4

This engaging, hands-on treatment is for the desktop publisher learning and using the Windows edition of Ventura. It covers everything from working with the Windows interface, to designing and printing sophisticated publications using Ventura's most advanced features. Understand and work with frames, graphics, fonts, tables and columns, and much more.

Mastering Ventura 3.0 Gem Edition

Matthew Holtz

650pp, Ref. 703-7

The complete hands-on guide to desktop publishing with Xerox Ventura Publisher—now in an up-to-date new edition featuring Ventura version 3.0, with the GEM windowing environment. Tutorials cover every aspect of the software, with examples ranging from correspondence and press releases, to newsletters, technical documents, and more.

Understanding Desktop Publishing

Robert W. Harris

300pp. Ref. 789-4

At last, a practical design handbook, written especially for PC users who are not design professionals, but who do have desktop publishing duties. How can publications be made attractive, understandable, persuasive, and memorable? Topics include type, graphics, and page design; technical and physiological aspects of creating and conveying a message.

Understanding PFS: First Publisher

Gerry Litton

463pp. Ref. 712-6

This new edition of the popular guide to First Publisher covers software features in a practical introduction to desktop publishing. Topics include text-handling, working with graphics, effective page design, and optimizing print quality. With examples of flyers, brochures, newsletters, and more.

Understanding PostScript Programming (Second Edition)

David A. Holzgang

472pp. Ref. 566-2

In-depth treatment of PostScript for programmers and advanced users working on custom desktop publishing tasks. Hands-on development of programs for font creation, integrating graphics, printer implementations and more.

Up & Running with CorelDRAW 2

Len Gilbert

140pp; Ref. 887-4

Learn CorelDRAW 2 in record time. This 20-step tutorial is perfect for computer-literate users who are new to CorelDRAW or upgrading from an earlier version. Each concise step takes no more than 15 minutes to an hour to complete, and provides needed skills without unnecessary detail.

Up & Running with PageMaker 4 on the PC

Marvin Bryan

140pp. Ref. 781-9

An overview of PageMaker 4.0 in just 20 steps. Perfect for evaluating the software before purchase—or for newcomers who are impatient to get to work. Topics include installation, adding typefaces, text and drawing tools, graphics, reusing layouts, using layers, working in color, printing, and more.

Your HP LaserJet Handbook

Alan R. Neibauer

564pp. Ref. 618-9

Get the most from your printer with this step-by-step instruction book for using LaserJet text and graphics features such as cartridge and soft fonts, type selection, memory and processor enhancements, PCL programming, and PostScript solutions. This hands-on guide provides specific instructions for working with a variety of software.

OPERATING SYSTEMS

The ABC's of DOS 4

Alan R. Miller

275pp. Ref. 583-2

This step-by-step introduction to using DOS 4 is written especially for beginners. Filled with simple examples, *The ABC's of DOS 4* covers the basics of hardware, software, disks, the system editor EDLIN, DOS commands, and more.

The ABC's of DOS 5

Alan Miller

267pp. Ref. 770-3

This straightforward guide will haven even first-time computer users working comfortably with DOS 5 in no time. Step-by-step lessons lead users from switching on the PC, through exploring the DOS Shell, working with directories and files, using essential commands, customizing the system, and trouble shooting. Includes a tear-out quick reference card and function key template.

ABC's of MS-DOS (Second Edition)

Alan R. Miller

233pp. Ref. 493-3

This handy guide to MS-DOS is all many PC users need to manage their computer files, organize floppy and hard disks, use EDLIN, and keep their computers organized. Additional information is given about utilities like Sidekick, and there is a DOS command and program summary. The second edition is fully updated for Version 3.3.

The ABC's of SCO UNIX

Tom Cuthbertson

263pp. Re. 715-0

A guide especially for beginners who want to get to work fast. Includes hands-on tutorials on logging in and out; creating and editing files; using electronic mail; organizing files into directories; printing; text formatting; and more.

The ABC's of Windows 3.0

Kris Jamsa

327pp. Ref. 760-6

A user-friendly introduction to the essentials of Windows 3.0. Presented in 64 short lessons. Beginners start with lesson one, while more advanced readers can skip ahead. Learn to use File Manager, the accessory programs, customization features, Program Manager, and more.

DESQview Instant Reference

Paul J. Perry

175pp. Ref. 809-2

This complete quick-reference command guide covers version 2.3 and DESQview 386, as well as QEMM (for managing expanded memory) and Manifest Memory Analyzer. Concise, alphabetized entries provide exact syntax, options, usage, and brief examples for every command. A handy source for on-the-job reminders and tips.

DOS 3.3 On-Line Advisor Version 1.1

SYBAR, Software Division of SYBEX, Inc.

Ref. 933-1

The answer to all your DOS problems. The DOS On-Line Advisor is an on-screen reference that explains over 200 DOS error messages. 2300 other citations cover all you ever needed to know about DOS. The DOS On-Line Advisor pops up on top of your working program to give you quick, easy help when you need it, and disappears when you don't. Covers thru version 3.3. Software package comes with 3½" and 5¼" disks. **System Requirements:** IBM compatible with DOS 2.0 or higher, runs with Windows 3.0, uses 90K of RAM.

DOS Instant Reference SYBEX Prompter Series

Greg Harvey
Kay Yarborough Nelson

220pp. Ref. 477-1

A complete fingertip reference for fast, easy on-line help:command summaries, syntax, usage and error messages. Organized by function—system commands, file commands, disk management, directories, batch files, I/O, networking, programming, and more. Through Version 3.3.

DOS 5 Instant Reference

Robert M. Thomas

200pp. Ref. 804-1

The comprehensive quick guide to DOS—all its features, commands, options, and versions—now including DOS 5, with the new graphical interface. Concise, alphabetized command entries provide exact syntax, options, usage, brief examples, and applicable version numbers. Fully cross-referenced; ideal for quick review or on-the-job reference.

The DOS 5 User's Handbook

Gary Masters
Richard Allen King

400pp. Ref. 777-0

This is the DOS 5 book for users who are already familiar with an earlier version of DOS. Part I is a quick, friendly guide to new features; topics include the graphical interface, new and enhanced commands, and much more. Part II is a complete DOS 5 quick reference, with command summaries, in-depth explanations, and examples.

Encyclopedia DOS

Judd Robbins

1030pp. Ref. 699-5

A comprehensive reference and user's guide to all versions of DOS through 4.0. Offers complete information on every DOS command, with all possible switches and parameters—plus examples of effective usage. An invaluable tool.

Essential OS/2 (Second Edition)

Judd Robbins

445pp. Ref. 609-X

Written by an OS/2 expert, this is the guide to the powerful new resources of the OS/2 operating system standard edition 1.1 with presentation manager. Robbins introduces the standard edition, and details multitasking under OS/2, and the range of commands for installing, starting up, configuring, and running applications. For Version 1.1 Standard Edition.

Essential PC-DOS (Second Edition)

Myril Clement Shaw
Susan Soltis Shaw

332pp. Ref. 413-5

An authoritative guide to PC-DOS, including version 3.2. Designed to make experts out of beginners, it explores everything from disk management to batch file programming. Includes an 85-page command summary. Through Version 3.2.

Graphics Programming Under Windows

Brian Myers
Chris Doner

646pp. Ref. 448-8

Straightforward discussion, abundant examples, and a concise reference guide to graphics commands make this book a must for Windows programmers. Topics range from how Windows works to programming for business, animation, CAD, and desktop publishing. For Version 2.

Hard Disk Instant Reference SYBEX Prompter Series

Judd Robbins

256pp. Ref. 587-5

Compact yet comprehensive, this pocket-sized reference presents the essential information on DOS commands used in managing directories and files, and in optimizing disk configuration. Includes a survey of third-party utility capabilities. Through DOS 4.0.

Inside DOS: A Programmer's Guide

Michael J. Young

490pp. Ref. 710-X

A collection of practical techniques (with source code listings) designed to help you take advantage of the rich resources intrinsic to MS-DOS machines. Designed for the experienced programmer with a basic understanding of C and 8086 assembly language, and DOS fundamentals.

Mastering DOS (Second Edition)

Judd Robbins

722pp. Ref. 555-7

"The most useful DOS book." This seven-part, in-depth tutorial addresses the needs of users at all levels. Topics range from running applications, to managing files and directories, configuring the system, batch file programming, and techniques for system developers. Through Version 4.

Mastering DOS 5

Judd Robbins

800pp. Ref.767-3

"The DOS reference to keep next to your computer," according to PC Week, this highly acclaimed text is now revised and expanded for DOS 5. Comprehensive tutorials cover everything from first steps for beginners, to advanced tools for systems developers—with emphasis on the new graphics interface. Includes tips, tricks, and a tear-out quick reference card and function key template.

Mastering SunOS

Brent D. Heslop
David Angell

588pp. Ref. 683-9

Learn to configure and manage your system; use essential commands; manage files; perform editing, formatting, and printing tasks; master E-mail and external communication; and use the SunView and new Open Window graphic interfaces.

Mastering Windows 3.0

Robert Cowart

592pp. Ref.458-5

Every Windows user will find valuable how-to and reference information here. With full details on the desktop utilities; manipulating files; running applications (including non-Windows programs); sharing data between DOS, OS/2, and Windows; hardware and software efficiency tips; and more.

Understanding DOS 3.3

Judd Robbins

678pp. Ref. 648-0

This best selling, in-depth tutorial addresses the needs of users at all levels with many examples and hands-on exercises. Robbins discusses the fundamentals of DOS, then covers manipulating files and directories, using the DOS editor, printing, communicating, and finishes with a full section on batch files.

Understanding Hard Disk Management on the PC

Jonathan Kamin

500pp. Ref. 561-1

This title is a key productivity tool for all hard disk users who want efficient, error-free file management and organization. Includes details on the best ways to conserve hard disk space when using several memory-guzzling programs. Through DOS 4.

Up & Running with DR DOS 5.0

Joerg Schieb

130pp. Ref. 815-7

Enjoy a fast-paced, but thorough introduction to DR DOS 5.0. In only 20 steps, you can begin to obtain practical results: copy and delete files, password protect your data, use batch files to save time, and more.

Up & Running with DOS 3.3

Michael-Alexander Beisecker

126pp. Ref. 750-9

Learn the fundamentals of DOS 3.3 in just 20 basic steps. Each "step" is a self-contained, time-coded lesson, taking 15 minutes to an hour to complete. You learn the essentials in record time.

Up & Running with DOS 5

Alan Simpson

150pp. Ref. 774-6

A 20-step guide to the essentials of DOS 5—for busy users seeking a fast-paced overview. Steps take only minutes to complete, and each is marked with a timer clock, so you know how long each one will take. Topics include installation, the DOS Shell, Program Manager, disks, directories, utilities, customization, batch files, ports and devices, DOSKEY, memory, Windows, and BASIC.

Up & Running with Your Hard Disk

Klaus M Rubsam

140pp. Ref. 666-9

A far-sighted, compact introduction to hard disk installation and basic DOS use. Perfect for PC users who want the practical essentials in the shortest possible time. In 20 basic steps, learn to choose your hard disk, work with accessories, back up data, use DOS utilities to save time, and more.

Up & Running with Windows 286/386

Gabriele Wentges

132pp. Ref. 691-X

This handy 20-step overview gives PC users all the essentials of using Windows—whether for evaluating the software, or getting a fast start. Each self-contained lesson takes just 15 minutes to one hour to complete.

Up & Running with Windows 3.0

Gabriele Wentges

117pp. Ref. 711-8

All the essentials of Windows 3.0 in just twenty "steps"—self-contained lessons that take minutes to complete. Perfect for evaluating the software or getting a quick start with the new environment. Topics include installation, managing windows, using keyboard and mouse, using desktop utilities, and built-in programs.

Windows 3.0 Instant Reference

Marshall Moseley

195pp. Ref. 757-6

This concise, comprehensive pocket reference provides quick access to instructions on all Windows 3.0 mouse and keyboard commands. It features step-by-step instructions on using Windows, the applications that come bundled with it, and Windows' unique help facilities. Great for all levels of expertise.

UTILITIES

The Computer Virus Protection Handbook

Colin Haynes

192pp. Ref. 696-0

This book is the equivalent of an intensive emergency preparedness seminar on computer viruses. Readers learn what viruses are, how they are created, and how they infect systems. Step-by-step procedures help computer users to identify vulnerabilities, and to assess the consequences of a virus infection. Strategies on coping with viruses, as well as methods of data recovery, make this book well worth the investment.

Mastering the Norton Utilities 5

Peter Dyson

400pp, Ref. 725-8

This complete guide to installing and using the Norton Utilities 5 is a must for beginning and experienced users alike. It offers a clear, detailed description of each utility, with options, uses and examples—so users can quickly identify the programs they need and put Norton right to work. Includes valuable coverage of the newest Norton enhancements.

Mastering PC Tools Deluxe 6 *For Versions 5.5 and 6.0*

425pp, Ref. 700-2

An up-to-date guide to the lifesaving utilities in PC Tools Deluxe version 6.0 from installation, to high-speed back-ups, data recovery, file encryption, desktop applications, and more. Includes detailed background on DOS and hardware such as floppies, hard disks, modems and fax cards.

Norton Desktop for Windows Instant Reference

Sharon Crawford
Charlie Russell

200pp; Ref. 894-7

For anyone using Norton's version of the Windows desktop, here's a compact, fast-access guide to every feature of the package—from file management functions, to disaster prevention tools, configuration commands, batch language extensions, and more. Concise, quick-reference entries are alphabetized by topic, and include practical tips and examples.

Norton Utilities 5 Instant Reference

Michael Gross

162pp. Ref. 737-1

Organized alphabetically by program name, this pocket-sized reference offers complete information on each utility in the Norton 5 package—including a descriptive summary, exact syntax, command line options, brief explanation, and examples. Gives proficient users a quick reminder, and helps with unfamiliar options.

Norton Utilities 6 Instant Reference

Michael Gross

175pp; Ref. 865-3

This pocket-size guide to Norton Utilities 6 provides fast answers when and where they're needed. Reference entries are organized alphabetically by program name, and provide a descriptive summary, exact syntax, command line options, brief explanations, and examples. For a quick reminder, or help with unfamiliar options.

PC Tools Deluxe 6 Instant Reference

Gordon McComb

194pp. Ref. 728-2

Keep this one handy for fast access to quick reminders and essential information on the latest PC Tools Utilities. Alphabetical entries cover all the Tools of Version 6—from data recovery to desktop applications—with concise summaries, syntax, options, brief explanations, and examples.

Understanding Norton Desktop for Windows

Peter Dyson

500pp; Ref. 888-2

This detailed, hands-on guide shows how to make the most of Norton's powerful Windows Desktop—to make Windows easier to use, customize and optimize the environment, take advantage of shortcuts, improve disk management, simplify disaster recovery, and more. Each program in the Norton Desktop gets thorough treatment, with plenty of practical examples.

Understanding the Norton Utilities 6 (Second Edition)

Peter Dyson

500pp; Ref. 855-6

Here is a detailed, practical sourcebook for PC users seeking to streamline their computing and extend the power of DOS with Norton 6. Features hands-on examples and up-to-date coverage of such topics as file management and security, hard disk maintenance, disaster recovery, and batch programming. Includes a complete command guide.

Understanding PC Tools 7

Peter Dyson

500pp; Ref. 850-5

Turn here for a complete guide to taking advantage of the new version of PC Tools for DOS 5 and Windows—with hands-on coverage of everything from installation to telecommunications. Special topics include networking; data security and encryption; virus detection; remote computing; and many new options for disk maintenance, disaster prevention, and data recovery.

Up & Running with Carbon Copy Plus

Marvin Bryan

124pp. Ref. 709-6

A speedy, thorough introduction to Carbon Copy Plus, for controlling remote computers from a PC. Coverage is in twenty time-coded "steps"—lessons that take 15 minutes to an hour to complete. Topics include program set-up, making and receiving calls, file transfer, security, terminal emulation, and using Scripts.

Up & Running with Norton Desktop for Windows

Michael Gross
David Clark

140pp; Ref. 885-8

Norton's new desktop utility package lets you customize Windows to your heart's content. Don't miss out! Learn to use this versatile program in just 20 basic lessons. Each lesson takes less than an hour to complete, and wastes no time on unnecessary detail.

Up & Running with Norton Utilities 5

Michael Gross

154pp. Ref. 819-0

Get a fast jump on Norton Utilties 5. In just 20 lessons, you can learn to retrieve erased files, password protect and encrypt your data, make your system work faster, unformat accidentally formatted disks, find "lost" files on your hard disk, and reconstruct damaged files.

Up & Running with Norton Utilities 6

Michael Gross

140pp; Ref. 874-2

Come up to speed with Norton Utilities 6 in just 20 steps. This slim volume covers all of Norton's constituent programs (for both versions 5 and 6), provides command line syntax and options, and spells out the differences between versions 5 and 6 with special upgrade notes.

Up & Running with PC Tools Deluxe 6

Thomas Holste

180pp. Ref.678-2

Learn to use this software program in just 20 basic steps. Readers get a quick, inexpensive introduction to using the Tools for disaster recovery, disk and file management, and more.

Up & Running with XTreeGold 2

Robin Merrin

136pp. Ref. 820-3

Covers both XTreeGold 2 and XTreePro-Gold 1. In just 20 steps, each taking no more than 15 minutes to an hour, you can learn to customize your display, archive files, navigate the user interface, copy and back up your files, undelete accidentally erased files, and more.

CorelCHART Main Menus*

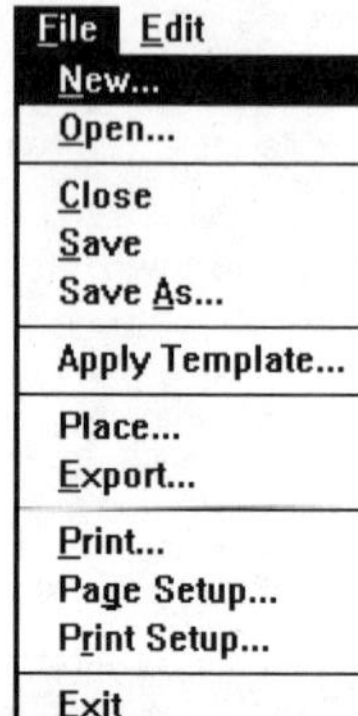
File
Edit
New...
Open...
Close
Save
Save As...
Apply Template...
Place...
Export...
Print...
Page Setup...
Print Setup...
Exit

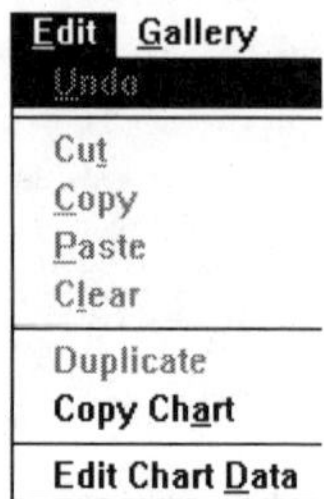
Edit
Gallery
Undo
Cut
Copy
Paste
Clear
Duplicate
Copy Chart
Edit Chart Data

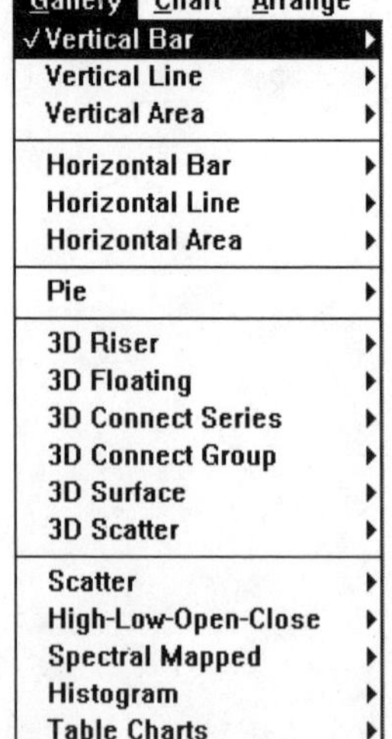
Gallery
Chart
Arrange
√Vertical Bar
Vertical Line
Vertical Area
Horizontal Bar
Horizontal Line
Horizontal Area
Pie
3D Riser
3D Floating
3D Connect Series
3D Connect Group
3D Surface
3D Scatter
Scatter
High-Low-Open-Close
Spectral Mapped
Histogram
Table Charts

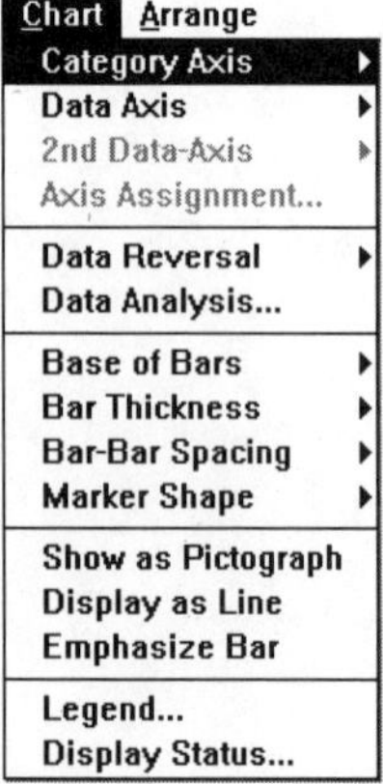
Chart
Arrange
Category Axis
Data Axis
2nd Data-Axis
Axis Assignment...
Data Reversal
Data Analysis...
Base of Bars
Bar Thickness
Bar-Bar Spacing
Marker Shape
Show as Pictograph
Display as Line
Emphasize Bar
Legend...
Display Status...